KIDFOOD

D1600706

KIDFOOD

◇

How to Get Your Kids to Eat *Right* Right from the Start –and Like It

Lisa Tracy

A DELL TRADE PAPERBACK

*For all the parents and kids who helped,
and especially our friends at TOTS.*

A DELL TRADE PAPERBACK
Published by
Dell Publishing
a division of
Bantam Doubleday Dell
Publishing Group, Inc.
666 Fifth Avenue
New York, New York 10103

Designed by Richard Oriolo

ISBN: 0-440-50245-4

Printed in the United States of America
Published simultaneously in Canada

October 1989

10 9 8 7 6 5 4 3 2 1

MV

CONTENTS

◇

ACKNOWLEDGMENTS

Kidfood appears thanks to the cooperation and assistance of experts at various organizations and experts in the home. Special thanks to the American Academy of Pediatrics for making available expert opinions on children, child health, and nutrition in the form of various publications, to Dr. Laurence Finberg, chairman of the AAP Committee on Nutrition and to Carolyn Kolbaba, media coordinator, AAP; to Dr. Brian Morgan of the Institute of Human Nutrition at Columbia University College of Physicians and Surgeons; to Pepper Leeper of the National Research Council of the National Academy of Sciences; to Phyllis Brogen and the Greater Philadelphia Area Celiac Sprue Support Group; to Drew DeSilver of *Vegetarian Times;* to Larry Clark of the Himalayan Institute; to Sandra Hvisten of the American College of Nurse Midwives; to Dr. D.W. Bronner of Nutrition West; and to our own incomparable pediatrician, Dr. Matthew Boulis.

Special thanks to the parents: Margaret Brossy; Chris Burger; Margaret Mary Carroll and Larry Stoiaken; Betty DeRoo; Nancy and

Stephen Doyne; Cathy Hall; Meg Herron; Amy Huntoon; Linda Kranzfelder; Karen Parker; Judith Tafelski; Mary and Cabell Tutwiler; Linda Wengerd; to all those who gave generously of time, information, and recipes, including Mary Cross, Carol Mayer, Gwen Rosvold, and Betty Linville of the TOTS Coop Nursery staff; and to our friends Laverna Dawley, Bridget and Tina Duffy, Mary Flynn Day, the Paul Lynch family, the James Linville family, and the Mary Kinter Mills family, who helped with their time. Thanks to our family for recipes, time, and good times shared over and about food.

Thanks to my agent, Herbert M. Katz, without whom it would all have been impossible; and to Jody Rein, Dell executive editor; her assistant, Jeanne Cavelos; and Chris Benton, copy editor, for their care and many good ideas.

And finally, thanks to people like the National Resources Defense Council, the Environmental Defense Fund, the Center for Science in the Public Interest, and Consumers Union—people who give their time and energy to see to it that the public's food supply will be made safer and healthier for all of us.

INTRODUCTION

As parents today, we live in a world of abundance, an age of un-precedented choices for our children in every part of their lives. Not the least of these is food. Supermarkets and specialty stores offer us a range and variety of foods undreamed of fifty years ago. Restaurants, manufacturers, and retailers cater to the growing segment of our population that eats out or takes out because we are too busy to cook every meal at home. Television feeds us a continuing stream of encouragement to buy new and competing food products.

But abundance is a mixed blessing. Sometimes there's too much of a good thing. In the past decade a congressional report, the National Institutes of Health, the American Cancer Society, the American Heart Association, and other health organizations have all brought us the same message: it's time to cut out the fats, sugars, salt, and stimulants our culture so abundantly provides. And what goes for us certainly goes doubly for our children, for whom we wish the very best, the nutritional edge, from the beginning of their young lives.

With abundance comes choice. How do we explain to our kids that the pink marshallow cereal they see on TV, advertised as a "complete breakfast," isn't necessarily the best selection? Do we just put our feet down and say no, or do we give in and hope that they will come to their senses someday and eat shredded wheat? Chances are we do both. Choice is there—flexibility is the key to getting through all the options and selecting something for everyone, but without abandoning good nutrition.

Good nutrition isn't all that hard to come by, if you just know how to put it all together. Here choice plays a really positive role: we have become such smart food consumers—with a little help from the NIH and others—that we demand better food, and we're getting it. A spokesman for a leading supermarket chain tells me that the aisle the markets count on to draw customers into the store is the fresh fruit and vegetable aisle, of all things. As busy as we all are, we are finding the time to feed ourselves better. Just as the experts told us to, we're eating more fish and chicken, more whole grains, more fruits and veggies, and less saturated fat. We must be demanding less sugar and salt too, because the low-salt snacks and the no-sugar-added juices are more and more available.

We're teaching our children how to eat this way, too—teaching them by example and by choice. We are selecting the best foods for them whenever we can. And if we give them a foundation of good nutrition, serving them a dinner from the supermarket freezer, or even taking a trip to the local fast-food restaurant on a night when everyone's busy, is not a disaster. That's flexibility, and we need it. Because—as I don't need to tell you if you have ever dieted—the best nutrition program in the world isn't going to work if you're too busy to use it.

So what we need is a program that gives us a solid base we can rely on most of the time. That's what *Kidfood* does for children and their parents. I tell you how, right from the start, you can use familiar, easy-to-fix foods to meet the Recommended Daily Allowances of essential nutrients for children of all ages, from infants to teenagers. I also introduce some less-familiar ingredients that are high in vitamins, minerals, and fiber and low in fat and cholesterol—

and I tell you where to find them and how to prepare them. I tell you how to get your toddler involved in cooking, what to do if you can't breast-feed your infant around the clock, what you might want to tell your seven-year-old when she goes to dinner at a friend's house, or what you might pack in your ten-year-old's lunch. And I talk about what to tell the baby-sitter about food for your nine-month-old and how to navigate special diets and the tricky teen-age years with your child.

Basic to my philosophy of how to feed the kids, based on years of studying nutrition, practicing good nutrition with my family, and writing and editing, is the concept of alternatives. Knowing what all the alternatives are lets you make the best choices for your children and yourself. Whether those alternatives are foods you've used for years presented in a new way or foods that are exotic to you, there's information on how to use them as well as recipes that incorporate them. Both are geared to make interesting meals with a minimum of fuss—meals that give your child the nutritional advantage.

Making good choices from the start can help your child avoid allergies and other health problems. Learning how to be flexible without giving up on good nutrition can keep you, and the kids, sane. Good choices, knowing your alternatives, and flexibility add up to a happy and healthy eating experience—right from the start.

I

◇

Eating Right:
The Hows and Whys

ONE

Getting from There to Here—From the Beginning

Dinnertime. Owen is eating homemade chicken soup. He's eating it out of several dishes—three, to be exact—because he eats more that way with less fuss. At four years old, he likes his noodles and chicken, but not necessarily in the same bowl as his broth.

I watch him and smile as I think how we got from there to here—from the beginning to age four and eating his broth from a cup, his noodles from a bowl, and his chicken from a saucer. I know, as my son does not, what good vegetables went into the broth. I know he is getting his protein from the chicken. I know he especially likes noodles and will have fun eating them. If it takes three dishes, I'm willing to play that game. We have years to polish the social graces. He already has his basic good table manners, but right now I'm really more interested in nutrition.

In the back of my mind, as I sit down to my own soup, I am carrying on a little mental arithmetic I do every day. What did Owen eat today, and how much of it? Has he gotten his vitamins and minerals? His protein? His fiber? How much dairy food has he eaten?

Does he get a cookie (or two) after dinner, or has he already had more than his share of sugar today? Should he have some milk with the cookie? I complete the tally and decide he might be a bit low on vitamin C today, so I offer him a slice of cantaloupe before dessert. Owen likes cantaloupe. He accepts. Because all the kids around us seem to have colds, I will probably give him some vitamin C drops before bed, too.

When I think about how we got from there to here, I know that a lot of things didn't turn out quite as I expected. Owen is our first child, and trying to feed him well has been a learning experience for all of us. What we have ended up with is a diet that matches our family's life-style and simultaneously provides Owen with the nutrition we think he needs.

As members of the health-conscious baby boom generation, we started with some pretty high hopes for our child's nutrition. At the same time, we recognized from the outset that we are living in a society that has a certain life-style, and that includes the foods we eat. From the beginning, we made a tacit decision to live in the mainstream. The result for Owen has been variety, a variety that ranges from brown rice to fast food. Through it all, we steer him to good-quality food wherever and whenever possible. Yet we recognize that the soul needs food, too, and that some of a little person's needs have to do with having the goodies that everyone else gets.

To some extent, I think we have to trust our children to eat what they need to eat. Studies have actually shown that a child—even an infant—will often balance out his or her diet over several days, eating more of this one day—or even three days in a row—then switching to more of that. There are parameters that need to be imposed, of course, and I will talk about them throughout Part I. But it is my firm belief that parents who are obsessed with food (whether in terms of feeding themselves or in terms of demanding that children eat a certain way and only that way) may create children who are also obsessed with food, and that can be unhealthy. That is why a little flexibility is good for the kids.

It's good for the parents, too. It takes the heat off in at least one area of our lives at a time when we are juggling many things, responding to many stresses. I draw not only on my own experience in writing about feeding children, but also on the experience of many other parents. We all have the same concerns, the same problems. We are trying to work, feed the kids, feed ourselves, feed our minds and spirits as well as our bodies, keep house, keep our sanity and our sense of humor—a tall order, and not necessarily in that order.

And sometimes we simply have to settle for less than the best.

I know there are going to be days when I'm working and we will all be eating fish sticks and french fries. This is an example of how things have not quite lived up to my ideal, but I am comfortable with the compromise because I am keeping an eye on the overall nutrition picture. My system for doing that, which I want to share with you, has to do with knowing what kids should eat, what they want to eat, and what they *will* eat. It's a system that involves knowing what the best sources of nutrients are, knowing how to present those nutrients to the kids, and knowing when to give in and let 'em eat cake. Because they will, sooner or later, no matter what we say. It's also a system for getting kids involved in preparing food, so that they actually enjoy it more. It's a system that aims at teaching children enough about good food sense to know, when the time comes, how to feed themselves right.

My quest for good food for the whole family with a minimum of fuss and bother grew out of a personal interest in food and writing about food. In my first book, *The Gradual Vegetarian,* I explored ways to eat a lighter and healthier diet without giving up the protein and other essential nutrients we need. Part of my philosophy is that it has to be easy or we won't do it. That's especially true for parents, whose time is at a premium, with pulls from so many directions. From a vegetarian and semivegetarian background, I also draw on a wealth of ingredients from cultures around the world; ingredients that are full of good nutrients and are now, thanks to technology, available at stores near most of us. We just have to know what to look for.

To research *Kidfood* I consulted the experts: pediatricians, staff and members of the American Academy of Pediatrics, nutritionists—and parents. Parents today are more aware than any previous generation of health concerns; they are the ones who are putting pressure on the schools to serve healthy snacks, on the networks to cut the candy advertising, on their kids to eat right . . . and on themselves to get all this done. Some are cooking special foods for kids with allergies; some are just reading the labels carefully, taking that extra ten seconds to screen the food for the little people they love.

Great Expectations—and How to Relax

One of the key things I've learned about feeding children in the last few years is that children know a lot more about you than you may think. If you care too much about what they eat, they won't. (If you eat chocolate chip cookies when they're not around, they'll want some, too, even though they didn't see you eat them and have no way of knowing the cookies are in the house. It's uncanny, I agree, but there it is.) So the first rule to remember in making any and all food decisions is to relax and realize there are years of eating ahead. As parents, we have many decisions to make, and we'll probably make some mistakes, but there *is* time to correct them. I had to learn this lesson myself—I'm one of those people who leaves written instructions for the baby-sitter even when I'm only going upstairs to my office.

What helps in making food-related decisions, right from the start, is to understand where we as parents are trying to go and what basic issues are involved. First of all, food is nutrition, but it's also a social experience. We need to keep both of those things in perspective. Then there may be factors from our family health history that we want to take into account. In my family, for instance, we have no history of heart disease, but we do have several people with allergies. So I was naturally more preoccupied with allergies in Owen's first year than with whether he was going to get too much cholesterol. Each family needs to think in terms of its own family medical history and the specific health needs its children may have—and what to do about them.

Then there's the world of nutrients. How do we determine a baseline for feeding the kids what they need to thrive? And then how do we get them to eat it? And what attitude should we take about all the attractively packaged nonnutrients out there, the TV commercials that sell them, and the countless other situations in which kids will encounter them as they grow?

Food as nutrition, food as fun, food as family tradition, food as a potential threat to our families' health—these are some of the concerns we parents have right from the start. Again, there is time to make decisions on all of these matters and correct our mistakes if necessary. *You can make a difference at any age.*

Of course it's important to start your children off right. Early nutrition—the needs of infants—is discussed in Chapter Two. But it's also important to remember that a child's body is constantly growing, creating new cells and discarding old ones. So whatever age your children are, there's truly no time like the present to take stock of how they are eating.

The next step in feeding your children is to ask yourself: Is there anything I can do, in the time I have available, to make the eating experience healthier or happier for my children? I suggest that you start as early as possible on that. In Chapter Three you'll have a chance to review what you already know about healthy eating for all ages and learn more about the key nutrients, such as protein, iron, calcium, vitamins A through E, including where to find them, with some sources you may not know about. Health problems including allergies are discussed in Chapter Four, with an emphasis on how to minimize or avoid problems by healthy eating. Chapters Five through Eight trace your children's progress through various stages of eating and involvement with food, from their first trips away from you to the baby-sitter or relatives to their earliest interest in helping in the kitchen, and on through finicky eating stages, early school experiences, and up to and including the teen years, where growing bodies demand the highest nutritional input ever and growing spirits just want to be on the go.

Chapters Nine through Eighteen comprise the recipe section of *Kidfood,* and this section comes equipped with suggestions on getting children involved in preparing foods, how to make a meal that will satisfy all members of the family at once (what I call "dovetail" meals), reminders about where the good nutrients are located, and recipes for parties, holidays, and just plain fun in the kitchen. There's also a section on comfort foods for when kids are under the weather. At the back of the book you'll find a list of resources, tips on breast feeding, and more suggestions on dealing with allergies.

The recipes and suggestions are there to help you implement the healthy eating you choose for your family. The decisions you make about healthy eating take effect almost immediately to improve your lifestyle. So let's get started on the first steps!

T W O

$\Diamond$

First Decisions: Feeding Your Infant

I s there a right way or a wrong way to start a baby off in life? In the beginning, babies are breast-fed or bottle-fed. First-time parents are often surprised—as letters to Miss Manners and Ann Landers attest—by the inordinate curiosity of total strangers about how the baby is going to be fed.

That first decision is an important one, but it's not the only one you will make in the baby's first year. Solid foods enter the picture at around four to six months. You have to decide what kinds of food you want your children to eat and in what form—commercially prepared, homemade, or both? What foods do you absolutely want to avoid?

Meanwhile, the advice continues to flow, whether from established or self-proclaimed experts. It can all be pretty nerve-wracking. This chapter is for both new and seasoned parents. If you have a very young baby right now, it will serve as a guide to the first year of feeding your child. For parents of toddlers and older children, it's a review of those first basic nutritional building blocks of life. For those with new babies, there's no time like the present to think about how much good a little care and information about diet and health can do in the long run. For those with older kids, there's also no time like the present to think about how your early decisions have influenced your current attitudes toward food.

In the following pages you'll find information on the transition from mother's milk or formula to solid foods. Here you'll read about how to introduce foods gradually to prevent allergies, which first foods most babies will eat with relish and the essential nutrients those foods provide and which foods to avoid during this crucial first year of life. I also discuss the alternatives available to you in this health-conscious age.

Most likely the first decision you'll make—often well before your baby is born—is whether to breast-feed or bottle-feed. In fact, you may find that well-meaning friends and relatives will ask you about this as soon as they find out you're expecting an addition to your family.

To Breast-feed or Not to Breast-feed?

When Owen was a month old, he was a pretty crabby little baby. We took him for a checkup, and the doctor we were then seeing weighed him, frowned, and informed us that our baby wasn't getting enough to eat. I remember him saying "What happens is that these babies can starve themselves to death. . . ." (Actually, what *I* remember him saying was that *my* baby was starving, but Owen's dad assures me it wasn't quite that bad.) After that, I didn't hear too much about how or why except that the problem was that I was breast-feeding when I ought to be bottle-feeding. The doctor recommended that we at least "supplement" Owen's diet with formula.

I was in a panic. Everything I'd read warned against combining the two. Breast-feeding manuals indicated that if you bottle-fed your baby at all your milk supply would fail to develop, and that would be the end of your breast-feeding experience. Our pediatrician was telling me my baby would starve if I didn't feed him formula. But the literature I'd read noted professional studies that had shown formula-fed babies were up to twenty-seven times as likely to develop lifelong allergies—and, as I mentioned, allergies were a concern in our family. What were we going to do?

We went home miserable, and fed him a bottle of formula. He fell asleep with a peaceful look on his face, and we pondered our course. We decided to strike out into unknown territory: to try to have it both ways for the sake of our baby's health and our own peace of mind. We would feed him the formula, but I was going to continue to breast-feed to give him as much of the immunities, closeness, and other benefits of breast-feeding as possible. And we were going to find a pediatrician who would help us do that. We did. Thirteen months later, Owen was still breast-feeding, still drinking formula, and enjoying a pretty wide range of first solid foods. Three years later, he has come through with a good health profile: few ear infections, no discernible allergies, few colds, and no apparent digestive problems. I think we accomplished what we wanted, even though it was by no prescribed route.

I mention this because I think you ought to know that sometimes you just have to go with your *own* instincts, even though it can be frightening, especially when you're first-time parents. Your instincts are good, and your situation is unique. No one else can really know better than you what's good for you, your child, and your family. Yes, you take the expert opinions into account, but then you decide what will work best for your life-style. This is true about breast-feeding versus formula, about what foods you first feed your child, and about all the decisions that follow.

As for that momentous first decision for your baby's nutritional future, there's no doubt that breast-feeding is good for babies. The American Academy of Pediatrics has indicated that breast milk is the best food for babies up to six months, and recommends it for at least four to six months unless there are contraindications (like an infectious disease that could be passed through the milk) or other overriding reasons not to breast-feed. There are many reasons breast milk is the best food for babies, but basically it boils down to common sense: technology hasn't succeeded in supplanting or duplicating what nature has provided.

Technology has, however, given us formula, and it's the closest substitute for breast milk that we now have. It is a quantum improvement over the straight cow's milk that was fed to the baby boom

BREAST MILK NUTRIENTS

In an article called "Food for Thought," *Consumers Research* magazine calls breast milk "the ideal food for the first year of (human) life," citing the Committee on Nutrition of the American Academy of Pediatrics as its source (*CR* Sept. 1987).

Perhaps we shouldn't be surprised that nature tailors the mother's milk of each species to nourish that species best . . . but what is it that makes breast milk the ideal source of nutrients for babies, exactly?

According to the AAP's article on "Nutrition and Lactation" in *Pediatrics* journal, breast milk starts by providing especially protein-rich nourishment right away with the colostrum produced by women in the first five days after birth. Throughout lactation, women who eat a diet high in polyunsaturated fat produce milk that is high in unsaturated fat. Breast milk contains more cholesterol than cow's milk or a formula based on cow's milk; an adequate intake of cholesterol throughout the body's growth period is believed to allow the proper sheathing of the spinal cord and formation of essential bile acids and hormones (a reason why the AAP cautions strongly against limiting fat and cholesterol intake during infancy).

Colostrum also contains disease antibodies, including antiviral antibodies, that protect against specific infections during the first six months of life (including polio, various staph infections, Coxsackie B virus, and some intestinal infections). Beyond infancy, breast milk appears to aid in a lifelong resistance to allergies, because the proteins in breast milk are the most digestible for human babies. Undigested or partially digested protein molecules slipping through the intestinal lining are believed to be the culprits in starting damage to the immune system that may result in allergies or in increased susceptibility to infections. A study at Northwestern University School of Medicine showed that children who had been breast fed fully for six months or more had four times *fewer* ear infections and colds than children who were bottle-fed babies. Babies fed formula went on to have eleven times as many tonsillectomies, twenty times as many diarrheal infections, and up to twenty-seven times as many allergic conditions (Pryor, *Nursing Your Body*).

The AAP also reports on certain key nutrients other than protein. The calcium-phosphorus ratio of milk is 3-to-1, a good ratio for absorption of calcium. The iron in human milk is better absorbed than that from other milks. Human milk also has "a 50 percent better bioavailability" of zinc than cow's milk. Colostrum is high in vitamins A and E, and studies show that mother's milk provides ascorbic acid (vitamin C) even at the mother's expense. Availability of B vitamins in breast milk generally seem to reflect their presence in the mother's diet. The AAP summarizes its findings by saying, "The unique biologic advantages of human milk justify the promotion of lactation as the normal method of infant feeding."

generation when breast-feeding was out of fashion (the cow's milk that generation drank as babies may well account, by the way, for the number of allergies ailing us today). So formula is certainly something to consider if breast-feeding is not an option.

When is breast-feeding not an option? That's really up to you to decide. There can, of course, be medical reasons to opt for bottle-feeding. Current literature acknowledges the impracticality of breast-feeding for the mother who works outside the home. But what most of the books *don't* tell you, is that you *can* combine breast-feeding with formula. Sure, it will mean your milk supply isn't totally developed, but it will also mean your baby is getting some of the immunities discussed above as well as the perfectly balanced meal that breast milk offers. If you're working from home or part-time, you can work breast-feeding around your schedule. If you're taking the first six weeks off and then plan to return to full-time work, breast-feed for the first six weeks and then go to formula. The point is, you can mix the two systems.

Breast-feeding offers comfort, convenience (you don't have to go to the store for it), and a sense of accomplishment. Bottle-feeding too offers convenience: it allows other people, like Dad and other relatives, to feed the baby, which means more rest for the mother, and provides flexibility in leaving the baby with sitters. Bottle-feeding these days is also pretty simple, devoid of complicated sterilization procedures in most areas. Your local pediatrician should know whether the tap water in your area is safe for babies and will advise you accordingly.

If you choose to breast-feed, you should learn about the new technology in terms of breast pumps and milk storage that has developed since the mid-1980s in response to the large number of working mothers who want to breast-feed their babies. There are also organizations to turn to if you need help, support, or advice: (see Appendix B). La Leche League and other groups can put you in touch with local chapters of mothers who can answer questions and help you with breast feeding.

Making the Transition to Solid Foods

Breast or bottle or both, the first decision you make in feeding your baby carries you for four to six months. During recent decades it has been the fashion to start feeding babies solid foods quite early, sometimes when they were only a few days old. When Owen was a month old, one friend of mine asked whether he was eating solid foods yet and was scandalized when I said he wasn't. I was scandalized, too, because the literature I'd been reading suggested quite the opposite—no solids at all for months. Fashions do change, and not without reason.

One reason babies were fed solid food early in past decades was that the technology for presenting safe commercially prepared baby foods had been developed and the food companies were touting it. Another reason that solid food has been pushed early is the supposition that it will help baby and, more to the point, parents, sleep through the night.

There are, however, some good reasons not to hurry with solid foods, too, and one of the them is allergies.

In this chapter I'll point to some basic methods for avoiding allergies and discovering whether your child has an allergy to a specific food. For more detailed information on "preventive nutrition"—how to deal with allergies and other matters of concern in your family—see Chapter Four.

Before your baby has reached the age of four months, be aware that his waking up through the night is *not* necessarily a signal to feed him solid foods. It's just a signal that your child's hungry—again. If it's a hassle, minimize it: keep the baby in your bedroom, in a bassinet, a portable crib, a cradle, or your bed. If it's formula you're feeding, invest in a supply of sealed individual containers just for nighttime. Sure, they're more expensive, but they are only for a feeding or two a day. Keep them next to the bed so you can just open one up if you need it, providing a sterile, ready supply.

Somewhere between the four-month checkup and the six-month checkup, your pediatrician will probably discuss introducing solid foods. The pattern that's typically recommended is to begin with one food that is easily digested and unlikely to produce allergies. This is usually rice in baby-cereal form, mixed with formula or breast milk. Parents are advised to try the new food for a certain length of time—a week or more—before introducing the next new food. This "week test" allows you to spot at once any potential digestive or allergy problems. The introduction of new foods moves through cereals to mild vegetables and fruits to higher-protein foods like meat, eggs, and dairy products.

In a way, this is a relaxing time, because you can proceed slowly with lots of guidance available. There are no multicourse meals to prepare, and if your baby shows lack of interest or outright dis-taste—which the infant will express adamantly by making a dis-gusted face or spitting the cereal right back at you—you can simply return to breast milk or formula only for a few weeks; there's no rush. If you are breast-feeding, you may even choose, and there are experts who will support you, to delay introducing solid foods until your baby is at least a year old.

The Signals That Your Baby Is Ready

Your baby will help you know when to start feeding solid foods, by giving you certain signals. You might notice that some time around the age of four to six months, your baby begins to take an interest in your eating habits. What is this stuff Mom and Dad are putting in their mouths, anyway? This coincidentally is often about the time when the first teeth are appearing. Both of these events are impor-tant clues that your baby is getting ready for a new phase.

At this time much of your baby's nutrition is still coming from breast or bottle; solid foods are not the main food. They are chiefly a novelty for your baby, as any parent who has witnessed the look of utter bewilderment on the face of a baby taking its first bite of cereal can attest. So the quantity of food your baby is eating shouldn't be your chief concern as long as his or her height/weight curve shows consistent progress, as it most likely will. Your monthly checkup meetings with your baby's health care provider will reassure you that all is well.

Begin Planning Now

At the same time, this can be your period for planning—there is a lifetime of meals, snacks, and "nonfoods" ahead of you. This is a time when you can and should give some thought to the way you plan to feed your child in the all-important next few years of growth. What do you want your child to eat—and avoid? Who else will be feeding your child, and how will you handle controlling the food supply when you're not around? To what extent do you plan to use prepared foods? Homemade foods? Now is the time to look at the whole world of foods and think about which ones you want your child to learn to like. These are the foods you will introduce and emphasize in the next year and a half. They are the foods you should eat yourself whenever feasible—children learn by watching you. And they are the foods you will pack to send along with your child to the baby-sitter or ask your relative to feed the baby when you're not there.

Then there are the foods you *don't* want your child to eat. Here too you'll want to plan your strategy. There are some foods you might want to forbid altogether. Do it. Later on, when Jennifer or Jonathan is three, you may grit your teeth as soda and candy are demanded. But for right now, you are in absolute control. Make the most of it. This can include never having the forbidden foods around; making your preferences very clear—in a polite way—to any and all baby-sitters; and being cheerfully firm with those, including relatives, who think they know better than you what to feed your child. *No one* knows better than you.

In the last analysis, most people will recognize your right to raise your own child. They may secretly think your ideas are crazy, but they won't argue with you when they see your mind is made up. Sometimes the baby's grandparents can be especially gracious about letting you have your way. First of all, they know this is one child they aren't responsible for. In the second place, they've lived long enough to see how fashions change. They had their ideas about what foods were good and bad, and you have yours. It can be helpful—and also tactful—to back your preferences with expert opinions about nutrition, of course.

Nutrients: Carbohydrates, Proteins, and the Rest

Infants need large amounts of protein to grow, and they need carbohydrates to sustain their daily activity level. In the beginning they mostly grow. Their activity per se is limited largely to sleeping. In fact, they sleep all the time—except when they're eating or demanding to eat. Even that takes carbohydrates, of course. And they get their carbohydrates, protein, and vitamins and minerals from breast milk or formula.

As they grow, they begin to need more carbohydrates to sustain their greater activity level. That's where the solid foods come in. The cereals, vegetables, and fruits are high in complex carbohydrates that provide slow-burning energy and can be stored by the liver as glycogen for future use. These early foods are also the foods that are easiest to digest and least likely to cause allergy problems. Potential allergy problems are a major reason why pediatricians recommend that the high-protein foods be added last in introducing solid foods. The baby's intestinal tract is still somewhat immature and can tend to let undigested protein molecules slip through. These in turn have been connected with the creation of allergic reactions by the immune system. The milder carbohydrate foods are high in energy and contain vitamins and minerals that supplement and begin to replace those in the infant's breast milk for formula supply. Most of the baby's protein, meanwhile, is still coming from the easily digested breast milk or formula for the whole first year. There's no rush to introduce meats or dairy proteins—and perhaps allergies with them.

Your baby's health care provider may recommend a liquid vitamin supplement during the first year, and you may wish to consider it. Other than that, however, your baby's first nutritional needs will be met by breast milk or formula for protein, carbohydrates, vitamins and minerals; by grain foods (cereals) for carbohydrates and protein; and by vegetables and fruits for carbohydrate energy, vitamins, minerals, and bulk.

Making sure the baby gets a good supply of iron is a common concern among health care providers as the baby reaches six months, because the baby's own supply of iron, with which he or she was born, is generally considered to have been depleted at four to six months (although recent studies have indicated that babies who breast-feed get a break here, because the iron in mother's milk is especially well assimilated, so the baby can actually use more of it). The concern that babies get added iron at this age is one reason pediatricians almost universally recommend that the first solid food be a commercially prepared cereal: these cereals, besides being mild, are iron-fortified.

Introducing Solid Foods Step by Step

In Chapter Three I will go into more depth on the roles of the essential nutrients and how to see that your infant or toddler gets enough of them. For now, you should be concerned with giving your child the best possible introduction to solid foods.

Cereals

Among the three most common allergy-provoking foods is wheat. That's why your health care provider will not recommend wheat-based cereals as a first food. Remember, your baby's digestive system is maturing daily, and the longer he or she can go without encountering any allergens, the better your chances for an allergy-free child.

Rice is the most digestible, least allergenic grain and is usually the first cereal recommended. Most pediatricians will suggest you use the commercial brands, which today are marketed without sugar and salt in response to society's greater nutritional understanding about what's healthy for children. These cereals come with instructions for mixing the cereal with breast milk or formula for the essentially liquid consistency the baby expects at this point. Don't feed your baby pureed or liquefied solids from a bottle. Part of the eating experience an infant is ready for at this stage is a spoon, held by you. Also the unfamiliar consistency, presented in a bottle, could cause choking.

The next two nonallergenic cereals likely to be recommended are oatmeal and barley. Again, these are available commercially, and the commercial versions are quick and easy to prepare. Alternatives to commercial cereals are discussed later in this chapter.

Use the "week test" to introduce each of these cereals; if your family has a history of allergies, spend more time with each one. What you should look for with each new food is any instance of intestinal discomfort, constipation or diarrhea, rash, or major respiratory discomfort (excessive mucus, stuffiness, etc.). In all probability your baby won't have a problem with these first foods.

By the time you've gotten through the cereals, trying them one at a time, your baby will be almost a month older. Now you can move on to a new category of foods.

Vegetables and Fruits

Pediatricians sometimes suggest that you feed your baby vegetables before fruits to get the baby used to the vegetables, since the fruit taste is sweeter and presumably will be preferred (for more on why children like sweets, see Chapter Seven). Most experts suggest starting with the sweeter vegetables, which are sometimes referred to as the "yellow" vegetables. These include carrots, sweet potatoes, and winter squash. They should be cooked and pureed if you are making your own (for commercial food alternatives see "Alternatives" later in this chapter). Don't feed your baby raw vegetables of any kind at this point; the cellulose in them needs to be broken down by cooking so that an infant's digestive system can handle it.

After the yellow vegetables, the green vegetables are often recommended. By now, proceeding on a week-by-week basis, at least six weeks have elapsed since you started cereals with your baby, so the child is certainly more than six months old, if you started solids as early as four months, and may be almost eight months old. There are minor caveats about the green vegetables. Peas and beans, if not adequately pureed and strained, contain seed hulls that may be irritating. Large amounts of spinach and some other greens shouldn't be fed to your baby because of their high oxalic acid content, which interferes with absorption of calcium, so important for bones.

So you may want to skip the green vegetables for now, going right to fruits after the sweet or yellow vegetables, especially if it's summertime and hot. Mashed fresh bananas and avocados and cooked and blended apples and pears are mild and nonacidic first fruits. Avoid acid fruits, including citrus, berries, and peaches, until the age of a year.

Somewhere between six and eight months your baby will also become interested in self-feeding. This is no time for you to be squeamish about the condition of the dinner table. Put down some newspapers under the high chair and let the baby eat finger foods—small pieces of those foods you have already tried that are soft enough for the baby to "gum" or chew on with those first few teeth. Cubes of soft fruit or vegetables (cooked carrots or sweet potatoes are good) can keep your child occupied and intrigued while the rest of the family is having dinner. You may want to "administer" the other needed nutrients, such as cereal, beforehand or at another meal. If you have one of those really independent-minded souls who wants nothing to do with the spoon once she has discovered her fingers, that may be a sign that it's time to stop pureeing and add some finger foods as well.

Proteins

By the time you have explored vegetables and fruits, your baby is perhaps nine months old. At this age the proteins—eggs, poultry, and dairy foods—may begin to be introduced. Eggs should be fed to your baby without the whites first. Eggs, wheat, and dairy foods are the three most common allergy producers among foods, and egg whites appear to provoke allergic reactions more than the yolks. Some experts recommend avoiding introducing the whites until your baby is at least a year old for this reason. Again, there's really no rush, and avoiding allergies is a good reason to defer. Egg yolks are often recommended for their iron content. All eggs should be cooked; salmonella bacteria, which can be devastating to a baby's intestinal tract, are not uncommon in raw eggs.

As for dairy foods, cow's milk is a major allergy producer. It is also a good source of protein; you may want to consider using it in more digestible forms, like yogurt. If allergies are a concern, read more about dairy allergies in Chapter Four.

Most babies like cottage cheese and yogurt, and both of these forms of cow's milk are more digestible than the plain milk itself. Yogurt is almost a predigested food because of the acidophilus cultures in it. It can be commercial or homemade, but by all means use plain, not sweetened, unless you add your own unsugared fruit to it. This way you get your baby used to a taste that will come in very handy later when you're looking for wholesome snacks or even meals. It's a good food for filling out your child's daily protein needs, now *and* in the years ahead. Hard cheese is probably a little rich for a baby under a year, and you can supply your child with enough dairy food without it.

By ten months, your baby is no longer a bewildered novice in the food department. He knows what mealtime is about and wants to be part of it. His continuing growth and iron needs prompt most pediatricians to recommend meats, poultry, and fish at this time, if not before. By now the digestive system is more mature, and the risk of developing allergy is greatly reduced. So introduce the high-protein animal foods at this point unless you have a philosophical objection to them (see "Alternatives"). You can puree beef stew, which can include vegetables introduced earlier, or make Chicken Oatmeal Soup (see recipe in Part II) out of leftovers. Fish is soft enough to puree easily with leftover grains or vegetables, but you must go carefully through the cooked fish pieces you are using with your fingers to be sure there are no bones. Shellfish is usually put off until after age one because of allergies.

If you have a baby who has voted for finger foods, any protein that is soft enough—whether it's egg yolk or shreds of meat from a well-cooked stew—can be a finger food (but note the warning about hot dogs in "Food to Avoid"). People often mention that babies enjoy bologna at this point, because they can pick up the pieces and chew them, but you should know that processed meats contain a lot of additives, not the least of which is salt. Consider fish, egg yolks, cooked ground beef, and maybe even small shreds of meat or chicken instead.

Babies also really like the firm variety of tofu, which can be steamed to provide a fine, tasty high-protein dinner. Check it out as you would any other food, by giving it the "week test." If your baby tolerates it well, you know that good-quality soy products are fine. Uncooked tofu is not raw, by the way, but it can cause gas, so cooked is better. And speaking of finger foods, cottage cheese *is* a finger food, though you may not think so—as, you may discover, are applesauce, soup, yogurt, and so on. Look on the bright side. Your baby still has the uninhibited joy of eating. Spread more newspapers.

Alternatives

Among adults, alternatives to mainstream eating most often come from a desire to eat more natural, less processed foods or from a philosophy about eating such as vegetarianism or macrobiotics, or from a health need, such as a restricted diet. What alternatives are available if you don't want your baby to eat processed packaged foods or if at some point you want to steer your children away from the mainstream program of eating?

Here too, your choice doesn't have to be either/or, though it may be. You may, for example, choose to combine as much infant "home cooking" as you can with some prepared products. And you may make some choices based on health factors, some based on philosophy and others on the basis of both. Keep an open mind and be ready to try new things, and you'll get the widest possible range of healthful foods for your child to choose from when it gets to be the *child's* turn to name the alternatives.

Alternatives can begin at the earliest stage. If, for instance, you're not thrilled about packaged baby cereal, you may try First Rice Cereal (see recipe in Part II). It includes a macrobiotic ingredient readily found in health food stores that is rich in minerals and fortifies the cereal naturally with iron. After First Rice, you may move on to substitute oatmeal, barley or millet in the same recipe.

This brings us to the first, and perhaps most common, alternative to commercial baby foods—home cooking for infants.

Homemade Baby Food

If you're taking the home-cooked route, try the recipe mentioned above when the baby is still at the cereal stage.

Your next natural foods are the sweet vegetables; one family we know add onions here, cooking them with carrots for added flavor after the carrots have passed the "week test." Then come other vegetables and the fruits. You're following the conventional diet here but doing it yourself. Look for the signals discussed earlier that a food may not be acceptable to your baby's digestive system at this time. It's also wise to avoid foods that can cause gas or other intestinal discomfort even in adults (see "Foods to Avoid").

At first, cook and puree all your fruits and vegetables except avocados and bananas, which may be mashed raw. Later, pieces of cooked fruit or soft fruits may become finger foods.

Some families resist the home-cooking alternative because all that pureeing seems like a lot of work. It's true that it's not as quick initially as opening a jar. But with home-cooked foods you can save work by pureeing a batch of a vegetable and freezing it in serving-sized portions. Then your work is done for a week (or even a month), and you don't have the bother of running to the store because you're all out of baby food. So it's a trade-off. And don't forget, you can use both options: homemade foods at home, commercial foods for convenience on excursions. If your baby-sitter or other caregiver lives nearby, it may be practical to pop a couple of portions of your frozen home food into a plastic container to take along. Basically any food that you can buy you can also make. As with adult meals, freezing allows you to work ahead when you have time. But you may also want to stock the baby-sitter's shelves with a few jars or boxes of your preferred commercial brand. (One way of making sure people feed your baby what you want them to is to provide it.) There may also be hectic days at home when you're glad you can grab a jar of your baby's current favorite off the shelf.

HOME-COOKING TOOLS
AND TECHNIQUES

To puree early foods:
Use a blender to puree early foods, adding a little formula, breast milk or water to aid in pureeing. If you have any doubts about texture, dilute the puree again with a little liquid and reblend or force the puree through a sieve. Babies' first foods should be truly liquid, blended at the highest speed; the blending can produce progressively more grainy, less smooth textures a few weeks later, as the eating adventure proceeds. The hand-worked baby-food grinders are extremely handy for producing the grainier textures, but they don't grind food finely enough for the first solid foods.

To freeze pureed foods:
Freezing is easy—just use extra plastic ice trays for serving-sized portions of cooked fruit or vegetables, then pop them out, and store them in a bag in the freezer (see Almost-Instant Baby Food Cubes in Part II).

To serve homemade baby food:
Thaw frozen portions in the microwave or by adding a little hot water to the cubes and letting them sit. Always taste or touch your baby's food to be sure the temperature is okay (it should be just tepid) before serving.

After your baby progresses beyond pureed foods, you can freeze portions of finger foods, such as cubes of cooked vegetables, to avoid waste. But with finger foods you'll often be feeding your baby little bits of what you're eating, as long as it's not too rich or spicy. If your baby continues to enjoy pureed foods, use the infant food mill (see sidebar) to grind up whatever meal is handy. And after you've given up pureeing, by the way, don't discard that infant food mill. It will come in handy when your child is a toddler with enough manual dexterity to help prepare his own meals—great for producing interesting-looking mashed potatoes or "soup."

The Vegetarian Infant

If your family follows a strict vegetarian diet, you should consider very carefully your baby's growth needs. Babies really need large amounts of protein, and the most concentrated proteins are in animal foods. That, of course, doesn't mean you have to feed them meat, but at least you should consider the milk-and-eggs route, coupled with conscientious use of complementary proteins.

Other Alternatives

You probably have a specific reason for seeking food alternatives for your baby, but in a more general sense, feeding your baby the widest range of healthful foods gives you and the baby all the available alternatives for obtaining the essential nutrients. As mentioned earlier, you have an incredible range of food choices today. Explore all the possibilities—including palatable and nutritious foods of other cultures and dietary philosophies. Foods that might seem "exotic" to you can supplement your mainstream diet and provide health benefits for the whole family. You'll find a list of some choices worthy of consideration in Chapter Three.

Experiment, find what you're comfortable with, and let your baby's other caregivers know what the plan is. The first year or two of life is your planning and foundation time.

Foods to Avoid

Food for babies under a year old should be mild. This may mean, as mentioned, avoiding foods with tough fibers or hulls (like beans, corn, peas, and celery) unless these are strained. Acidic fruits and vegetables (citrus, tomatoes) also may produce indigestion; go easy on their juices too. And you may want to hold off on the cabbage family (including kale, collards, mustard greens, broccoli, Brussels sprouts, and cauliflower as well as head cabbage) and dried beans; these two food families often produce gas.

Then there's the safety factor with infants—avoiding anything in pieces of a size that could get stuck in the throat or windpipe—notably hot dog slices, nuts (including peanuts), and pieces of hard raw fruits and vegetables. Another safety warning concerns honey: it is generally ruled out for babies of less than one year because it has been known to produce botulism in their immature digestive systems. Use apple or pineapple juice as a sweetner instead.

The chief allergy producers—dairy, egg, and wheat products—have already been mentioned. Corn and shellfish are two others. Corn allergies are the reason that the better commercial baby foods no longer are made with corn syrup. Unless you have a prominent family history of allergies, you may be feeding your child yogurt, cottage cheese, egg yolk, and cooked pasta (wheat and sometimes egg) before age one. Just use common sense and don't overdo it.

Being a Smart Consumer

One last precaution is to be a wise consumer and read the labels. All your care will do little good if the foods you buy to feed your baby are loaded with food-starch filler, sugar, corn syrup, salt, or heavy fats. I never buy a new food product of any kind for anyone in my family without reading the label. It's a habit that will serve you well.

The consumer movement of the 1970s targeted baby foods, which then contained both sugar and salt. The food companies responded to the logic and force of consumer demand and moved to eliminate these ingredients, which consumer advocates had pointed out were not only unnecessary but actually bad for children.

Fortunately, we in the United States do have labeling laws that require ingredients to be listed in descending order: from the major ingredient to the least ingredient (although the laws do have some loopholes). Check the labels of all commercial foods to see whether the food you think you're buying is what you're really getting:

* If you're buying a jar of pureed carrots, make sure carrots *are* the major—and preferably *only*—ingredient (besides water).

* Make sure the product includes no added sugar or salt. There is absolutely no reason babies should get used to these tastes at a early age; you'll have enough trouble keeping them away from the chips and the cakes when they're six.

* Be certain that no artificial flavors or colors have been added. Don't buy anything with blanket labeling, such as "some artificial flavor and coloring added," if you can avoid it—you have no way of knowing exactly what the added flavor or color is.

* Avoid foods that contain a lot of saturated fat (this includes hydrogenated oils and coconut and palm oil as well as animal fat. Again, there's no reason to start the kids out on something that you already know is bad for them. Commercial baked goods more often than not do contain saturated fats, and you often can't be sure from the label whether they are animal fats or vegetable, or what kind of vegetable fat, except that it is hydrogenated (therefore saturated). Getting in the habit of avoiding saturated fats is an important goal for families with a history of heart disease and/or weight problems.

Reading labels may not be enough to make you a smart consumer, unfortunately. A recent baby-food scandal involving incorrectly labeled apple juice made that abundantly clear. And we have had other unpleasant experiences with learning that a food we use a lot is not as safe as we thought. Food companies typically respond, at least verbally, to consumer concern; but to some extent you can only do your best, be reasonably alert for any food recalls or other problems, and be aware of consumer news items. Good sources of information about food products include *Consumer Reports* and the general news media.

Also talk to other parents. When there was first a flap about the chemical daminozide (trade name Alar) used to treat apples (that mainstay of the baby juice department), for example, many parents switched to other fruit juices. As the news continued to develop, certain juice companies were reported as not using the chemical, and some apples were reported safer than others. We followed this news and passed it on to our friends. We bought the juices that were rated safest and hoped for the best. In the world we live in, chemical

---

HAZARDOUS CHEMICALS AND WHAT TO DO ABOUT THEM

Attention became focused on pesticides in the foods our children eat in the mid-1980s when it was first reported that a carcinogenic substance called daminozide (trade name Alar) was being used to control the ripening and color of apples. When processed for apple juice, the chemical converted to an even more deadly carcinogen known as UDMH. The U.S. Environmental Protection Agency, after intense lobbying by environmental groups and reports in the *New York Times,* the *Wall Street Journal,* and on *60 Minutes,* announced in March 1989 its intention to ban daminozide.

In the interim, companies including Mott's, Red Cheek, Tree Top, and Very Fine had voluntarily said they would refuse apples treated with daminozide for their products. But in its report in February 1989, *60 Minutes* reported that traces of the chemical had been found in apple products from all major manufacturers.

The daminozide controversy focused national attention on the question of chemicals and what to do about them. Some, like daminozide, are called systemic—in other words, once applied, they permeat the fruit or vegetable and cannot be washed off. Others, like a pesticide called banamid (used on bananas), cannot be detected by current lab testing methods. Others can at least be removed by very thorough washing.

Current recommendations on how to deal with the problem come from the National Resources Defense Council:

* In the case of apples, use Granny Smith apples (green when ripe, not treated with daminozide). If buying other apples, buy locally grown fruit from people you can ask about it and whom you trust; buy organic products if you can be sure they really are chemical-free, as the word "organic" implies.

* Wash all fruits and vegetables in a diluted solution of a soap you feel safe about. (You may want to buy your produce detergent or liquid soap from the health food store.)

* Peeling is the route to take with waxed fruits or vegetables, as opposed to washing. Remember that neither peeling nor washing will remove systemic chemicals.

* Domestic produce (grown in the U.S.) generally contains fewer chemical residues than imported produce. Ask your supermarket produce manager to display labels that show country of origin for all fruits and vegetables.

* Produce grown under the Integrated Pest Management system has been raised under alternative methods of pest control that keep chemical use to a minimum.

* Ask your supermarket to buy organic produce. Write to corporate headquarters (see Appendix A for some major chain addresses) to express your concern.

* Grow your own. (Ask your county agriculture agent what tests are available for local soil where you live.)

* For information on where to write the NRDC and other organizations, and how to order a book on pesticides *(For Our Kids' Sake)*, see Appendix A.

treatment of food is an increasing concern; some of it is reflected in labeling, and some isn't. More recent developments have made consumers more aware of the Alar controversy than we were at first—and given us more ideas of how to respond (see Hazardous Chemicals sidebar).

A recent development, in response to the baby boom generation's demand for good food for its children, is small natural-food companies that are dedicated to producing organic alternatives. Earth's Best in Middlebury, Vermont, is one of these. It advertises that its jars of foods contain no preservatives or synthetic additives. Earth's Best delivers through diaper services and can be reached at an 800 number. Growing Gourmet in Walnut Creek, California, is producing a line of frozen toddler entrees that can be microwaved. Growing Gourmet at present distributes to California and in New England. Given the size of the baby boom's boomlet, it seems likely more such services may be on the way (see Source List, Appendix A).

The Next Step

The next step after introducing first foods and trying to avoid potential health hazards is practice. Your baby is about a year old and growing fast. That means you have a potentially good eater on your hands. Make the most of it: this is your chance to learn as much as you can about nutrition and discover the many ways there are to get the proper nutrients into your baby's diet. It's easy, it can be an eating adventure for you too, and it is one way of making sure you lay a nutrition foundation that will really work for you and the kids.

THREE

Building on the Foundation: Making Nutrition Work for You

When Owen was around two, I remember asking our pediatrician, not without trepidation, about food. It seemed we ate the same foods over and over again, and I was worried about whether our son was getting enough protein in the negligible bites that went into his mouth. "Does he eat mashed potatoes?" the doctor asked. Yes, I said. "Spaghetti?" Yes. "Cereal?" Yes. "Peanut butter sandwiches?" Yes. The doctor, our sane, well-educated pediatrician who is never at a loss for the most up-to-the-minute answer to any question, simply shrugged. Owen was on his height/weight curve. He was eating the things two-year-olds eat. We could feed him a vitamin supplement if that would make us feel better. We would all survive.

No matter what you do, the terrible twos will come. They may bring some trying times at the table. Just remember, tastes change. Children test their parents. The two-year-old is often likened to an adolescent. Be cool.

In the meantime, there is something you can do. At age one, you still have some months, maybe even a year, of grace. It's to your advantage to establish as many good eating habits as you can, drawn from as wide a background as possible. This means looking around outside your own eating style. Experiment with foods you may not have tried. Find out what other people are doing. Learn a little about how other cultures eat and what's good about those choices.

We were lucky when it came to establishing our sources of food, especially in light of the amount of taste-testing our son did. We were lucky because we had looked at the nutritional elements of a lot of foods that are not exactly what you would find in your local pizza parlor or fast-food franchise. I almost hesitate to mention macrobiotics in this context because I think a lot of people think it too esoteric or difficult to master or that it is a diet that is too restrictive to be useful to the average American family. There are, however, some really valuable foods and techniques that are common in other cultures of the world, but not in our own, and macrobiotics is a good *example* of such a system. I'm certainly not suggesting that you switch wholesale to another cuisine at this point in your life—or your child's. What I am suggesting is that you *borrow* from other cultures for good sources of protein, calcium, iron, and low-fat, high-carbohydrate energy sources. Macrobiotics, Middle Eastern, Hindu, and South American cooking—these may seem like exotic sources to consider when we are talking about feeding a one-year-old, but stay tuned.

The point, again, is alternatives—with a purpose. The purpose is to get your children to eat as many good-tasting, healthy foods as you can *while their tastes are still being formed*. I cross my fingers as I say this; Owen still drinks amasake, the naturally sweet rice-based drink I introduced as "milk shake" when he was one-and-a-half. Amasake contains no dairy food, no fillers, no chemicals, preservatives, sugar, or other sweeteners—just the naturally sweet rice, cultured in a way somewhat similar to yogurt preparation, making it a treat that's really a meal for young children—a liquid cereal. Older kids and grownups will love it too, with meals, for dessert, or as a sugar-free snack.

According to the prestigious Gesell Institute of Child Development, children of twelve to fifteen months eat three meals a day, although at twelve months they may be developing their gross motor skills so rapidly that they'll want to stand up to eat. They are still hearty eaters; at fifteen months they may drive you crazy with their determination to feed themselves and in the process spangle the kitchen and their faces with mashed bananas. But at eighteen to twenty months, "the robust infant appetite may already be decreasing, and the child does not necessarily eat three 'good' meals a day. The eighteen-month-old is still . . . rather accepting of the type of food that is offered [although he/she] may not consume as much as you think he should." By twenty-two months, the institute warns, food preferences may become "extremely strong and should be respected" (Gesell Institute, *Your One Year Old,* p. 55).

So, this is your chance to become educated in the nutrition basics you are going to carry with you. It's your time to learn where the nutritional goods are so that you can proceed to feed with confidence and pleasure as your child grows. Learn the basics, experiment with as many good foods as you reasonably can, and use this time to good advantage to make your child as good an eater as possible.

This chapter discusses "how to make nutrition work for you" by presenting you with alternatives in two senses: "sources" and "standbys." The source foods are the foods you will introduce into your child's diet—and perhaps into yours—because they are excellent, easy ways to get a day's supply of calcium, vitamin A, or some other nutrient and because *your child will like them.* In other words, they are the specific nutritious foods themselves. An example is carrots, an excellent source of vitamin A. The "standbys" are foods or ways of presenting foods that can fill a gap when your child suddenly decides he no longer cares for ground beef, milk, apples, liver, brussels sprouts, or some other source food.

Here's an example: At one point in Owen's third winter I was worried that he wasn't getting enough minerals and vitamins. After a little thought, I concluded that carrots would be the best strategy. But how could I get enough of them into his rather small stomach, and without making him tired of them? The solution was a juicer. We happened to have one, a fairly heavy-duty one. Every evening I juiced a bunch of carrots, together with apples for sweetness, and we all drank our "special juice" (a cup for us, half a cup for Owen). The pulp didn't go to waste, because we used it in muffins, which Owen was learning to help make (see Chapter Five for more on kids in the kitchen). That carrot juice became our standby for vitamin A. A juicer, by the way, is not a bad tool to have around. The fresh fruit and vegetable juices are a good source of vitamins, minerals, and the clean water your body needs to cleanse itself at the cell level to stay healthy. (Why don't these children ever decide they're not eating potato chips?) For instance, the apple-carrot juice essentially provided everything the apples and carrots had to offer (except their fiber, of course) but in concentrated form. If I wanted to, with the juice, I could feed my child the equivalent of half a pound of carrots at dinner, and forget about vitamin A for a week (yes, that's right—remember, vitamin A is a fat-soluble vitamin, which means it is stored in your body and not lost in sweat or urine; so whatever you absorb stays with you). The fiber he'd eventually get in a moist, delicious Apple-Carrot-Bran Muffin.* For another example, suppose you don't see how your child can possibly be getting enough iron. The most concentrated iron source is red meat (especially organ meats like liver), which she/he never eats. It helps to know where else the iron is: eggs, apricots, sweet potatoes, peas and beans, lentils, green leafy vegetables. You can then program your meals to include: eggs as eggs or in pancakes and french toast, or in potato salad; sweet potatoes baked or in a pie; apricot nectar; leafy greens in salad, soup, spanikopita, or Soufflé-stuffed Peppers;* peas, lentils, and beans in soup, including Miso Soup* (see New Ingredients box), which with its rich soy paste base is also a good protein source. When you know that your child only needs between 10 and 15 mg. of iron a day, you quickly see that just a few of these sources give you that. A helping of tofu (soybean curd, so it's a bean source) gives you 1.9 mg. A sweet potato would give you 1 mg. An egg would

*See recipes in Part II.

be between 2 and 3, and a slice of spanikopita might offer 5. If your child doesn't have a weight problem, he might also snack on unsalted pumpkin and sunflower seeds, also good iron sources. Traditionally, nutritionists caution that iron is best absorbed from red meats, but recent studies have also shown a good rate of iron absorption among vegetarians. For more information see box on Getting Enough Iron. So you see, we can do ourselves and our children a favor by expanding our nutrition IQs even slightly, for the key ingredients that we worry about are not many, and it's easy to learn them. And it gives you such peace of mind to know that there's more than one way to feed a kid.

For source foods, the two key pieces of the puzzle are the nutrients children need most and the amounts they need. Knowing the RDAs of certain key nutrients for your child's age is a good place to start. The major nutrients of concern for children include protein, vitamins A, B, C, D, and E, and the minerals iron and calcium.

Beyond the key nutrients and their RDAs, it helps to know that some nutrients must be present in balances so that the body can absorb or use them optimally. Examples are calcium and magnesium, sodium and potassium, calcium and phosphorus, and the amino acids with each other, as we'll discuss shortly. It's also useful to know which foods can inhibit absorption of vital nutrients.

Getting enough calories is not a concern for most children in our culture, so the energy supply is there. Still, there is an alarming incidence of malnutrition among American children, and that results largely from the consumption of empty-calorie junk food—food that contains plenty of calories but few nutrients. So, it's important to aim for complex carbohydrates.

Once you understand which nutrients are needed by your child, it's not difficult to learn which source foods provide them; the following pages summarize some of the best choices, including many you will already be aware of and some that may be new to you. The more source foods you become familiar with, the greater your list of available standbys will become. If the kids won't eat one source of iron for their RDA, you will know there are a bunch of others. By knowing the familiar source foods for the key nutrients (the way everybody knows that there's iron in liver) and *then* knowing how to take a leaf or two from other cultures, you multiply the number of nutrient sources available—and that in turn increases your options for feeding your family well.

Nutrients of Major Concern

Protein, calcium, iron, and vitamins A, B, and C are probably the nutrients we worry most about for our children, though they are not the whole story. Even if your child is already past the magic age where he'll eat just about anything, read on. The more you know about where the good nutrients are "buried," the calmer you'll be about what the kids eat. And that will probably make them eat better.

Proteins

By now probably everyone knows about meat versus nonmeat protein sources, but a review can be helpful. The standard protein food for our culture for decades was red meat, but since the early eighties the emphasis has shifted because of the high fat content of red meats. Consumers have caused a boom in the chicken and fish industries; one major meat-packing company even bought up catfish farms while other meat packers were going out of business.

The point, of course, was the warning from the NIH and other researchers about too much fat and cholesterol in our diets. Much of the fat that is marbled through even the leanest meats can't be removed; it's *in* the meat. Chicken, on the other hand, has a layer of subcutaneous fat; much of the fat in chicken can be removed by taking off the skin. The fat in fish, in the form of monounsaturated oils, is actually good for us, according to recent information (although fat in any animal is always the collection point for toxins the animal has ingested; that includes us and the fish we eat—if the fish contains PCBs, they will be in the fat).

I always think it's odd that people will go to great pains to drink skim milk, and have their children drink it, when an 8-ounce glass of *whole* milk actually contains only one-tenth the saturated fat of a 4-

Recommended Dietary Allowances

	Age	Weight Kg	lbs	Height cm	in	Energy* (calories)	Protein (grams)	FAT-SOLUBLE VITAMINS Vitamin A (RE)	(IU)	Vit D (IU)	Vit E (IU)
Infants	0–6 months	6	13	60	24	Kg × 117	Kg × 2.2	420	1,400	400	3
	6–12 months	9	20	71	28	Kg × 108	Kg × 2.0	400	2,000	400	4
Children	1–3 years	13	29	90	35	1,300	23	400	2,000	400	5
	4–6 years	20	44	112	44	1,800	30	500	2,500	400	6
	7–10 years	28	62	132	52	2,400	34	700	3,300	400	7
Males	11–14 years	45	99	157	62	2,800	45	1,000	5,000	400	8
	15–18 years	66	145	176	69	3,000	56	1,000	5,000	400	10
	19–22 years	70	154	177	70	3,000	56	1,000	5,000	400	10
Females	11–14 years	46	101	157	62	2,400	46	800	4,000	400	8
	15–18 years	55	120	163	64	2,100	46	800	4,000	400	8
	19–22 years	55	120	163	64	2,100	44	800	4,000	400	8
Mothers	pregnant					2,400–2,500	46–48 +30	1,000	5,000	400	10
	lactating					2,500–2,600	46–48 +20	1,200	6,000	400	11

	WATER-SOLUBLE VITAMINS						MINERALS					
(Ascorbic Acid) Vit. C (mg)	(Folic Acid) Fola- cin (mcg)	Vit B Niacin (mg)	Vit B Ribo- flavin (mg)	Vit B Thiamin (mg)	Vit B Vit B$_6$ (mg)	Vit B Vit B$_{12}$ (mcg)	Calcium (mg)	Phos- phorus (mg)	Iodine (mcg)	Iron (mg)	Magne- sium (mg)	Zinc (mg)
35	30	6	0.4	0.3	0.3	0.5	360	240	35	10	60	3
35	45	8	0.6	0.4	0.4	1.5	540	400	45	15	70	5
45	100	9	0.8	0.6	0.6	2.0	800	800	60	15	150	10
45	200	11	1.0	0.9	0.9	2.5	800	800	80	10	200	10
45	300	16	1.4	1.2	1.2	3.0	800	800	110	10	250	10
50	400	18	1.6	1.6	1.6	3.0	1,200	1,200	130	18	350	15
60	400	18	1.7	2.0	2.0	3.0	1,200	1,200	150	18	400	15
60	400	19	1.7	2.0	2.0	3.0	800	800	140	10	350	15
50	400	15	1.3	1.2	1.6	3.0	1,200	1,200	115	18	300	15
60	400	14	1.3	1.1	2.0	3.0	1,200	800	115	18	300	15
60	400	14	1.3	1.1	2.0	3.0	800	800	100	18	300	15
80	800	15–16	1.6–1.7	1.4	2.5	4.0	1,200	1,200	175	18 +	450	20
100	500	18–19	1.8–1.9	1.4	2.5	4.0	1,200	1,200	200	18	450	25

RE = retinol equivalents   IU = International units   mg = milligrams
mcg = micrograms
*based on RESTING metabolic rates
from *Recommended Dietary Allowances, 9th ed.* 1980 National Academy of Sciences—
National Research Council (10th ed. scheduled for release in Summer 1989.)

ounce piece of steak (and also contains a better ratio of protein for small children, for whom the relatively higher protein content of skim milk can put a strain on the kidneys). A 4-ounce piece of tofu, of course, compares even more favorably in the fat-vs.-protein sweepstakes, but let's not get ahead of ourselves. The point is, again, there are many ways to get adequate nutrition, and that includes protein sources. More to the point about meats is that children often don't seem to like them very much, especially young children. And that may make you worry about whether they're getting enough protein.

Let's look at the statistics. The protein RDA for children aged one to three is 23 grams. It goes up by 5 to 10 grams about every three years to a top level of 56 for adult males (age eighteen) and 46 for adult females. So, from what foods can we get these 23 grams? Consider the alternatives. The first rank of alternatives is the other animal foods, because they give you complete protein, i.e., protein with all the amino acids in a balanced form so the body can use them. Here we have eggs, milk, cheese, yogurt, and ice cream; also any baked products, puddings, soups, salads, etc., that *contain* eggs and dairy products. Don't neglect to tally these when you look for your sources. Of course anything with a lot of sugar in it, such as ice cream, commercial pudding, and presweetened yogurt, is not the best source and shouldn't be your only source. But overall, the grams do add up. If, somewhere in the course of a day, your child eats an egg (french toast? pancakes?) and a container of yogurt, that's already 11 protein grams, almost half the RDA. Add a cup of milk, and you're up to almost 20. Add a slice of banana bread, and you've got 23. That was relatively easy, and it was accomplished without meats and even without the powerful complex carbohydrate protein sources, whole grains and beans.

This is just one example among many possibilities. You might not want to lean on dairy foods as heavily as this example does, such as in the case of allergies. The point is that the RDA for a nutrient such as protein can add up more quickly and easily than you might have thought.

Now look at the potential of grains and legumes (peas and beans).

Taken separately, grains and legumes are incomplete; together they are complementary proteins; that is, grain or seed plus legume equals total protein. Protein Pancakes (see recipe in Part II) will give you complete protein in the form of soy flour (the soybean is a legume) mixed with wheat flour (the grain). If your child eats two pancakes, he or she could be getting 10 grams of protein. Add a quarter cup of split pea soup and a slice of bread, and you have another 6 grams. A peanut butter sandwich would be around 6 to 8 grams of protein. That puts the child's intake at 22 to 24 grams. And there are countless other alternatives: a handful of sunflower or pumpkin seeds for 6 grams; small slice of tofu and 3 tablespoons of cooked brown rice with soy sauce for 8. So, on a given day, even if you avoid dairy foods *and* meats altogether, you child could still get the 23-gram RDA without exploring all the available options.

Considering the meats option, 3 ounces of lean beef will provide 17 grams; the same amount of fish, 16 to 20 grams; the same amount of chicken breast, 24. So, if you can get your child to eat 3 ounces of chicken in a day, your problem will be solved right there. Then again, 3 ounces of anything looks like a lot to many two-year-olds, so you'll probably find the grains and legumes a boon to your quest for low-fat protein.

Don't forget these grain and legume protein sources:

• all nuts

• all soy products, including miso (discussed below)

• any bread or cereal

• peanuts, chick-peas, azuki beans, and lentils, as well as the more familiar beans

• all seeds, including sunflower and sesame

• barley, buckwheat, and bulgur wheat, as well as the more familiar grains.

Here are a few other protein source foods you may not be in the habit of using but should investigate: There's a protein source called *amaranth* that is now being grown experimentally. Amaranth was a grain used by the Aztecs; it contains protein that vies with soybeans and milk in quality and is available in cereal form in health food stores. Unfortunately, I must admit that I had some and didn't find it very interesting—but I'm sure someone is working on a better version. Meanwhile, you can mix it with other things. If you have a Greek market handy, you may be able to purchase amaranth's spinachlike leaves in a form called *vleeta.*

Speaking of mixing, don't forget nutritional yeast (available in health food stores). Sneak a teaspoon of it into your child's food, and you add a protein gram or two. The best way to introduce it is to add a tablespoon or so to any hearty soup your family will eat. If it passes undetected, add some more.

Miso works in a similar way. This soy paste (easily found in many supermarkets as well as in health food stores and Japanese markets) can go in any hearty soup or be made into a soup of its own. It is worth mentioning separately because babies definitely like it, and the noodles that go into Basic Miso Soup (see recipe in Part II) make it a complete protein (noodles for the grain, plus miso for the legume). Also, like yogurt, it's a cultured food, and that makes it very digestible. It's a good thing to start children on at an early age.

Miso paste *is* very high in sodium, an objection people often raise to soy sauce, also called "tamari" (the name used in health food stores for naturally fermented soy sauce). But these two soy foods are very concentrated, which means you won't be using them undiluted. Their sodium content will be much lower when spread across a bowl of soup or another dish. Therefore, the sodium content of the basic paste or sauce should not be an issue.

Iron

Earlier I mentioned iron as an example of how to expand your "nutrition IQ" beyond the most familiar source foods. In addition to meats, rich sources of iron include apricots, leafy green vegetables, sweet potatoes, darker meats of chicken and fish, nuts and seeds, beans, dried peas and lentils, beets, and seaweeds (more about seaweeds below).

In addition, cooking in iron pots adds dietary iron, so make that spaghetti sauce in an old cast-iron skillet or kettle or buy a new one and season it.

GETTING ENOUGH IRON

There are two types of iron in dietary sources: heme and nonheme. Heme iron is found in meat, and up to 25 percent of it can be absorbed; nonheme iron, found in grains, fruits and vegetables, is believed to be absorbed at a rate of about 5 percent. Ferric iron is the most common nonheme form in plant sources, and it is bound up by fiber and by compounds called phytates and polyphenols, thus reducing its absorption from plant sources by the human body.

But medical studies reported in *Vegetarian Times* (April 1989) show that vegetarians actually often get more iron than nonvegetarians, in spite of the fact that they don't eat meat. That's because, according to two studies reported in *VT,* they "consume higher levels of iron and other minerals than non-vegetarians, thereby compensating for any absorption inhib-itors in their diets." One factor that helps when the major sources of iron and fruit and vegetables is vitamin C. Vitamin C (absorbic acid) and other acids in fruits and vegetables aid iron absorption; so when you eat those sources (broccoli and other greens of the cabbage family, for example, are high in iron but also in vitamin C), you absorb more of the available iron.

Other research suggested that fermented soy foods con-tained much more bioavailable iron than nonfermented soy foods (phytates and other inhibitors are high in soybeans per se). So the miso soup and the tamari soy sauce are sources to use.

Excess iron can be toxic; iron poisoning, according to *VT,* is most commonly reported in children under 5. So keep iron supplements out of children's reach, and don't use them for children without your pediatrician's advice.

Some tips on iron and iron absorption:

• Since the form of iron contained in greens is sometimes absorbed incompletely by the body, eat those nonanimal (or nonheme iron) sources with an animal (heme iron) source to increase absorption.

• In breads and cereals, look for fortified products that list iron on the label.

• Chocolate, like tea and coffee, contains substances that prevent iron absorption, so keep it away from your iron-rich meals.

• Remember that foods high in vitamin C enhance the body's absorption of iron.

• Although red meats are often labeled the best source of iron, poultry and seafood contain it, too. Dark meat of poultry is higher in iron than white.

• Cooking in iron skillets or other pots is a traditional way of getting extra iron.

• Calcium and phosphorus inhibit iron absorption even more than phytates, according to *VT;* so if you want the kids to get their iron, don't serve iron sources and dairy products at the same time.

• Excess consumption of sugar reduces copper levels in the body, and copper deficiency decreases iron utilization in the body, and can in fact lead to anemia.

Children between the ages of one and six have among the highest needs for iron, second only to teenagers. A quarter pound—4 ounces—of calf liver provides 10 milligrams (the RDA for children

4–10 years old) of iron, and that's why it's the cliché source of this mineral. But how often are you going to get your three-year-old to eat 4 ounces of calf liver and meet the RDA in one swoop? (As the cow grows, by the way, the liver takes a nutritional nosedive; a pound of beef liver has only 6 milligrams, but note that a pound of chicken livers has 36.) Get your child to nibble away at the RDA, though, and it will be reached with ease. A quarter cup of pumpkin seeds has 4 milligrams, an egg perhaps 3, a cup of raisins or prunes perhaps 6, a cup of prune *juice* 10. Even a cup of apple juice, which the average child well may drink in a day, has 1.5. Breads and cereals also contain iron, and the cereal manufacturer will often conveniently give you a serving-sized nutritional breakdown on the package—although again, anything packaged with a lot of sugar may not get full absorption in the digestive system.

Now to seaweed. It's certainly at the opposite end of the spectrum from raisins and nuts—you aren't going to get the children to scarf seaweed down by the handful. But seaweeds are very rich in minerals, and they are sold dried in health food stores so that they are no problem to store. Of course they may be eaten plain, though this is an acquired taste. More to the point, they can go into soups, where they will disintegrate quietly or blend in with other ingredients. See the "New Ingredients" sidebar for information on how to incorporate these foreigners (to our culture) into your cooking. Rich in iron are agar-agar (or kanten); arame; hijiki; nori, used in sushi; and wakame, a mild-flavored seaweed.

Calcium

Yes, milk is our number one source of calcium, but it's not the only one. And if you are trying to avoid excess dairy food, what *do* you do to get those 500 to 800 milligrams a day into your child's meals?

First of all, the benchmark: a cup of whole milk has 291 milligrams, a cup of skim 302. Low-fat yogurt provides 415, skim-milk yogurt 450. So two containers of plain yogurt a day will certainly solve this problem, if your child will eat them. (Don't forget, by the way, that if you don't mind using dairy products, digestible yogurt can be added to soups, milk shakes, salad dressings, baked goods, and more.)

Then there are the leafy greens, traditionally touted for their calcium content. True, they have it, but the absorption of calcium from greens is a matter of some controversy owing to the presence in greens of those natural chemical compounds called *phytates*. Various kinds of greens provide as much as 200 milligrams of calcium per cup, cooked. We all know, however, that most kids just aren't going to eat a cup of collards, cooked or raw. So, what to do?

For one thing, let us now praise the sesame seed. A half cup provide almost 1,200 milligrams of calcium. No way, you say? Not a half cup on any day, let alone every day? Take heart: the sesame seed is an incredibly versatile little character:

- It goes into sesame butter—mix it half and half with peanut butter.

- It's the principal ingredient in tahini—spread it on a cracker or make Sesame Chick-pea Spread (see recipe in Part II) with it.

- It's in Gomasio, a sesame seed-salt condiment that is much better for your family than plain salt (see recipe in Part II).

- It can be added to granola, cookies, cooked oatmeal, and salads.

- And it is ideal as a simple, tasty condiment. Keep a jar of toasted sesame seeds in your kitchen and sprinkle them on cereals, salads, sandwiches, soups, and just about anything else (but see caveat below).

Caveat: Calcium is no good if you can't absorb it, and you can't absorb it unless it's in the proper balance with phosphorus. Meats happen to be very high in phosphorus, so if you are eating calcium-rich foods and meat at the same time, the phosphorus in the meat will block absorption of much of the calcium. In fact, one nutritionist who was discussing this with me said that if he were giving people advice about how to get enough calcium, he wouldn't begin by telling them to drink a quart of milk a day. His first recommendation would be to avoid eating meat and calcium foods at the same meal. Only then would he discuss specific sources of calcium. So, don't add sesame seeds to your meat loaf.

Calcium is best absorbed when the ratio of calcium to phosphorus is one to one or more (more calcium per unit of phosphorus). In milk the ratio is roughly one to one, with calcium slightly ahead. In tofu the ratio is one to one. In leafy greens, the ratio is often three to one. In sesame seeds it's two to one. In meats the phosphorus outstrips the calcium by fifteen to one and more.

Tofu is a reasonably good source of calcium; a 4-ounce serving provides 140 milligrams. Two other sources are also worth considering: seaweed and bones. The seaweeds are generally mineral-rich, and all of them are good calcium sources. Kombu and agar-agar (see "New Ingredients" sidebar) are especially easy to use, and both are good sources of calcium; the kombu goes into soups, where it actually helps make bean and pea soups more digestible, and agar-agar helps desserts to jell. As for bones, sardines and herring (with the bones still in, but soft) are great calcium sources if you can get your child to eat them. Another trick is to make soup stocks with bones: Fish bones give up their calcium fairly easy. Dr. Lendon Smith suggests adding vinegar to animal bones in a stockpot to draw out the calcium. You can also throw eggshells into the stock for added calcium, provided you strain the stock before you go on to make the soup.

Vitamin A

"Eat your spinach!" is the parents' weary battle cry. But why? What do green vegetables, which kids so often seem to hate, offer? Vitamins, minerals, fiber, and water. The fiber they'll also get from bread and cereal; the liquid, vitamins, and minerals they can just as easily get elsewhere too. We've already seen how this is true with calcium and iron. It's true with the vitamins too. Vitamin A is well-known for its presence in the leafy greens (2,500 to 3,800 international units in a quarter cup of cooked greens, when the RDA is

2,000 for toddlers—the rest will be stored, remember). But it's also found in carrots (11,000 IUs in one large), pumpkin and sweet potato (about 4,000 in one cooked), tomatoes (1,300 in one medium), egg (600–700 in one cooked), milk (500 in one cup), ice cream (about 250 per serving), and liver (as high as 25,000 IUs per quarter pound of calf liver). Like other fat-soluble vitamins, vitamin A can be toxic in excessive amounts, but it must be ingested in amounts considerably larger than the RDA before it becomes a problem (so yes, it is okay to have liver and ice cream too). It would seem in the case of this vitamin that there are so many sources that there shouldn't be any fear of deficiency in our culture. But in fact the body can't absorb all of the vitamin A that comes to it from vegetables: it typically manages to convert about one-third of the vitamin-A precursor carotene from root vegetables, and about half the carotene from green vegetables. The need for vitamin A increases when there is pollution (including cigarette smoke) in the environment; it also may increase when the body is fighting an infection. Vitamin A helps build bones and blood, and maintain good eyesight, good digestion, and healthy mucous membranes. A daily dose of 18,000 IUs-plus, on a steady basis, can be toxic for infants. Again, it's *very* unlikely you'd ever get that much from foods; I just mention it as a caution to keep vitamin A supplements out of children's reach.

Vitamin A, like D and E, is fat soluble, which means that it is stored in the fat of our bodies and that if we take in an excess amount on one day, it doesn't just wash through our systems as B and C vitamins do.

Being fat soluble also means that some animal fats are a good source of the vitamin, including butter and of course cod liver oil (11,900 IUs in a tablespoonful).

B Vitamins

The B vitamins include thiamine (B_1), riboflavin (B_2), pyridoxine (B_6), B_{12}, niacin, folic acid, PABA (para-aminobenzoic acid), and pantothenic acid. The B vitamins are water-soluble, meaning they cannot be stored by the body, so adequate amounts must be provided—ideally, daily. The B complex functions in an interdependent way; getting excess amounts of one B vitamin (as in individual supplements) can interfere with the absorption of others. Stress increases the need for B vitamins, and children need them for growth. The B vitamins facilitate metabolism of proteins, carbohydrates, and fats and keep the nerves healthy.

The complex as a whole is found in liver, whole-grain cereals (including breads and the grains themselves), and nutritional yeast. These may not seem like very many sources, but the B vitamins are also produced in the intestinal tract when it is healthy. The intestinal bacteria are fed by milk sugar, and cultured foods like the soy products miso and tamari soy sauce are beneficial.

Because there are so many Bs, and because the RDAs are often in tenths of milligrams or even micrograms, it's not easy to pinpoint the exact point where the RDA is reached. A deficiency of riboflavin, or vitamin B_2, is said to be the most common dietary deficiency in the United States, for instance (Kirschmann, *Nutrition Almanac*, p. 24), indicating that we can't afford to be smug about these vitamins. This is the perfect example of why eating a wide variety of good foods is a kind of nutritional insurance policy. That way, if the kids won't eat liver, at least you know they are getting their B vitamins when you give them amasake (cultured rice drink), Cheerios, whole-wheat bread, miso soup, fortified pasta, and that tablespoon of yeast that was lurking in the minestrone. Just keep the source foods coming. Like chicken soup, it can't hurt.

Vitamin C

Water-soluble vitamin C has gotten so much publicity that we all probably know more about what it is, what it does, and where it comes from than about the other vitamins. Some of the sources you might think of less often than citrus fruits are cantaloupe, strawberries, the cabbage family, tomatoes, and peppers—there's even a traditional cold remedy that consists of brewing hot peppers, garlic, and honey together. As noxious as that sounds, it really works, but you may find in the short run that a bottle of vitamin C drops is easier to live with. (By the way, you can use cayenne or hot pepper sparingly in recipes for children as young as a year, and older children seem to like it a lot; but don't give it to babies. Sometimes even the smell of it cooking will set them crying because it burns their nose and throat.)

Once Owen got past infancy, the only vitamins I kept in the house were the liquid vitamin C drops. They come out at the first sign of cold symptoms or sometimes even of gray skies in winter. The drops are easy to administer. The established RDA for vitamin C for children aged one to ten is around 40 milligrams. Of course we all know people who take thousands of milligrams daily for colds, even though this is not completely noncontroversial.

According to Dr. Brian Morgan of the Institute of Human Nutrition at Columbia University, studies have shown that too much vitamin C (for adults, more than 200 milligrams a day, according to the studies) can impair the functioning of the immune system. He adds that while vitamin C has not been shown to reduce the number of colds a person may contract, it does reduce symptoms by as much as one-third. Dr. Morgan points out that a safe ceiling level of vitamin C has not been established for children. I would recommend liquid vitamin C drops, available from the health food store, to be used at the recommended dosage for both healthy and sick children.

As for the food route, some data: a half cup of most kinds of berries or a slice of most medium melons will provide 10 to 15 milligrams of vitamin C. A half cup of grapefruit juice has 48. A quarter cup of coleslaw (cabbage) has about 8. A quarter cup of cooked kale (cabbage family) has 26, and so has a quarter cup of sliced green peppers. A cup of orange juice has 46.

Other Nutrients

Other nutrients, including vitamins D and E and the trace minerals, are of major importance but do not really need to be scrutinized if you are paying attention to the source foods for all the nutrients discussed above. If your child is eating the foods that contain those nutrients, he or she is quite likely to be getting these additional nutrients as part of the bargain. For example, vitamin D is present in fortified milk (and via sunshine, which activates oil in the skin to produce it). Vitamin E is present in grains and grain oils. The trace minerals follow along where the major minerals exist: in seeds, in seaweeds, in greens, and in yeast. A few additional notes follow.

Vitamin D

This vitamin is produced more readily in the skins of lighter-skinned people in northern climates. A darker-skinned person in a northern climate in winter should have an additional source. If milk isn't tolerated, cod liver oil will serve as a standby. Vitamin D aids calcium absorption. It is fat-soluble, can be stored, and can be toxic in megadoses (a megadose would only occur from misusing a vitamin supplement).

Vitamin E

Vitamin E helps prevent harmful oxidation in the body whereby toxins are released. It has been associated with cancer prevention. To protect vitamin E in food sources, it's important to keep oils and flours from becoming rancid. Storage in a cool place is the key. Good-quality vegetable and nut oils provide vitamin E. Extra-virgin olive oil is a possible supermarket source of vitamin E. Most other supermarket oils are overprocessed. Cold-pressed oils (available in health food stores and some supermarkets) are preferable for salads, cooking, baking, and other uses. Vitamin E is fat-soluble.

Mineral Balances

The importance of the calcium-phosphorus balance has already been mentioned. Other crucial balances include calcium-magnesium and potassium-sodium. The calcium-magnesium ratio should be two to one; magnesium will be supplied in adequate amounts if nuts, greens, soy products, corn, and apples are in the diet. The potassium-sodium balance should be 5,000 milligrams of potassium per 2,100 milligrams of sodium (the amount in a teaspoon of salt). There is no formal RDA for sodium, but a suggested one has been 1,100 milligrans daily (*half* a teaspoon) for *adults*. Americans ingest up to nine times that amount daily. This is a reason to avoid soft drinks, which may contain sodium not shown on the label, when feeding the kids. Don't let them get that habit; diet sodas are often especially sodium-rich. Instead, if they crave fizz, make them sodas out of sodium-free seltzer and fruit juice. As for potassium, it's hard to imagine a toddler not getting plenty, since most of them love bananas. Oranges, potatoes, greens, grains, and seeds are other good sources.

Looking Ahead

At this point it's wise to consider the longer view in getting your children acquainted with these source foods. They may not always be willing to eat all of them, but if you provide enough options you can hope at least that you have covered the bases. Over the long haul these foods can help inhibit or prevent the degenerative diseases that are the real killers of our society. The links between foods and health are becoming clearer as research uncovers connections like the ones between beta-carotene (vitamin A), vitamin C, and vitamin E and cancer prevention; oat bran and heart disease prevention; fiber and lowered cholesterol—the list goes on and on. With a notion of what your child's RDAs are, what the source foods for them are, and what foods can stand in for others, you are well equipped to deal with your child's food preferences and a diet for a lifetime.

NEW INGREDIENTS

What exactly are the contents and uses of such ingredients as agar-agar, kombu, tahini, and kuzu? Herewith a little glossary of foods that may be unfamiliar. Some have been discussed in this chapter; others will occur in Part II, the recipe section, and in our discussion of allergies and other health problems (Chapter Four).

Amaranth and quinoa: Two grains that were grown in ancient Central and South America; good sources of protein and good substitutes for those who must avoid other grains because of allergies. Available in flour, cereal, and pasta form in health food stores.

Amasake: A sweet, cultured, nonalcoholic rice drink also used in cooking and baking; may be used in desserts or as a dessert in itself. A good protein source, and a good milk and ice cream substitute.

Azuki (or aduki) beans: Small, earthy beans used in Japanese cooking. They take less time to cook (they don't have to be soaked first) and are more digestible than other beans.

   Daikon radish: Used in Oriental cooking and traditionally considered a digestive aid, it also is the source of the enzyme diastase, used in commercial digestive aids.

Ginger: Traditionally used to aid digestion in Oriental cooking.

Gomasio: A salt-sesame seed mixture that is a good salt substitute. Heat 1 part salt in an iron skillet until it gives off a mild chlorine smell. Add 10 to 15 parts seeds. Roast until golden; grind up in a mortar and pestle or blender.

Kuzu: A root that is used as a thickening agent in Japanese cooking and is somewhat interchangeable with arrowroot; must be added to cold water or other liquid to dissolve it before heating it.

Millet and bulgur wheat: Grains used in Middle Eastern and Eastern cooking. Millet is the most alkaline of the grains, and is therefore considered especially easy to digest; a good non-allergenic grain. Bulgur wheat is actually a wheat product; it's cracked wheat, so it can be prepared very quickly with little or no cooking. It's good in salads. Both are good complementary proteins and help vary the grains in your diet.

Seaweeds: Generally rich in minerals; according to some studies, they also have the ability to remove toxic heavy metals from the body or else to neutralize their effect.

Agar-agar or kanten—negligible in calories, good source of calcium and iron; may be used to thicken or jell desserts.

Arame: Very rich in calcium and iron; a dark, threadlike seaweed when dry, used in soups, chili, etc.

Dulse: Good source of calcium and iron; use in soups, etc.

Hijiki: Richest source of calcium and iron among seaweeds; similar to arame in appearance and taste and used in same ways.

Kombu (or kelp): Rich in calcium; cooked with beans and peas to make them more digestible (prevents gas).

Nori: Good source of calcium and iron; used to wrap sushi.

Wakame: Good source of calcium and iron; used in soups, etc.

Sesame seeds: Good calcium source used roasted in salads, soups, cereals, breads, etc. Also available in the forms of tahini, a rich sesame and oil paste that may be used in desserts, salad dressings, or hummus; and sesame butter, which may be used instead of tahini or spread on bread or crackers or rice cakes like peanut butter for a lunch or snack. Sesame oil is a good light cooking oil.

Shiitake mushrooms: Used in Japanese cooking and traditionally considered an aid in digesting protein, they have recently become popular in this country; sold fresh or dried.

Soba and udon: Two Japanese noodles that are good in soups. Soba is buckwheat-based and also contains a little wheat, but not much. Udon is a wheat noodle but is made without eggs. Both are good partial protein sources that are potentially helpful alternatives for those with allergies.

Tofu, tempeh, miso, and tamari: Traditional Oriental treatments of the soybean, which in its unadulterated state is hard to digest. Tofu is the white chunk of bean curd, usually coagulated by adding a mineral called *nigari*. Tempeh is a cultured product (like yogurt) that makes a good ground beef substitute and is rich in vitamin B_{12}. Miso is a dark fermented paste that is a good meat stock or bouillon substitute and is rich in protein and B vitamins. Tamari is good-quality, naturally aged soy sauce.

FOUR

◇

Preventive Nutrition: How to Minimize Allergies and Other Health Problems

When Anne's second baby, Zachary, was born, she already had an idea of what to expect. Her first child, Elizabeth, had developed pronounced allergies as soon as the first solid foods were introduced. Anne's family had a history of hay fever, and her husband had food allergies. She'd done a lot of reading after Libby's allergies showed up, and she knew that one in four parents with allergies could expect to have a child with allergies. And she and John *both* had them.

"Zachary was a big baby, and I was having a hard time keeping up with his appetite just nursing," she recalls. "So we tried solid foods at four months, and the rice cereal went okay. But when we started to move along, trying new foods, nothing else worked. He had a rash with everything." With Elizabeth, not even the rice cereal had worked. Three days after they started it, there was the rash, and it reappeared with each new try.

With both babies, Anne followed her pediatrician's advice and tried different foods, one at a time, waiting each time to see if the food would "take." When nothing seemed to work, she dropped solids for a few months and stuck to nursing alone. Towards the age of one year she started to introduce solids again. "With Libby, I think it was lamb and pears," she recalls with a laugh. "I know that sounds like an odd combination, but the doctor said we might have better luck with foods I didn't usually eat a lot of" (because the baby would not have been sensitized *in utero* to foods the mother rarely ate).

With Zachary, Anne learned a few more things about allergies, even though she'd been through it once before. At two months he was a colicky baby and a fitful sleeper until she cut chocolate and milk from her own diet. "It was horrible for me, but because I was nursing him, the things I was eating were passed to him in my milk. After I stopped milk and chocolate, he slept much better."

She also remembers that her health care provider suggested she cut out milk and eggs in the later months of pregnancy. She didn't, because she was worried about getting enough calcium and protein. In retrospect she thinks she might do things differently if she could do it again. But at eighteen months Zachary can now eat everything except dairy products; his sister has no restrictions. Anne thinks the continued nursing plus her own patience in trying out foods may have made the difference for her children.

Today's childhood diseases are not the same as those of earlier times. Antibiotics and inoculations largely control illnesses like diphtheria, scarlet fever, and whooping cough. Instead we worry about conditions that may be genetic, including allergies and degenerative diseases, such as cancer and heart disease. We want to give our children an edge in life, and that includes forestalling as much as possible the diseases or conditions we know our genetic makeup may have made them susceptible to.

Among the conditions that are inherited that we positively know food can affect are allergies, obesity, and heart disease. Of these, the first two show up early enough to make childhood miserable for the afflicted ones. For heart disease, the frequent precursor is an elevated cholesterol level, which can now be detected as early as age two.

We do not entirely know what role diet may play in other degenerative diseases or in other diseases that involve the immune system, as allergies do. Studies done with adults, for example, have shown the positive effects of diets low in animal fats. Rates of obesity and cancers of breast, colon, and prostate are lower radically in populations where less meat is eaten. (Some of these studies, done among a Seventh Day Adventist population, also showed the positive correlation between lower animal fat consumption and lower rate of heart disease; this connection at least is firmly established for adult males.) These studies are part of the background that led to NIH recommendations in the early 1980s that Americans eat less fat, sugar, salt (sodium is high in meats and soda beverages as well as in the saltshaker), caffeine, and alcohol and more complex carbohydrates—grains and legumes, fruits and vegetables. Subsequent studies showed that monounsaturated oils were actually helpful in promoting a healthy circulatory system.

So we do know that diet has a positive effect in preventing certain diseases or conditions, and the link with other diseases or conditions is in the process of being established. This chapter is placed early in the book because parents today are well aware of and concerned about whatever their family's genetic legacy to their children may be. We want to know *now* what we can do to ensure their better health. Besides allergies, we will consider some conditions that the American Academy of Pediatrics has targeted as being of special concern: potential obesity, hypertension, or cholesterol problems, as revealed in family health history; family history of heart attacks or diabetes; and the role of good nutrition in preventing these. Our chapter on preventive nutrition concludes with a consideration of some of the health-sickness signals we may get from infants and toddlers who can't really tell us what is wrong in words; and some ideas about comfort foods and helpful foods for children who are sick with minor ailments.

Allergies

Allergies were addressed briefly in Chapter Two because it is believed that allergies are linked to early digestive problems. Statistically, a child who reaches the age of one year without developing allergies is much less likely to develop them at all. It is in the early months of life that they seem to develop most readily, and it is believed that the immature infant digestive system plays a role here. Allergies are one of the immune system's responses to unfamiliar substances. The frequent villains are protein molecules, such as those in cow's milk, that slip undigested through the lining of the immature digestive tract. The body sets up a defensive reaction to these undigested food molecules, and sensitization sets in. Cow's milk is often implicated because it is an early food, either as such or in formula; but protein molecules could derive from the cereals offered as early solid foods as well. After the six-month mark, babies are much less prone to develop allergies. Again, the appearance of teeth may be your best clue to the maturity of your child's eating and digestive apparatus. As mentioned earlier, there is no reason to rush solids, and if your family has a history of allergies you should approach solid foods with caution and forethought.

Minimizing the Chances

Specifically, here are steps to consider if you want to minimize the chances of allergies:

Prebirth The nourishment a mother provides her baby, both *in utero* and through breast milk, can strengthen the baby and its immunities to allergy and disease. If you know you might have an allergy-prone child, look for alternatives to milk, especially, and to other possible allergy producers, during your pregnancy.

I was an example of a pregnant woman with a family (and personal) history of allergies—mostly respiratory ones. I had read that a pregnant mother should drink a quart of milk a day. Given my family history of hay fever and colds, there was no way I could do that. In addition I knew that the heightened hormone levels of pregnancy aggravated nasal stuffiness in many people, a condition that milk would only make worse, because milk products could create more mucus for the respiratory system to deal with. My health care providers just didn't know what to do with me; I was a vegetarian to boot, and milk was a major protein source.

What I did for myself and my baby was essentially to follow the steps recommended in Chapter Three: I sought out all the possible alternative sources of calcium, iron, and protein and ate those instead of milk and meat. I took the high-potency pregnancy vitamins prescribed by my health care providers. When I did use dairy products as a source of calcium and protein, I used cheese and yogurt, two forms of milk that are more digestible for some people than straight milk. Mind you, I had never shown any allergy to milk myself, not in an overt form anyway. Skin tests had shown I had inhalant but not food allergies. But I wasn't taking any chances. If you want to restrict your intake of milk, other calcium sources include calcium supplements (available at health food stores) as well as the food sources listed in Chapter Three. Getting your daily calcium entirely from nondairy sources entails some work. Make up the difference with forms of milk that are easier to digest, such as yogurt. If you want to drink milk, but are worried about its effects, you might also consider acidophilus milk, available in many supermarkets, or milk treated with the enzyme lactase to make it more digestible. Lactase-treated milk is marketed as Lact-Aid and is available at some supermarkets or through health food stores.

Breast-feeding   Breast milk is the ideally balanced food for babies; its protein, iron, and other nutrients are more readily absorbed than when those nutrients come from other sources. Babies that nurse beyond three months show significantly less tendency to develop allergies than babies who stop short of that mark. If you have a family history of allergies, breast-feeding exclusively up to six months is a good idea. Besides the ongoing immunities that breast milk is known to confer on babies, the easily absorbed nourishment it provides gives the immune system a break. So if possible, nurse your child past three months. Even a combination of nursing and bottle-feeding may be enough to do the trick. If you opt for this path, introduce bottle-feeding a little at a time. If your baby is colicky or not a good sleeper, take that as an indication that dairy products are affecting the child, either through your milk (in which case, go easy on the dairy products yourself) or through formula (you may try a nondairy formula).

Living with Your Child's Allergies

In the long run minimizing you child's chances of having allergies to milk, eggs, wheat, and other foods—which are so much a part of our standard diet—is worth the trouble of taking certain precautions. But what if, in spite of everything you do, your child does have allergies? First, be attuned to your child. Excessive ear infections or nasal congestion or colic could be a sign of allergies in the making. Don't dismiss the possibility. For those who have established that their child does have an allergy here are some diet suggestions:

Wheat Parents of allergic children quickly learn that there are many analogues or substitutes for wheat flour, which may be the most inconvenient allergy of all because it cuts out practically all baked goods. See Appendix C for suggested substitutes for commercial bread, a guide to adapting recipes in *Kidfood* and elsewhere, and equivalents, cup for cup, of nonwheat flours.

One problem with wheat allergy is that sometimes in fact it is an allergy to gluten, which is the portion of the wheat that interacts with yeast to produce the rising action in bread. Gluten is found in other flours too, though not in significant amounts. For many people, just avoiding wheat products is enough. Gluten is also found in rye, oats, malt, barley, MSG, hydrolyzed vegetable protein, durum flour, dried peas and beans, and millet. Substitutes for those with a gluten allergy can include sago (a starch made from the pith of a sago palm), tapioca, rice, corn, potato, soy, arrowroot, buckwheat, and soft wheat (pastry flour). Health food stores offer various pastas made with little or no wheat. (For more information, see the Sources List, Appendix A.)

Milk and Eggs Getting around milk and eggs for the very young obviously knocks out two good sources of protein and a major source of calcium. Here's where using the alternatives suggested in Chapter Three and the recipes in Part II may be of help. Also, one thing that has been noted by various allergy specialists is that we often seem almost "addicted" to the foods we are in fact allergic to. By extension, we can relieve our allergies by eating foods we are not accustomed to. Here's where venturing into a whole new cuisine— using azuki beans instead of the beans common in our culture; using grains from the Middle East and the Orient, such as millet rice, and buckwheat; learning to enjoy amasake, Rice Dream (a brand name for a rice-based ice cream substitute), and other macrobiotic treats—can be of help.

GLUTEN INTOLERANCE: WHEN ORDINARY BAKED GOODS ARE NO GOOD

Celiac disease, once know as *sprue,* is an intestinal disorder caused by intolerance to gluten. Gluten is a protein found in many cereal grains, especially wheat, rye, and barley. Gluten is the factor that enables dough to rise when yeast is added; the more gluten in a flour, the better it rises (to state it simply). So you can imagine that it is inconvenient, to say the least, to try to get along in our bread-eating, cereal-loving, pasta-consuming society without the glutenous cereal grains. But it can be done, as any parent who has a child with celiac disease can attest.

In celiac disease the gluten irritates the intestinal lining, so that eventually the body cannot absorb vital nutrition or liquids at all or cannot absorb them well. In severe cases a sufferer can become undernourished through a form of slow starvation. Signs of the disorder include weight loss, diarrhea, gas, abdominal pain or cramps, and anemia. A related vitamin B_6 deficiency that sometimes occurs with celiac disease can add vomiting and eczema to these symptoms.

I know one couple who finally learned their child had celiac disease after an alert pediatrician suggested this might be the cause of their preschooler's failure to gain weight over a period of more than a year. The child had also suffered from repeated respiratory infections but had not shown the classic symptoms of celiac disorder. Now on a gluten-free diet, he is healthy again and more energetic than before the disorder was treated.

Although avoidance is not always easy, it is a small price to pay for those with this disorder. And once a gluten-free diet is established, no other treatment is necessary. The flours recommended as substitutes are rice flour, corn flour, and potato flour. For an equivalency chart, see Appendix C. For information and sources of gluten-free products, see Appendix A.

Multiple Allergies   For children with multiple allergies, a specialist is the only answer. In addition, you have to learn to read labels very carefully and even read between the ingredients listed (corn, an allergen for some people, can be found in everything from baking powder to chewing gum to gummed envelopes and stamps!). You also have to practice an "elimination diet," which an allergy specialist will explain, not unlike the "week test" for introducing solid foods to babies, to identify your child's allergens. Once the allergies are established, you learn what other foods may belong to the family the child has tested allergic to (the Asthma and Allergy Foundation, in its *Allergy Encyclopedia* [see Appendix A], groups fruits, vegetables, grains, nuts, and seeds by family, enabling you to avoid allergens you might not even have suspected).

MILK: AN ALTERNATIVE VIEW

Rudolph Ballentine, in his classic *Diet and Nutrition,* discusses milk and milk products from the point of view of Aruyvedic medicine, a system developed in the Hindu philosophy:

> Many persons avoid milk and milk products in their diet because they say they are "mucus-forming," and it is true that some people can notice an increased amount of mucus in the throat, nasal passages and bronchi when they use greater quantities of milk. Milk is a body builder. Its basic nature is to promote the growth of flesh. It is designed to be the most efficient food possible for the rapidly growing animal. In Aruyvedic terms, milk is said to promote *kaph.* This is the solid, substantial aspect of the human being. . . . During periods of growth, when recovering from an illness, or when one needs to gain weight, milk can be a very valuable addition to the diet. If the body does not need to increase in *kaph,* however, or if it is for some reason unable to properly assimilate it, then it is thrown off as waste. . . . Unusable *kaph* is what is known in the West as mucus, and our English word "cough" takes its origin from the Sanskrit term.*

Ballentine states that experiments have shown that pasteurized milk is basically indigestible, and that this might explain the intolerance many people have for milk (and presumably the products made from it). (There are, however, certainly other genetic forms of lactose intolerance as well.)

He suggests raw milk as an alternative but points out that simply drinking raw milk as is is not always wise, since one cannot always be sure of the cleanness of the herd from which

*Reprinted by permission of the Himalayan Institute (see Appendix A).

the raw milk is taken. Theoretically, of course, certified raw milk is a sign of a healthy, government-inspected herd. However, a lingering, flulike condition can be contracted from raw milk from dairy herds infected with a disease called *brucellosis*. Ballentine's suggestion is to sterilize raw milk by boiling it at home.

Allergies and Stress

Hans Selye's famous pronouncement that allergies are really a reaction to stress should not be overlooked. Allergy specialists have signaled the healing properties of a really restful night's sleep. In deep sleep the pituitary gland releases growth hormones and stimulates bone growth in children; adrenal hormones that help digest proteins and fats are also released. In sleep too the mucous linings of the body are repaired, the blood pressure and metabolic rates are lowered, the nervous system and muscles are relaxed. All these functions aid the body in resisting infection and stress. In addition, exercise can play a key role in building the body's resistance to stress and allergies.

A Review

Again, your best chance with allergies is to try to avoid them altogether, so keep these suggestions in mind:

1. Try for a pregnancy free of as many common allergies as possible—even if you don't have an allergy to a particular food.
2. Breast-feed if possible, still avoiding the allergy foods yourself.
3. Go really slowly in introducing solid foods, sticking to the simplest foods up until a year (these include nonwheat grains, vegetables, fruits, and cautious use of protein foods).
4. Try to utilize alternate sources wherever feasible to give your child the widest variety of healthful foods available.
5. Avoid foods with additives such as dyes—both during pregnancy and in feeding your child.

6. Don't stress your system or your child's with rich foods or foods containing much sugar or salt.
7. Try to avoid, and have your child avoid, foods that he or she really "craves." At least rotate them with reasonable substitutes.

Fat, Cholesterol, and the Threat of Heart Disease

Until recently children weren't even considered in connection with cholesterol levels, heart disease, and the relation of diet to both. The whole issue is still distinctly controversial; it has by no means been proven, for instance, that a diet that helps adults reduce their cholesterol levels is appropriate for children. In fact, the American Academy of Pediatrics feels that it is not.

Nevertheless, if your family or your spouse's family has a history of coronary problems, you want to do *something*. What you can do, without severely limiting your child's intake of nutritious foods, is to try to emphasize a wide variety of foods, especially those that will help you lay the foundation for a low-fat diet later in life.

This in fact is the recommendation of the AAP, which kicked off the whole discussion in 1983 with a statement entitled "Toward a Prudent Diet for Children." After this statement came varying recommendations by others, including the American Heart Association. The AHA recommends that total fat intake for children be about 30 percent of total calories consumed daily, with the fat split evenly among saturated, monounsaturated, and polyunsaturated. An NIH panel recommended that "all Americans (except children younger than two years of age) . . . be advised to adopt a diet that reduces total dietary fat intake from the current level of about 40 percent of total calories to 30 percent . . . and reduces daily cholesterol intake to 250 to 300 mg or less" (quoted in the APA's "Prudent Lifestyle for Children," *Pediatrics* Sept. 1986).

First of all, please note the exception of children under two. It's very important, because after all these reports came out, news stories followed that reported on overconscientious parents adopting adult low-cholesterol diets for their infants, who then exhibited a failure to thrive that was alarming to pediatricians. When the children were removed from no-fat or very low-fat diets, they returned to a normal growth pattern in both weight and height. The AAP specifically recommends that dietary fat *not* be restricted for children under one year old. So if you're feeding your eleven-month-old cow's milk, it should be *whole* cow's milk. The AAP is also concerned that the best sources of iron, calcium, and protein for older children will be removed if their diets are too restrictive.

Recommendations from the AAP for eliminating or reducing any tendency in children to develop heart disease include the following:

* After age one, children should have a varied diet. "The key is balance from variety," states "Toward a Prudent Diet for Children."

* Pediatricians should use height-weight curves and blood pressure tests as early warnings of potential obesity and hypertension.

* Children with a family history of coronary problems should be screened at age two to have their serum cholesterol checked.

* As childhood progresses, children should be counseled about exercise and ideal body weight. Teenagers should be counseled on the association of smoking and heart disease. For parents of children at risk for coronary disease, please also remember that if you smoke, you increase their risk—because "passive smokers" also inhale, and tobacco smoke has been indicated as a factor in coronary disease.

* For children, fat should comprise 30 to 40 percent of the total calories of the diet. (Please note that in this the AAP is at odds with the AHA, which recommends no more than 30 percent. The AAP is anxious that parents not overdo it. If you don't have a family history of heart disease or obesity, you may want to be a bit lenient in this department.)

In general it seems that the current thinking is that you need worry about your child's diet only if there is a reason to—such as a family history of obesity, heart problems, diabetes, or some other diet-related condition. Specifically, for those with a history of coronary disease, saturated fats must be targeted as an area to reduce.

In fact, this is something all parents probably should think about. In spite of our increasing enthusiasm for fitness and health foods, Americans continue each year to consume record amounts of fast food, much of it containing and/or cooked in saturated fats. One prominent fast-food chain was noted in recent years for deep-frying in tallow (beef fat). You could taste it on the french fries. Saturated fat, whether it's lard, palm oil, or hydrogenated vegetable oil, is virtually omnipresent in such seemingly innocuous items as crackers and commercial pie crust, to say nothing of cookies, candies, cakes, chips, and the host of other junk snack foods. Your family might not have a history of heart disease, but it may develop one before this generation is done chowing down on the munchies.

Certainly, if your family does have a history of cholesterol problems, obesity, or coronary disease, you have to watch the saturated fats. The key in the long run is to get children involved. Explain why your family wants to be especially health-conscious about certain foods and how this can actually be a bonus in other areas: a healthy heart for a lifetime may go along with a thinner body that has more endurance, to give a simplified example. Explain to your child that this nutrition information is relatively new, that not everyone knows about it, but that fortunately your family does. You can, and should, add that while this may mean you as a family will be eating a little differently from some other people, it is something you will all be doing together. Always talk to your child about any proposed changes in diet. Explain the objectives and ask for input into how to achieve them. Emphasize that the whole family will be trying something new. For younger children, discuss the kinds of foods you want to eat versus the kinds of foods that are out there and that perhaps most people are eating.

If you think your child might be in the high-risk category, you'll want to have him or her tested. A pediatrician or the local AHA chapter can explain what kind of test is needed (it's a relatively simple, two-step procedure) and possibly even direct you to a free screening. These are periodically offered by hospitals and other interested groups.

Meanwhile, heed the AAP's advice. Let your child's height/weight chart be your guide and aim for a wide diet rather than a restrictive one. Don't restrict fats for children under two unless your doctor advises it. Do contemplate the following.

Put Your Family on a Quasi-Vegetarian Diet

By this I mean limiting animal foods to chicken, fish, turkey, and reasonable amounts of dairy foods and eggs. Much chicken fat can be removed by stripping away the skin. Turkey is very low in fat. White meat is less fatty than dark, in both fish and fowl. Cold-water fish, such as salmon and mackerel, contain a special category of fat (or oil) that is polyunsaturated: eicosapentanoic, or EPA (which means "having to do with fish oil"). The EPA, when tested, actually appeared to lower cholesterol levels. The EPA are a form of Omega-3 fatty acids. In addition, a quasi-vegetarian diet puts the emphasis on the vegetable kingdom, where there is no cholesterol (but beware on one point: hydrogenated vegetable oils and such heavy oils as palm and coconut are saturated fats—and these actually can elevate the cholesterol level). For the most part vegetables are not only cholesterol-free but also fat-free. The fats they do contain are poly-unsaturates or monounsaturates. Use fatty foods like red meat and hard cheeses sparingly; a little can go a long way in a salad, stew, soup, taco, or casserole.

Draw Up a Family Meal Plan

This should include both meals eaten at home and meals eaten elsewhere. Establish quotas for such items as snack foods and fast foods. You might allow a trip to a fast-food restaurant once a week (or once a month, depending on your situation). You might make an agreement that cake and ice cream are allowed at other people's birthday parties, in small amounts. (For your own parties, you know you can serve Rice Dream—available in health food stores—and make your own cake the low-fat kind.) If your family includes snack and sweets addicts, make agreements about making and carrying your own with you or establish rules about what can be bought (such as fruit rollups, yogurt, rice cakes, and all-fruit frozen confections).

Getting Wise to Oils and Fats

Be sure the peanut butter your children are eating is the kind with no added sweeteners or hydrogenated oils. Peanuts in fact are a source of good monounsaturates, which have been shown to reduce cholesterol levels in the body; so is olive oil, which is handy, because the extra-virgin olive oil available in supermarkets is one cooking oil you can buy without worrying about its fat content or what the processing has done to it. I buy all my other cooking oils at a health food store, where cold-processed oils are available. (Oils processed at low temperatures are less likely to be partially hydrogenated; also, cold-processed oils are less likely to have the chemical residues found in most commercially prepared oils. Extra-virgin olive oil purchased at supermarkets has probably been processed at low temperatures and is all right to use.) Peanut oil is recommended as a cooking oil for those restricting cholesterol in their diets because it is monounsaturated.

Favor Foods Associated with Lower Cholesterol Levels

Oats, and especially oat bran, have gotten a lot of good press in this department. There's something in the oat bran fiber that binds with bile (which carries cholesterol) in the intestines, enabling it to be excreted. The pectin in some fruits, including apples and berries, has the same effect. So do fibers in dried beans and peas. All of these can take more of a leading role in your family's diet. Oatmeal (or oat bran, if you prefer) is especially versatile: it can be eaten as a meal, put into any number of baked goods, and even included in soups. I use it in lentil loaves and patties, because it's an excellent binding agent in lieu of eggs. My brother-in-law makes dynamite pancakes with ground oatmeal (see Breakfast Recipes in Part II).

The cholesterol-lowering properties of certain oils have been noted earlier. Also, one study has suggested that some forms of milk, especially fermented ones, might actually lower cholesterol, though to date no one is exactly sure why. Again, it can't hurt to substitute yogurt, buttermilk, or kefir (a yogurt-like drink) for milk in your cooking or in ordinary consumption. In the meantime, watch for updates on this subject.

Also remember that while eggs don't lower cholesterol levels, all the cholesterol is in the yolks. Consider using just the whites in cooking; that's where most of the protein is located anyway.

Avoid Sodium

Up until now we've talked mostly about fats and cholesterol in connection with cardiac health. Hypertension (high blood pressure) also affects the heart's health, and the connection between sodium and hypertension is well established. Besides table salt, processed foods are almost uniformly high in sodium unless they are "dietetic" (in which case you should still read the label). Processed foods include favorite commercial cereals. Other sodium-rich foods you may not have thought of include oil-packed tuna, processed meats, ham, and many cheeses. Sodium is an ingredient in baking powder, baking soda, and club soda (unless labeled "low-sodium"). Commercial baked goods tend to be high in sodium. And some vegetables, including spinach, celery, and beets, are naturally high in sodium.

Obesity and Diabetes

The AAP recommends that its member pediatricians include in the family histories of their young patients information on the incidence of premature heart attacks or strokes, hypertension, obesity, diabetes, and hyperlipidemia (elevated fat levels in the blood). We've talked about the conditions that affect the heart, which leaves diabetes and obesity—both of them incidentally not unrelated to healthy circulatory systems. Oddly enough, the type of diet that will help children at risk for heart disease is the very diet for preventing and treating these remaining two disorders.

But not diabetes, you may say. Yes, current thinking about diabetes is that a diet high in *complex* carbohydrates (versus simple sugars) is both the best medicine and the best prevention. Diabetics are prone to coronary problems, so the very same low-fat, low-cholesterol diet works for them. In addition, of course, refined sugars must be avoided, but since these are so often coupled with saturated fats in our culture (as in baked goods), the cholesterol-fighting diet is low in commercial sweets too. The complex carbohydrates provide the energy your child needs in a slow, steady stream, which is ideal for the diabetic patient as well as for the healthy child. A diet high in carbohydrates instead of simple sugars is your best protection for children at risk for diabetes.

For children with a weight problem, the quasi-vegetarian, high-carbohydrate, junk-free diet is ideal. Again, talking about it and planning it out *with* your child is essential, both to get the child involved and to stress the relative healthfulness of foods rather than abstract caloric values. Understanding that various aspects of health, such as weight maintenance and a healthy heart, are interrelated, may make a healthy diet (as opposed to dieting) more palatable to a child. Again, you need agreement among the family members about what foods are allowed, how much, and how often. And it will help if the whole family changes diet together, instead of leaving it all up to the child.

I have already warned against sodas because of their sodium content, but they are also a poor choice of beverage for the child with a weight problem. Commercial soda drinks are also high in phosphorus, which will cancel out the calcium all children need. And this caveat includes diet sodas. Artificial sweeteners aren't necessarily an improvement over sugar; in some cases they are labeled as potentially hazardous to your health. (In our house, we make our own soft drinks with fruit juices and low-sodium seltzer water. Adults actually prefer the less sugary taste, and children will accept it.) If you have a child who's trying to lose weight, using a chemical-laden diet drink as a crutch is not really doing that child a favor. Part of losing weight is letting the body cleanse itself from the level of the individual cell on up. Excess sodium, for one example, can inhibit this process by upsetting the sodium-potassium balance on which cells rely to cleanse themselves of toxins. Chemical additives to food haven't really been around long enough for us to know what effect they may have, so keep your child's diet as simple and clean as possible.

This suggestion extends to all kinds of processed foods: keep them out of your child's diet if you want him or her to lose weight. Processed foods often mean empty calories with little nutritive value. Real food, in the form of whole carbohydrates, for example, takes longer to eat and longer to digest and provides energy longer for fewer calories.

Feeding Problems:
Infant to Toddler

Be alert to the fact that some health problems could be a signal to you to change your child's diet. For example, constipation, diarrhea, or, in very young infants, colic may be a sign that something in the feeding process needs adjustment. And, of course, your baby's height/weight curve might indicate a need to reexamine your baby's diet, but your pediatrician will no doubt provide guidance on this.

Around the age of toilet training chronic constipation may develop. In part, this may be the result of the child's efforts to gauge just what control is, and it sorts itself out. In some cases it is a child's form of unconscious protest, especially if there's some unwelcome change at home, like a parent returning to work full-time. The only real danger is that hard stools can cut or scrape the mucous lining of the anus, making the process even more uncomfortable and difficult. What sometimes works is a tablespoon of good-quality vegetable oil taken by mouth, a lot of patience (sometimes ignoring the situation is the best medicine), and added fiber in the diet to make sure the problem doesn't recur. Avoid rice, cheese, and fruits with pectin (e.g., apples) for the duration of the problem—these foods can be "binding," which only exacerbates the constipation. Get your child to drink plenty of liquids. Keep feeding the vegetable oil if needed. Doctors will often recommend mineral oil (made from coal tar), but olive oil or another vegetable oil works just as well. Vegetable oil doesn't leach nutrients out of the body the way mineral oil does.

Obviously, you will consult your health care provider in the case of problem constipation or diarrhea (which can dehydrate a child's body if it goes on for long). Classic treatment for mild diarrhea is a diet of bananas, apples, and rice. For diarrhea after a round of antibiotics, ask your doctor to prescribe Lactinex to restore the intestines' depleted supply of helpful bacteria.

A Word on Exercise

Exercise is one of the keys to preventing and combating all the conditions we've been talking about. And just as diet alone is not as effective for adults as the combination of diet and exercise, your child needs exercise along with good nutrition, too. Exercise is not only good for the circulatory system, but it helps combat allergies, too. For one thing, improved circulation helps carry away the waste products that would otherwise accumulate in tissues and irritate them. For another thing, exercise stimulates the mucous lining of the respiratory tract, where inhalant allergies attack. The mucous lining becomes more moist, and antibodies in the lining become more active. This puts the respiratory system, a weak spot in people with inhalant allergies, in a better condition to resist infection. The role of exercise in reducing stress is well documented, and this also helps combat allergies and degenerative diseases.

Weight-bearing exercise stimulates bone growth, putting that calcium you've been dishing out to good use.

Vigorous exercise actually promotes healing. It causes the body to secrete large quantities of norepinephrine, which stimulates the immune system in a positive way, and epinephrine, which stimulates the metabolism (an aid in some weight problems).

As with food allergy, an ounce of prevention is worth a pound of cure. Especially if you know you have a family history of coronary disease, other degenerative diseases, obesity, or allergies, get your child started exercising very young, before the problem develops—and so that exercise can be a lifelong habit. As with diet, everybody wins.

When Kids Get Sick:
Comfort Foods

What can you do to make a sick child feel better? After you've consulted your doctor and taken whatever steps are needed to ease the crisis at hand, you're left with a mopey or crabby child and a few shut-in days ahead of you.

First, you can treat your child to the novelty of not eating in the usual place. Spread a bath towel or plastic tablecloth over any area that you don't want to spill on. The child will appreciate your company and the fact that he can remain cozy under the covers (on his bed, your bed, or the sofa) instead of dragging to the table. After a day or two at the most, the child will welcome—conversely—the novelty of getting bathed and dressed and returning to civilization.

Good things to feed ailing children depend on the ailment. For sore throats, real-fruit frozen treats or a nondairy pudding (see recipes in Part II) may be welcome (with respiratory ailments, avoid dairy products that will cause excess mucus to form). Or you can make or purchase amasake. Or the mildly salty taste of a simple miso soup with noodles (see recipe in Part II) may be comforting.

If there's been nausea or vomiting, you are cautiously trying clear liquids, to see what will stay down. This is the time for mild carbonated beverages like ginger ale (an exception to the no-soft-drinks rule in this case)—not fruit juice or milk, which may make things worse. Thaw a quart of Basic Chicken Stock (see recipe in Part II) and serve a cup of it warm, but not too hot. After a day, or when things seem to have stabilized, move on to Chicken Oatmeal Soup (something in the oatmeal seems especially soothing to irritated mucous linings of the throat, stomach, and digestive tract; see recipe in Part II). If there is nausea but no vomiting, Bancha-Ginger-

Plum Drink (see recipe in Part II) may relieve it. Ginger seems to have a settling effect on the stomach, and this drink is comforting in cases of mild flu or when your children (or you) "just aren't feeling well." A weak mint tea with a little honey also can be soothing to the stomach; mint is rich in magnesium, the mineral commonly found in over-the-counter digestive aids.

Also in the clear liquids category is Kanten Gel (see recipe in Part II), a good substitute for commerical gelatins with their food dyes. When children are sick with a fever or any kind of respiratory or stomach infection, one of your main goals of course is to get as many liquids as possible into them without irritating the system. The liquids help prevent dehydration in the case of fever, vomiting, or diarrhea; they help the body clean itself internally; and generally they provide the extra fluids to replace those lost under the stress of infection. That's why soups, mild drinks, hot cereals (on the thin side—more liquids), and frozen fruit bars are all helpful. In the case of a cold, obviously, hot liquids are more comforting; with a fever, cold drinks (sipped through a straw to prevent guzzling) and frozen fruit cubes or even crushed ice may be more comforting. Two added thoughts: If you're trying to avoid milk, add amasake to the hot cereal in lieu of milk and sweetener; and for mild, easily digested frozen treats, freeze amasake or Kanten Gel in Popsicle form.

And don't forget the vitamin C.

We've talked in these first few chapters about what we as parents can do to try to ensure the best health for our children. But the time comes when they have to be responsible for their health themselves. How do we get them through the finicky years when they turn up their noses at good food . . . and through the school years when we can't be there to look over their shoulders while they eat . . . and through the teen years, when they are more independent and more nutritionally needy all at once? How do we make food fun and healthy all at the same time? These are some of the questions we must now address. Let's start with those first few forays away from home, and take it a step at a time.

FIVE

Away from Home

I already mentioned that I'm the kind of person who leaves written instructions (well, maybe by now we could call them *suggestions,* but I'm more relaxed now that Owen's older) even when the baby-sitter is downstairs and I'm only a flight of steps away. Perhaps that seems extreme, but I care what Owen eats, and leaving instructions on paper is also my way of getting this concern off my mind. If I'm working, I don't want to be interrupted unless it's important. A snack certainly is important to a hungry toddler, but it's not something I want to be interrupted for when I can plan it in advance.

Looking back, I also remember the first few times Owen and I were separated because I had to go somewhere. From the beginning, I was a planner. I didn't want to leave my child's nutrition to chance, and no doubt neither do you. Sooner or later the moment comes when your child is dining without you. During the first four to six months, you probably will plan your outings for between mealtimes or leave your baby-sitter with instructions and a bottle.

In this day of the spread-out extended family, you probably also will travel as a family at some point when your baby is very young—

say on a trip across the country to visit grandparents. You might also take business trips together. If you're breast-feeding, the baby's meals cause little extra planning and if you're bottle-feeding, traveling is also relatively carefree.

Life does, however, get more complicated when the world of solid foods comes into view. This chapter offers suggestions on sticking to your well-thought-out food game plan in two challenging situations: when you're away from your child and when the whole family is on the road.

When You're Away from Your Child

Everybody has a different view about what is good food for a baby, and you'll be surprised, intrigued, shocked, and/or scandalized by the things people will feed to babies—your baby in particular, unless you plan otherwise.

One mother was telling me about the first time she and her husband visited his parents after the baby started eating solids. Annabel had been breast-fed, so her grandparents had never really had the pleasure of feeding her—and they'd missed that. The grandmother, a great Italian cook, met them with pureed meatballs, rich in garlic and spices. Annabel was still at the cereal stage, and her mother had to explain that she wasn't up to meatballs yet. But at age two plus, Annabel's mom says, she eats them with gusto, probably as a result of having been introduced to them pretty early (though not at six months!).

More insidious than entrees are the snacks that people—including relatives—will feed the children. These are insidious because people won't count them as real food, won't think they're all that important, and won't think to ask you or tell you beforehand that they're going to feed your child potato chips and sandwich cookies while you're gone.

Whether someone else is caring for your child at your home or elsewhere, there are two ways to ensure that your child eats only what you have in mind, and they go together. First, you make food available, whether that entails bringing things along or just making sure your kitchen is well stocked. Second, you provide instructions on what you've made available. Whether it's a jar of commercial baby food or a homemade dish, you show it to your caregiver and tell that lucky individual when it can/should be eaten, whether it needs to be heated or refrigerated, what should be done with leftovers, and with what utensils (spoon, bare hands, or whatever) the food should be presented.

If you're talking to a paid baby-sitter, you can give explicit instructions. If you're talking to a relative, you can engage in a dialogue, solicit an opinion, and offer your philosophy (you should do this sometime beforehand, not when you're already late for your train). Talking general philosophy with relatives can include making tactful but firm statements like "Jamie's just eating this baby cereal right now. The doctor says we can try pureed vegetables next week," or "We've decided not to feed Jackie anything with sugar in it until he's at least a year old—and it's a little tricky, but we feel good about it. We don't want him to get used to having stuff that will ruin his teeth." When your child is older, you can offer actual evidence from your own observations—many parents do report that they can see the difference in their children's behavior after the kids go on a Halloween candy binge or eat something with food dye in it. This can be especially noticeable with younger children, whose systems have not gotten accustomed to chemical additives and excess sugar. Artificial colors that have been linked to cancer in laboratory animals are still currently used in our food supply. In addition, both high sugar levels and the effects of artificial colors have been linked to delinquent behavior in older children. So no, it's probably not your imagination: your child really is acting up, and the candy may be the reason why.

If your baby-sitter, friend or relative demurs that "we never bothered about that sort of thing," you can tactfully but truthfully point out that there are a lot more junk foods, additives, and whatnot now than there were thirty years ago, and so you have to be careful—or that we have all learned so much about junk food, sugar, salt, and very-low-density lipoproteins in the last ten years.

We're talking about general philosophy here. When it comes to specifics, like how and when to feed what, don't be surprised if your caregiver's eyes glaze over a bit as you rattle on and on, especially if that person has raised a child or two. In my own experience, my baby-sitters' eyes often glaze over, but I guess they figure that it's their job to give me peace of mind, so they humor me. They report on what they feed Owen in a detail that sometimes suggests I might be from an alien culture whose religion is food. (And perhaps they're right.) But they do as I request and that's the point. You probably chose this caregiver in the first place in part because that person respects your concerns. If all else fails, invoke the experts, such as Dr. Spock, Dr. Brazelton, or the NIH.

Sometimes the people you dread confronting most about your food preferences are the grandparents—your own parents, who, after all, fed you, or your spouse's parents, who you think might interpret your whims as a rejection of their lifestyle. Don't worry. As I said before, they're the grandparents, and they can afford to rest on their laurels. At worst they will think you're silly or just plain wrong, but this is one child they don't have to tell: "Finish your peas." And as your child gets older, you might allow them the pleasure of breaking the rules now and then. Children can delight in forming a secret alliance with the grandparents behind your back, and there's no harm in this within reason. Also, you may find that children in the fussy stages of eating will actually eat better for anyone but you.

If it's snacks and sweets you're concerned about, you can do two things. First, establish the outer limits if necessary. If you want to caution a relative or baby-sitter about how much will be too much, do so. Then let the child eat cake, within reason, behind your back. This can be filed under the rule of "NIOH"—"Not in *our* house." For children beyond babyhood, this can sometimes be a very useful principle. Let them have some fun with the baby-sitter and relatives, as long as it's understood that the rules are still the rules when they get home—or when you get home!

Play Group

As your child's horizon expands, you might also be involved in a first socialization experience, the play group. Parents often get their children together in play groups as young as four to six months— and play groups typically continue to meet until preschool is well established, say, age three. Sometimes parents "co-op" the running of the play group, actually dropping their children off and leaving them in the care of other parents in the group; in other play group arrangements, each child has one parent or other caregiver stay where the group is in session. If you are thinking of enrolling your child in a play group *not* run by parents but by professionals, be sure to ask about their snack policy and state *your* preference.

Whichever kind of group it is, the play group usually involves a snack of some kind. Unless the plan calls for the parents to bring along their own snacks and juice, it is important to establish a snack ground rules.

In a play group run by parents snacks typically are provided by the parents on a rotating basis: if the group is meeting at my house, I provide the snack. Or, if we meet at a playground or some other public spot, we agree each week about who will bring the snack next time. Snacks are kept simple: juice and some kind of munchy, like crackers, plain cookies, or some kind of muffin or quick bread. Agreeing on rules usually isn't difficult, since most parents are as anxious as you to avoid excess sugar, salt, and fat. But it's a good idea to have a discussion to rule on what the kids are *not* going to eat (no juices with sugar added or artificial coloring, for instance, or no chocolate, or that certain kinds of cookies are off limits, or nothing with salt in it). Some good possibilities include

   unsalted crackers (Red Oval Farms is made without animal fat)
   arrowroot cookies

    animal crackers (Barbara's is one sugarless brand)
    low-salt pretzel sticks or bread sticks (nice for teething)
    homemade bread or muffins (you control the salt and sugar)
    rice cakes (Chico San, Pritikin, and Quaker all make these)
    raisins
    something for the adults (coffee, tea, a snack)

When the kids are still play group age, you might cultivate the system of diluting the juice fifty-fifty with water. Many parents do this as a rule, and it's a good idea, especially in the summertime when you want them to drink plenty of liquids. For one thing, you don't want them getting all their calories from juice, even healthful juice. For another, diluting the juice helps keep the sweet tooth at bay, because the children don't get used to the more concentrated sweet taste of juice as it comes from the bottle. (Frozen juices should be made according to directions and then diluted again.) Until the EPA bans Alar and systemic pesticides, you should consider using only organic fruit juices.

The play group is a good place for parents to swap nutritional information and pick up new ideas about how other people feed their kids—as well as a place just to relax while the kids do their thing.

Television

Yes, television does have something to do with how you prepare others to feed your kids. For one thing, television is almost like another person in your kids' lives, once they start watching it. Commercial television is like an adult who has different food values from you and is pushing them on your children. And unless you sit through programs with them (not a bad idea in the beginning), it is presenting its food values while you're not there.

Our solution, and that of many other parents, was to go really slowly with television. In our home, up until the age of four, it was a very rare occasion when Owen watched anything but public television, which of course is commercial-free and generally presents solid food values. As with food, we expressed that preference to whoever was watching him. This works up to a point, but eventually the kids are going to start spending time at friends' houses, and the rules there may be different. One thing you can do is to continue to hold the line on television watching in your own house. I think it hasn't dawned on Owen yet that the things he sees on TV in other people's houses could be available in ours. When it does, of course, it will be time to discuss the rule of "not in our house" and how it might apply to junk food seen on TV.

When You're All Away—Together

Some of my fondest food memories have to do with traveling with Owen. I think I treasure them because we took on the experience of travel with a small child with optimism but with no real idea of how we would handle it, and we found we handled it well. That made us feel terrific.

We were often traveling on business, so our time and energy weren't entirely our own, nor were we at our most relaxed. It was a big plus that feeding Owen at the age of two in an assortment of strange hotels and restaurants was virtually never a hassle. Wherever we were we found something he could and would eat.

And then there was the relief of discovering that peanut butter was readily available in English convenience stores and that village stores in rural Ireland sold juice boxes with straws that a toddler in the infant seat of our rented Ford could negotiate. On occasion there was the pleasure, after days in hotels, of finding ourselves somewhere with a kitchen where we could make our own chicken stew.

Eating varies, of course, depending on where, how, and how long you're traveling. When we're making an eight-hour trip by car in summer, for example, we usually pack a cooler and a blanket to sit on and look for a park or other public green place to eat, stretch legs, and play in. (Parks are good because they often feature a water supply for cleaning up after lunch and replenishing the water jug we carry in the car; they also offer more of a chance to let off steam than a restaurant, and that makes kids behave better when they get back on the road.)

If we're going to be somewhere for a few days, we go out when we get there and find a place to buy the don't-leave-home-without-it peanut butter and other nonperishables, such as fruit, for lunches on the go. Hotel rooms with even a small refrigerator are always a special plus when traveling with a baby, because they enable you to keep additional items like late-night milk or a supply of juice on hand—much more convenient than getting it from room service.

With a small child in tow, we did tend to rely on room service a good deal for our meals and also to use our hotel room as something of a total living quarters. We found that the staffs of hotels were most often very accommodating, especially the housekeeping staff, who usually knew where the nearest convenience store was to be found and would even sometimes supply a diaper in an emergency.

When Owen was two and younger, room service often provided us a more relaxed setting than a restaurant or hotel dining room. Room service or restaurant possibilities that work well for under-twos, we found, included bland soups, cooked cereal, fresh fruit, muffins, mashed or baked potatoes, other side dishes (vegetables, applesauce—smaller portions and less expensive than ordering a meal that won't be eaten anyway), crudités, and appetizers, as well as table food from the adults' plates.

When traveling, one problem with feeding children can be irregular schedules: by the time the food comes, they may be climbing the walls from fatigue, excitement, and the strange surroundings. That's why it's wise to get in the habit of requesting something be brought right away, while the rest of the meal is being prepared. Fresh fruit, juice, or cold cereal can be easy to get quickly at breakfast; soups or crudités at dinner; on-the-table crackers or bread sticks can also stave off disaster. For lunch in cities away from home we usually leave our lodgings with a sandwich in tow for Owen, so that wherever we find ourselves at midday he'll be taken care of. Then whatever else he eats, he has that food under his belt.

And if he gets hungry before we do, he can munch while we are on the move.

Then there's the wonderful world of fast food. We tried to keep knowledge of it, like sugar, a secret for as long as possible, so for us it wasn't even an option at age two. But as children become older, it becomes the sometimes inevitable if not elegant solution of where to eat. Why not? The kids like it; it's clean, predictable, and less expensive. And it turns out fast food, while it's not something you would want to base your whole diet on, isn't always as bad as you may have thought. Fast food is surprisingly high in protein, though also above the recommended level of fat. The average fast-food entree, whether chicken, fish, or a burger, provides at least three-fourths of the average RDA of protein for a child of three (half the RDA for a child of six and a third of the RDA for teenagers). Fast food tends to be high in sodium; it's also low in iron and vitamins A, C, and D, but you can always buy the kids milk or orange juice instead of soda, and these days fast-food establishments also offer salads. We're talking a meal or two on the road, not a daily diet. Among the not-totally-unnourishing options are chicken, fish, salad, pizza, fruit juice, milk, and ice cream; the fried food may not be ideal, but of course the kids will eat it. A meal here and there won't hurt them. And you can always bend the rules with the understanding that "we're doing this because we're away from home."

Trips by Car

If you're on the road for any length of time, fill the nutritional gaps with out-of-hand snacks like fresh fruit, yogurt, rice cakes, Cheerios (or health-food Oatios), and unprocessed cheese—things you can buy as you go along, eat, and be done with or that you can carry along without making a mess. We have a friend whose whole family piled out of the car at a supermarket in Bakersfield, California, bought yogurt, and devoured it on the spot. They were so hot that it seemed like the only thing to do. They may have been responding unconsciously to a craving brought on by calcium depletion in the heat, too. Veteran travelers, they had their plastic spoons with them. A knife, even a plastic one with serrated edges, is also a good thing to have along, for dealing with cheese or for peeling fruit you've just bought when you're not in a position to wash it. Needless to say, travel wipes, napkins, or (in the car) a whole roll of paper towels is handy. Things like a spoon and a knife take up no room, even if you're traveling light, and they can increase your impromptu options.

When driving long distances, food is great for keeping a one- or two-year-old occupied, especially if the child is in the back seat and you're in the front. You can entertain the back-seat contingent by periodically handing out little snacks like a salt-free rice cake, a pretzel stick, a quarter of a sandwich, Cheerios (or health-food Oatios) in a bag, health-food animal crackers, or a small box of raisins. A juice box is great if your child has mastered the straw and swallowing while in motion. Apple juice is less messy than grape, which stains. For the dry snacks, using a Dust Buster at the end of the trip restores your car to habitable condition. Reserve messier items like frozen fruit bars for your out-of-car travel breaks. For infants, pack a traveling meal supply of jars of food (organic? See Appendix A), dry formula if needed, and a safe supply of water (distilled or from your own tap).

Traveling by Air

For plane trips it's a good idea to find out in advance whether a real meal will be offered. A meal can be a great pastime. It provides relief and distraction from the monotony of sitting still. You may, through a travel agent or the airlines reservation desk, be able to order a special meal for your child, or a meal for yourself that you know he/she will eat part of. But you can also ensure peace by packing food to tide your infant or toddler over. Older children can deal better with the close quarters, the concept of the time the trip will take, and the strange food. For them, it's likely to be great fun, a novelty. Your toddler needs more of your help to get through, and snacking is one way to do it. Again, carrying your own dry snacks and a juice box can ensure peace and quiet even if there is a meal or snack being offered, because it often takes the flight attendants a while to serve everyone.

On takeoff and landing, giving the kids something to suck or chew on can help relieve pressure on the eardrums. Babies can nurse or take a bottle. Children old enough—three or four and up—can have gum. Two-year-olds might find a sugarless lollipop or even some raisins helpful. Try any food that engages their saliva glands enough to cause plenty of swallowing, but don't give them a cup of juice, for it might spill or make them choke as the plane lurches on takeoff.

Parents who have flown with small children know that any ploy, including food, is fair game to keep them quiet. But if you are seeking alternatives, non-food entertainment can start with feeding your child's enthusiasm by talking about the trip in advance and then pointing out novel sights (for the very young, these can include airline baggage trains, road construction trucks, piggy-back trailers, and farm animals). Bring favorite toys for peace of mind, and any games that can conveniently be played sitting still. Our favorite travel pastime since Owen was two has been a pad of paper and anything to draw with. I can't say how many plane trips and restaurants have been made bearable by crayons or even a pen or pencil and the back of a placemat. For older children, of course, the placemats often come equipped with games. But for toddlers, you can pass the time by asking them to draw you certain things, or drawing things for and with them, including simple mazes and tic-tac-toe, even though they won't understand exactly how to play. I'll often produce a new pack of crayons after we are in the air; sometimes a small new toy pulled out at a key moment can save the day.

Comfort is the other travel essential: something for cleaning up crumbs and stickiness and a change of clothes for spills and accidents. Travel wipes are handy, but I often pack a washcloth too, in case water (even a glass of it) is available, because I think it's a more refreshing cleanup for the child. (A dry, clean washcloth can also, believe it or not, double as a diaper for babies in an emergency.)

Train Travel

I haven't even mentioned train travel, surely the most pleasant mode known to man. Common sense will tell you that what applies to our two most common means of travel, cars and planes, is also good for trains, buses, and boats. Trains offer the added advantage of fairly free movement; they offer scenery to amuse the children and a certain glamour of their own. Motion sickness is minimal on a train. Train food is variable in quality, sometimes quite good, sometimes awful, sometimes prepackaged and expensive, but again, you can bring your own. And the adults can relax and enjoy the scenery or play games, too.

Motion Sickness

However you travel, motion sickness may become an issue. You can get medicine from your pediatrician if you suspect it will be a big problem. But for simple discomfort from travel motion, food is often the best solution, especially dry snacks, gum, or a mild carbonated beverage like ginger ale.

S I X

◇

Kids' Play
in the Kitchen

"Hey, Mom, did ya ever make a carrot telephone? Well, you take a carrot that doesn't have a bite taken out of it, and you tie a string to it, and then you tie another carrot to the other end. . . ."

The four-year-old imagination is on the loose again. These are raw carrots Owen is demonstrating with, and an imaginary string, so I don't mind too much. The carrots jog my memory, reminding me that at four he is probably old enough to advance to a new stage in the kitchen: using a scraper. Kitchen knives will definitely be off limits for several more years, but the blade of the scraper is pretty self-contained, and he's at a good age now to get some new chores.

Actually Owen has been helping with the real food in the kitchen since he was two, and it hasn't been much of a chore at all. In fact, it's been a pleasure. Two was the age when we started making muffins and low-sugar cookies together, and by now he can help with just about anything that involves a mixing bowl. He's also beginning to be allowed to approach the stove top under close supervision (we have a gas stove with an open flame, but hot electric coils can be treacherous too, needless to say). And he can do other simple activities that help us in the kitchen, first by keeping him busy, but even more because they make him feel good about himself, and that helps him grow.

I believe children should be comfortable from a very early age with the things they are going to deal with for the rest of their lives. For our children's generation that includes computers and space travel, and we're working on those, but I think it should also include kitchens. Kitchens, used properly, can be safe and fun, and they are a rich source of hands-on activities that make children feel independent and self-confident. Of course children love to eat some of the things they get to cook with adults—like cookies (and the grown-ups do too)—but beyond that they are totally fascinated with how things *work,* and there are so many things at work in a kitchen.

Early Cooking Experience

Baking is a good place to start with your child in the kitchen, because it doesn't involve the stove top. Most everything that you do in the baking process is preparation on a table or counter; the hot part comes only at the end, when everything goes into the oven. And then the child can go play while waiting for the cooking to finish, savoring those wonderful baking aromas. Part of the play can actually be helping Mommy or Daddy clean up the mess—if Mommy or Daddy is a very patient adult.

Making Muffins

Muffins are a good place to start in the world of baking because they don't require rolling the dough, they are quick to make, and the ingredients are easily combined. Part of the secret of good muffins, in fact, is not to mix the dry and liquid ingredients too thoroughly, so muffins are ideal for a first taste of cooking: preparation is done before the child is bored or you're totally exasperated, your child gets a chance to do a little at each stage, and about 15 minutes later you can actually eat the product. You have just enough time, in fact, to get the kitchen clean enough to eat in and maybe brew a pot of tea for yourself to go with the muffins.

Muffins are also a good place to start if you are not an experienced baker yourself. If you prefer to try using mix first, by all means do. Homemade muffins are really just about as easy, however, as you'll quickly see after you do it once or twice, and making your own from scratch gives you more say about the ingredients.

Muffins are also an ideal thing to make in the morning when you have time. It wouldn't make sense, for instance, to make cookies in the morning, because of course everyone would want to eat them right then. (We discourage sweets before lunch—by making mornings off-limits to sweets, we keep that part of the day free of questions and arguments about snacking.) But with muffins, you can let the kids have a little cereal to stave off starvation until the muffins are ready. The adults may just want to wait and make the muffins their whole breakfast.

Muffins are also a great way to use up odd leftovers (leftover fruit or even vegetables, leftover cooked oatmeal) or to work in a little extra nutrition (soy flour, bran flakes, nuts, and fruit)—see recipes under Bread in Part II. And who can resist them warm from the oven with a cup of milk or juice?

There is one drawback to baking, and that is that it almost always involves flour. And whenever you have flour and a child together in the same room, the child and the room are going to get some flour on them. Don't be compulsive about neatness at this point. Dry flour can be dusted off or swept up; once it gets wet, preferably in the mixing bowl, it stays where it is and doesn't get all over everything. Approach the cooking adventure with the expectation that you'll end up with a little bit more of a mess than if you were cooking all by yourself. It's not a big deal, and the kids can always start learning how to clean up, too.

Before you even start, you should both wash your hands. It's a good habit when working with food, of course, but especially since your child will probably want to make at least one handprint in the flour.

Always start your joint cooking ventures by assembling your ingredients ahead of time and putting them somewhere that is convenient but out of reach. In our kitchen we work on the table in the middle of the room. I keep the ingredients on the counter between the sink and the stove—an arm's reach for me, but where no one who is less than four feet tall can really reach them. The next step is to preheat the oven and get out the utensils. This is also a good time to grease the pans—by yourself. Any utensil that is not sharp or breakable can go on the table to be checked out by little hands and eyes. Now you're ready to start. With your child up on a chair, you measure the dry ingredients into the bowl, letting him or her watch and even help. Then the two of you mix the dry ingredients. This takes some motor control, but children get better at it with practice and as they get older. At first you may have to hold the spoon or fork with your child throughout the stirring, but with time you will get an assistant who can actually mix up all the dry ingredients without tossing them out of the bowl while you fetch the wet ingredients. Owen likes to use the fork he mixes the dry ingredients with as a power shovel, making appropriate noises as the machine backs and fills, lifting up "rocks" and "cement" and moving them around.

With the dry ingredients thoroughly mixed, you get the wet ingredients together in a separate bowl or cup and mix them quickly. If you're working with a very young child who is new to flour and may make a mess before you can turn around, you may want to premix the wet ingredients just before the two of you start on the dry ingredients. In that case, just mix the wet stuff in its own bowl and set it out of the way until you need it. That way it will be ready instantly when you do want it. Your child may help pour the wet into the dry; then, after careful but quick mixing by both of you, it's time to fill the muffin pans.

For your child, a small spoon will probably work best. Explain that the object is to lift a spoonful of batter and put it into one of the cups of the pan and that each cup needs more than one spoonful (say "stop" when the cup is about half full and tell your child to start another one). If you're making a dozen or more muffins, you will probably want to fill most of the cups yourself with a tablespoon while your child works on one or two. Then presto, into the oven (which your child of course knows not to touch), and in a very short time your muffins are ready to eat.

Other Baking Adventures

After muffins Owen and I branched out into biscuits, because he was still pretty young and I didn't want to open the Pandora's box of cookies just yet. Buttermilk Biscuits (see recipes in Part II) can also be pretty simple and quick to prepare, and they are great with soups. They do represent a small advance in expertise in that they involve rolling the dough, but this is a good skill for everyone to learn, and biscuits are a good way to learn it because they are very sturdy and won't fall to pieces on the rolling board like pie dough or cookie dough. I used to let Owen mix the dry ingredients, then I cut in the shortening, then we mixed the liquid in together, and then I rolled the dough out most of the way. He had his own little cookie cutters that he'd gotten for Christmas or a birthday, and he was thrilled to be allowed to cut out little dogs and tiny gingerbread man shapes, which I then put on a separate plate, and we dusted them with cinnamon sugar. This was Owen's idea of a homemade cookie for a long time.

From there we moved on to drop cookies and then to cutout cookies for holiday gifts. He and his father took on homemade chocolate chip cookies when he was three and became experts at making them from scratch on long winter afternoons indoors. Somewhere along the way Owen also began helping make pan-cakes—only the mixing end of it, not the cooking (the stove top still being off limits). And need I say he learned to lick the spoon and scrape the bowl without any help at all?

Kitchen Safety

If you have a toddler, you've already taken many precautions in kitchen safety: moving all the cleaning liquids out of reach, baby-proofing off-limits cupboards with fasteners, and getting in the habit of turning pot handles inward on the stove so they can't be reached from below. I think whatever access a very young child can have to the kitchen, like playing on the floor with pots and pans, is good. It creates a feeling of at-homeness that ultimately can contribute to your child's good feelings about the kitchen and what comes out of it. But you do have to set limits. The first time Owen reached for the knobs on the stove he was less than two. In retrospect, who could blame him? They were eye-catching. But I didn't think about that. Instead I swatted his hand; the stove was about the only place in the house that was totally off limits. He was outraged, of course, and the result was that I made a stove of his own for him out of a cardboard carton that afternoon. It has been in our kitchen most of the time since then and is well worn.

Children can be directed to play alongside you if you give them the equipment, and it can be simple and an effective way of keeping them out of your hair while you cook. Nesting pots or a pot and a spoon to bang with work for one-year-olds; other toddlers can stir dry beans or even play in the sink or tear up lettuce. But for cooking together, there are a few additional safety measures. Children need to understand clearly that the stove top and oven are off limits and that they are not allowed to handle sharp knives or scissors or electrical appliances. A good way to enlist cooperation rather than tempting them to defy you is to qualify the "don'ts": "until you're older" or "unless Mommy or Daddy is here in the kitchen with you." A good rule of that kind is that drawers are off limits. When a child is one and two, they should simply be inaccessible, probably with a baby proofing device, and any attempt to go into forbidden territory should be met with a firm "No." When he or she is three and four, that won't work, and it's time to introduce the rules. Keeping the drawers off limits at first—when they're old enough to understand rules—removes the temptation to reach in and maybe run into something sharp. Once you are confident that they do understand, you may segregate all the dangerous utensils in one drawer and keep that off limits. You may want to keep electrical appliances unplugged, or store their blades high out of reach, except when you're using them. I know one litle girl who got her pigtails caught in the mixer while her mom's back was turned. She was rescued without injury but at the expense of about a foot of hair (and a batch of cake, but that was the least of it). At the very least, keep these tools pushed far back on your counters, and keep an eye on your child's skill in climbing. If they're old enough to drag a chair up and go climbing in search of snacks, it's probably time to go over the safety rules again.

Helpers in the Kitchen

As your child grows, keep an eye out for things he or she can do in the kitchen. At three, for instance, you can enlist their help in fixing their own meals, and this is a good way to co-opt the fussy eaters. If they help fix it, they'll probably be more interested in eating it. Did you have a baby food mill? This is the time to get it back out and let your youngster use it to grind up his own mashed potatoes or sweet potatoes, or puree a little split pea soup (a.k.a. "green soup" in our house, another of many foods that masquerade under innocent-sounding names) or homemade applesauce, or to grind up nuts for baking. The more solid foods, like potatoes, come through the mill the way they do through a ricer, which you can also let them use if you have one. The little strips are neat looking, and children are interested in seeing the process at work and being part of it. The soup also seems to change its form as it goes through the mill. It's hard to tell whether they are more interested in the changing shape of things or in the idea that they are actually making their own food. Present it casually ("Here, you can make your own mashed po-tatoes"). Then show them how it fits together and turns, and hold the base steady while they do it.

With a little help kids of four can use other simple hand-worked kitchen equipment: a hard-boiled egg slicer, which may also be used to slice up apple sections or bananas; an apple corer, and a peeler for carrots and potatoes. These humble gadgets may not be in modern kitchens, but keep an eye out for them in discount stores. They can make things more interesting for your fledgling cook. Does anyone still own a hand-worked meat grinder? That use to be a real treat in my mother's kitchen—to be allowed to grind up the leftover meat for hash.

Another childhood experience I recall vividly was helping our next-door neighbor, who had a garden, shell peas and snap the ends off the string beans. Snapping the beans or shucking fresh corn is still a treat for today's children as long as you can keep it a novelty or a Mom-and-me (or Dad-and-me) activity. Children look at these chores as privileges as long as you keep it fun.

At four, they want to spread their own sandwiches. Peanut butter, jelly, honey, cream cheese, and other spreadables are all fair game. They should understand that they are being *allowed* to use the table knife only because Mommy or Daddy is there. A neat twist on the peanut butter sandwich is the Peanut Butter Caterpillar or Turtle (see recipes in Part II). Make the caterpillar by alternating banana slices (perhaps sliced by the child) and peanut butter layers and threading these on a toothpick. The turtle is made of apple slices and peanut butter, steadied by a toothpick, with grapes on tooth-picks for the head and feet and a carrot curl for a tail.

Another activity this age can do with toothpicks is making ice tray Juicesicles (see recipe in Part II). Fill the cubicles with several different juices, letting your child choose which juices go where but pouring or at least steering the bottle yourself. Then set toothpicks at a slant in each cubicle and freeze to make bite-sized frozen treats. Owen loved these for dessert at age three, and in hot weather I would let him have seconds without any quibbling, which he thought was a great treat. For a really hot day a nice lunch or dinner course is a chilled platter of sliced fruit (cantaloupe, berries, apples, grapes, peaches) sprinkled with lime juice, with ice tray Juicesicles added at the last minute.

Children aged three or four can also learn to use a hand-held eggbeater with a little help to prevent splattering. Let them help with batters, eggs, and soups that need pureeing. Of course you probably have a food processor or an electric mixer, and they will learn to use them in time, too. For right now, work in the low-tech basics whenever it is convenient. At four or five children can help make a salad (by all means give *them* the chore of scrubbing the vegetables, with a sturdy chair or stool at the sink and an apron of their own), set the table, mash potatoes, make pancake batter (they love to break the eggs) and, with *very* close supervision, stir pudding at the stove. They are fascinated by physical changes like jelling, by the way, so let them in on the pudding and the chilled kanten pies (see recipes in Part II). If they are going to be allowed near the stove, to make their own pancakes, help scramble eggs, or stir things, get them in the habit of working with hair pulled back, sleeves rolled up, and apron on, and no strings, ribbons, or jewelry that could get caught, heat up, or burn. Give kids their own tools, including an apron and anything else that is cheap and practical. They can have play utensils and dishes as young as two, real ones as they grow older, although those aged five or six will still enjoy play dishes, especially if you let them have a tea party with dolls or bears.

At four and five children are reaching the age where they can get their own cold cereal for breakfast. They like to have the responsibility, and you can help by storing the cereal down low and putting a small pitcher of milk in the refrigerator where they can reach it (to avoid spills from the larger milk carton). Under supervision *only* they can also make their own toast and spread things on it. The toaster can also be used to heat up frozen leftover french toast. Plain toast can make a whole breakfast if they spread it with peanut butter, cream cheese, or some other protein food.

Eating Games

"Don't play with your food" seems to be the constant refrain around our house. So why would I suggest eating games? Eating games are not the same as playing with your food. They are games to eat by and sometimes games that allow the chef to get dinner on the table.

Probably all of us have some kind of eating game. Children not only love to play; they *live* to play. It's been said that play is a child's work, and you can put that sense of play to work for you to get your child to buckle down and eat.

Eating games of course must be conducted within the bounds of dining etiquette. Throwing food is not an eating game. The kinds of games we use to help mealtime progress without terminally boring the children include "I Spy" sorts of games. Our current favorite is one that starts "If you're big and you know your alphabet, you'll find a letter A somewhere on this table." (This game does not work, incidentally, nor is it appropriate, for candlelight meals in formal settings. This is a game for dining at the table when there are things on it like milk cartons, juice containers, and perhaps part of today's paper.) The person who is "it" has spied the first letter of the alphabet somewhere within eyeshot (it could be anywhere in the room, as long as it can be seen clearly without leaving the table). The next person has to find the letter, and then it's his turn to be "it" with the next letter, which the third person must then find. While this is going on, two purposes are being served: The child is eating food without complaint, and at the same time interacting with the adults at the table.

Other possibilities are naming games where the food takes on a disguise. For example, you can serve your children Dinosaur Salad (see recipe in Part II) and have everyone decide what the components of the salad are: the broccoli spears are trees, the carrots are logs, the lettuce is grass, the sprouts are jungle vines—all of these being things that dinosaurs (the children) would love to eat. In similar games the mashed potatoes become clouds, the meatballs are boulders, the tomato wedges are boats, the string beans become

a logjam—the imagination of children gives you endless possibilities. You can even apply a form of Simon Says to the table,
where family members take turns saying what everyone is now going
to take a bite of.

Needless to say, the adults would go bonkers if these games went
on at every meal or during all of a meal, but they can help get
everyone through occasionally, and they do serve the major purpose
of making little children feel included in what otherwise seem like
interminable adult conversations. Children love to have their imag-
inations engaged, which is why the notion of foods turning into
clouds or trees pleases them, even though to adults it may seem
silly. Look at it as good exercise for the right side of your brain and
an opportunity for intergenerational communication.

Children have a sense of humor about it, too: they enjoy the
games even when they realize what the adults are up to. One night
Owen balked at applesauce, which I know he likes. He was just being
ornery. So instead of getting into a battle of wills with him, I said,
"Well, just a few bites." "One bite," he countered, prepared to haggle.
I waited. He took a bite. I found myself saying, in my best imitation of
the Count on *Sesame Street,* "One wonderful bite." He caught the
allusion and decided he would play my silly game. He took another
bite. "Two terrific bites," I said. Another bite. "Three thrilling bites
. . . four fabulous bites . . . five fantastic bites. . . ." In short order
the applesauce was all gone, and we had a good laugh.

Nonfood Kitchen Activity

Other activities that buy time for harried parents include finding
something the children can do while you're trying to fix dinner or
eat dinner. For fixing dinner with children under two, the best ploy,
as mentioned earlier, can be the time-honored method of letting
them range freely in the lower cabinets through the pots and plastic
bowls. It's educational play at age one to two for children to com-
pare sizes and volumes, and they will be fascinated by things that fit
inside of other things. From two to three, water play standing on a

chair at the sink may not be too messy. Or they can "cook" alongside of you at a play stove you keep in the kitchen. Or they can begin to occupy themselves for really appreciable amounts of time at the kitchen table with crayons or paints and paper, or with playdough, which they can help you make (see the Play Recipes section in Part II). At two to three, as discussed, they also begin helping with the real food, an activity that pays increasingly bigger dividends as time goes on.

If you want to have a nice quiet dinner in the dining room with adult conversation, the best way to do it in my opinion is to send the children somewhere else for dinner. But, as that's not always a practical option, your other choice is either to feed them early or excuse them from the table quickly. If you are not eating in the kitchen, you can then send them into the kitchen, where they will be close enough to supervise by ear but far enough away to allow you to talk. You can give them drawing and painting (or, better yet, pasting—that really absorbs their attention) activities at the kitchen table or let them play at the sink if you can trust them not to flood the house. In a pinch, dismissing the children to go watch a video is an option.

Holidays and Rainy Days

The kitchen can follow the calendar with a series of seasonal and holiday activities. These are a great way to pass rainy days as well as a natural for getting the kids involved in holiday preparations. The start of the (nursery) school year is a good point of departure. As leaves begin to turn, collect some on a walk. Wash them in a dishpan and blot them between paper towels. Let your child watch as you press them between sheets of wax paper (under a cotton towel) with a hot iron to make a door or window decoration. Preschoolers can use the finished product for show-and-tell. For older children who take lunch to school, let them help plan a week of menus and help you with the grocery shopping. The habit of involvement is one way you can try to ensure that the kids do eat what you send to school in their lunch boxes or brown bags.

Late fall is time for pumpkins. Pick your own at a farm if practical, as well as apples for lunches (involvement again) or a pie. Carve the pumpkin, with your child directing its facial expression (fierce or funny?). If you don't cut it until right before Halloween, and refrigerate it immediately afterward, you can bake it and use the flesh for pie or Pumpkin Eater Soup (see recipes in Part II), another cooking adventure the kids will enjoy.

For Thanksgiving, let the kids make a crookneck squash "turkey," with cranberries on toothpicks for head and tail, as a table decoration. You can bake pumpkin bread or pie for the holiday with some of the pumpkin you froze from Halloween (or some from a can). Make a big batch of cranberry sauce from scratch (see recipes in Part II) and freeze some until December, when the kids can fill jelly jars and decorate them with ribbon for simple presents. Another good present for the holidays are salt-dough decorations made with cookie cutters and painted. Or you can design your own patterns for holiday decorations and mold them from the salt dough. Insert wire hooks before baking, paint, and decorate with a ribbon. (See Play Recipes in Part II).

Home-baked cookies are another good winter holiday treat or present, of course. Take the kids on a mini-excursion to a hardware or discount store to look for seasonal cookie cutters and make old-fashioned Holiday Sugar Cookies (see recipe in Part II). This is one treat that won't work without the big S; we bend the rules for holidays, but we also balance our plates of cookies with healthier Oatmeal Cookies and Carob Chip Cookies (see recipes in Part II). Slices of homemade breads can also go on the paper plates you give to friends and neighbors, or you can get small disposable aluminum baking pans and give individual loaves covered with foil and topped with a bow. Cranberry, banana, nut, and pumpkin breads are all good treats for friends to enjoy with their holiday breakfasts.

Late winter is a time for enjoying hot carob cocoa or Hot Mulled

Apple Cider (see recipe in Part II) with cinnamon sticks and for making Valentine's Day presents out of salt-dough cutouts that the kids can paint. This is a good time to make a batch of playdough (see recipes in Part II) with the kids, too—it helps pass an afternoon when you're stuck indoors. Dye it with food coloring.

In late winter you can also plan a garden, even a window box if you live in an apartment, that will involve your child in another loosely kitchen-related activity—growing something that will later be eaten by all. Children love to play in the dirt, as we all know, and even if you just have a deck or terrace, there are herbs, flowers, and miniature vegetables that can turn into a spring and summer activity if you have a little time. Give your child his or her own territory, whether it's a corner of the garden, a window box of her own, or even a pot on the windowsill. An old tablespoon and a small watering can are the only tools the child will need to be happy.

Start children on gardening at whatever age you have patience to deal with; of course they get more coordinated as they get older, but things like squash vines, tomatoes, marigolds, and some of the herbs are pretty indestructible once they get going. You can start things like marigolds—the petals go into salads—squash, and pumpkins inside during late winter in sprouting trays fashioned from cardboard egg boxes, with dirt and seeds from a hardware store or garden center.

If you have a yard, even a small one, and are willing to make a one-time investment, you can even offer the family a lesson in completing the kitchen cycle with a compost bin. Before you protest that you don't have room, or the expertise, or that it will be too smelly, know that there are now relatively small, odor-free compost bins made of plastic that are available from most garden catalogs for about $100. Making compost involves physical and chemical changes that children find really interesting—to say nothing of helping the environment along a little and educating them about a bit of science.

Speaking of cycles, the garden brings us back to where we started. But before we leave summer, and the kitchen, how about starting one more activity that can become a family tradition? Invest in an ice cream maker or—for the low-tech version—teach the kids to make their own frozen yogurt bars or Frozen Fruit Parfaits (see recipes in Part II). Then let them help plan an end-of-summer picnic menu with a healthy homemade frozen dessert for the finale.

"Hey, Mom, know how ya make ice cream soup? Well, you take some vanilla ice cream and let it melt. . . ."

SEVEN

When Children Get Finicky

There is a huge teen-age population across the country that attests to the fact that children grow up to be healthy young adults with good teeth and strong bones on a diet of peanut butter and mashed potatoes. That's reassuring, but it doesn't necessarily ease your anxiety when faced with a finicky two-year-old.

At some point between the ages of two and six, it is very possible that your child's eating habits will surprise or even appall you. You may agonize over whether he or she could possibly be getting enough of the right nutrients. And since this is a crucial period both for physical growth and for establishing lifetime eating habits, it's important to be prepared.

Undoubtedly you will question the cause of this new development. Is your child (a) a fussy eater, (b) a child who knows his own mind, or (c) just going through a stage? It's (a) if you talk to his grandmother, (b) in your own opinion, and (c) according to his aunt. I think it's actually all three. I grew up in a generation where you ate what was put before you; you were supposed to be grateful for it, and absolutely no exceptions were made, not even if you were obviously about to choke on your liver and spinach. Ask your own parents' opinion, and they'll probably tell you you're spoiling the children. *Perhaps* that is true. But the question, it seems to me, is, what do you want to get out of an encounter at the table?

Do you want your child to be reasonably well nourished and to develop a favorable attitude toward food in general, a sense of confidence in his ability to feed himself, and a set of decent table manners? Or do you want to prove who's boss? (The child is. But more about that later.)

Children are difficult to feed at various points for a variety of reasons. It pays to keep cool about their eating habits, and it helps to know why they do the things they do when they do. The first major confrontations at the table can be especially frustrating. Not only are they likely to coincide with the "terrible twos," when your patience is apt to be short anyway, but they seem to occur at dinnertime, when most adults are already frazzled after a long day. Combined, these factors can make you come to dread even *fixing* dinner, let alone eating it.

Because toddlers are still largely preverbal—with the exception of their mastery of that maddening "No!"—your attempts at reasoning with them are limited. And you may be hard-pressed to reason with yourself. You're used to a hearty appetite, and you've watched your infant perhaps *triple* in size during the first year of life. Now, when your child seems to be eating less and less, you're apt to panic. What's going to happen to the toddler's height/weight curve?

Relax. Your child may very well be eating less, and that may be the best thing. Toddlers are supposed to grow more slowly than infants. They don't have to eat all the time just to sustain life and growth. Keep in mind that your eyes can be bigger than your child's stomach, and he or she may know more about portion control than you do. So be prepared to settle for small helpings.

Also keep in mind that the "terrible twos" may be a misnomer. It could be said that this age starts as early as eighteen months and goes on until four—at least. You might also feel funny about the word *terrible,* because it implies the child is somehow at fault. Of course that's not true. The phrase is just a description of a very real phenomenon of distancing that goes on in early childhood and again (hang on to your hat) in adolescence.

What looks like fussiness also may be caused by the fact that toddlers are learning to know their own minds. In early childhood, because food is such a large part of a child's life, much of the strife can revolve around food. So if you have a finicky toddler, you're not alone, and there are good reasons for this behavior. So keep it in perspective and don't get too caught up in what goes on at dinner.

Children do go through stages with food. They will love raisins for three years and then hate them for a year. They won't be able to get enough broccoli this week; next week they won't touch it. They'll eat spaghetti tonight and turn their noses up at it tomorrow. Going through stages does indeed sometimes make them into fussy eaters, but there's a positive side to this: This week they may not eat what they loved last week; however, they'll stun you by trying something you thought they hated. One couple I know had almost despaired of their child, who ate only mashed potatoes (what would happen the day he refused *those*?), when one night he requested *and ate* a meat-filled taco.

Still, putting up with a finicky eater from, say, age two to six is a terrifying prospect. When your child was a baby just learning to eat solid food, you were apt to be forgiving, but as your son or daughter grew older, you became more demanding. You *should* be more demanding, and your child should have more rights and responsibilities. Unfortunately, this means confrontations. These are normal and necessary, but they should *not* be allowed to erupt into a battle royal.

I mentioned earlier that when it comes to deciding what a child eats, the child is the boss. This may go against the grain—after all, *you* are the parents—but if you get into a battle of wills with the child, there is no way you can win in the end. You may force him to eat the beets, but he won't like them, and he won't like dinner. And if he *really* refuses to eat the beets, what choices do you have? Force-feeding? Starvation? Sure, but both are the makings of a no-win situation. Much better to head off the difficulty or have some win-win compromise up your sleeve when your child says no.

Also, you really do want your child to be on good terms with food. You *want* the child to be the boss, as much as is reasonably possible, so that he or she will eventually grow up eating the right foods and feeling good about it. The alternative—a child who is alienated from food—is a phenomenon we see increasingly in our society. Anorexia, bulimia, and obesity all are afflictions that have to do with a need to control one's life that is expressed in relation to food. Viewed in a more positive way, good feelings about food are good feelings about people, since eating is one of our most social human acts. So your job with a toddler at the dinner table is not only to nourish his body. It's to nourish his good feelings about himself and other people. As long as his pediatric checkups show he's progressing along his weight/height curve, and as long as there is no other reason to think he's malnourished, you can take the long view about what goes on at mealtime.

Raising a child to eat right and feel good about it is not achieved all at once and not without some blood, sweat, and tears. Fortunately there are a number of strategies for feeding recalcitrant children, making reasonably sure that their diet *is* balanced, and keeping your own sanity. These start, as mentioned in earlier chapters, when the child is an infant, and they don't stop until he or she sets up housekeeping elsewhere (some would say not even then). By then, ideally, you will have taught the kids not only what to eat but also how to fix it, so theirs will be a superior nutritional outlook. In the meantime, try some of the tactics that follow.

Throughout this chapter I've been referring to the dinner table, because dinner seems to be the most troublesome meal. Why? First of all, it's at the end of the day, and everyone is tired and perhaps a little cross. Second, it's the one meal where the whole family is most likely to sit down together, so it has special importance. Third, it's more likely to be the meal where adult tastes are catered to, with the result that the kids don't get fed kid food—unless you're willing to run a catering service. Finally, since it is the end of the day, you may be trying to fill any nutritional gaps left by breakfast, lunch, and snacks. It's a scenario full of Cecil B. De Mille potential for full-scale conflict over who's going to eat how much of what, so the following suggestions focus mainly on dinner.

Prepare Dovetail Meals

This strategy involves looking for places where a child's taste can fit into the meal the adults are having, like a dovetail joint at the corner of a building. Where tastes meet is your dovetail. This approach is so practical that you probably have already tried it, but if not, here are some examples of how it has worked for our family. Lots of little kids don't like tomato sauce, except on pizza. Maybe it's too acidic for their little tongues or stomachs—who knows? Whatever the reason, obviously you don't push it on them. Instead, give your child the spaghetti without the sauce for now and keep offering the sauce from time to time. A dovetail meal in our house is spaghetti with Parmesan cheese for Owen (he likes to sprinkle it himself) and Linguine with Red Clam Sauce for us. With it we have a Watercress Salad that includes seedless red grapes and orange slices. (See the recipes in Part II.) Owen gets the grapes and the orange slices and maybe a few carrot sticks. Presto—a meal we can all eat without protest, and it didn't mean *any extra work* (a very important principle) for the chef.

You know your child. Maybe she loves potatoes, but not au gratin in a casserole. Fine. After you slice the potatoes, set aside her portion, and just before everything else is cooked, throw them into boiling water or a steamer and then mash them. Say your child loves broccoli. If you're making a medley of vegetables with herbs, set aside some of the broccoli and cook it separately from the zucchini, mushrooms, and basil. If you're cooking carrots and your child hates carrots, save some raw ones. Keeping foods simple for fussy eaters also applies to fish, chicken, meat, and so on. Skip the seasonings and the problem ingredients and let the child eat the part of the dish he or she can deal with. It may take a moment of thought in advance, but the amount of extra preparation is minor, especially if you have a microwave. And *you* save on emotional wear and tear.

Focus on Food Appeal

One person's delectable is another's yucky. *Yucky* is a word we all come to know well in the child-rearing years, the ultimate in opprobrium. There's not much point in arguing about it, but it helps to know what brings it on. Children who are finicky, you may comfort yourself, are often the ones with the sharpest senses. They're attuned (sometimes too much so) to fine differences in texture, appearance, temperature, and taste that the rest of us sail right by.

Texture can be a special torment to the fussy child. Foods seem stringy, tough, scratchy, slimy, squishy, or a combination of these. It's better to let this child cope with each food separately and decide what to mix with what. It also helps to realize that children's palates often *are* more sensitive than ours, just the same way that a splinter hurts their tender fingers more. Whatever we can reasonably do to make the texture of food appealing is a help. Textures that are often appealing are crunchy, smooth, creamy, and firm. Raw vegetables that crunch may seem better than their cooked counterparts. If something is cooked, it will help if it doesn't have lumps. A squarely cut, firm chunk of chicken may win more plaudits than one that is falling apart, even though to our taste the one that's falling off the bone is the best.

In appearance, what's familiar is often best. If children can help you fix the food, that may help them, because they can see how it got to look the way it does. Sometimes making things into interesting shapes works. Sometimes your child may want vegetables raw, in sticks; other times only cooked vegetables in round slices will do. Who knows why? If giving the child a choice encourages eating, the reason doesn't matter.

For toddlers, an almost lukewarm temperature for cooked foods is usually okay, but some develop a fancy for foods that are cooler or warmer. Refrigerator cold is how they'll probably want their milk, juice, and yogurt—if it's not, then it's stale (or yucky). Their mouths are still sensitive to temperatures that are too warm, and one mouthful that's hot may put them off for the rest of the meal. If you're in a hurry to serve the oatmeal or other hot dish, put an ice cube or some compatible cold liquid into the child's portion and stir it around. He'll probably find this fascinating and want to help.

Taste is individual, but it helps to remember that young children generally prefer sweetness and have an aversion to bitterness. This is important enough to consider separately, since it can contribute to your meal planning.

And for those fussy eaters who just can't abide getting their hands sticky, wet, or whatever, an added ploy: try toothpicks. Cut the juicy foods into chunks and serve with toothpicks. For that matter, any reasonably acceptable food that can be eaten in chunks becomes more interesting when eaten with toothpicks. You can even let your young child put the picks in. But don't try to palm off any known-to-be-yucky foods this way, or you and the toothpicks will lose credibility. Children from age three up can handle the toothpicks safely, but you should watch them at first to be sure they have the hang of it.

Include Some of the Foods Kids Like Best

Kids seem to like foods that are crunchy; foods that are sweet; foods that are salty; sometimes foods that are oily, like fried foods; and foods that are familiar—comfort foods. Built-in tastes (for sweets and what's familiar) and distastes may be a survival mechanism intended to help our forebears avoid poisonous food. Well, kids might like junk foods like greasy french fries for a similar reason. Fast foods like french fries are mostly an experience in fat and salt. Both of these are overabundant in our culture, and we are all trying to limit our kids' (and our own) intake of them. But there *was* a time when salt was so rare that it was used for money—and salt in limited amounts is a necessary nutrient for humans and other animals. Likewise fat; during the Ice Age it was certainly essential to survival through long winters when food was scarce. Dietary fat provides a highly concentrated energy source—twice the energy, measured in calories, of either proteins or carbohydrates. Not only during the Ice Age, but indeed until modern post-industrial push-button times, getting enough fat in your diet could mean the difference between surviving and not surviving. It enabled people to do the hard manual labor required in everyday life. So it's no wonder we have a sort of built-in craving for it. You're not necessarily going to be able to program that out of your children, and you should know that. It may not make you any more inclined to give them those foods, but understanding why they crave them may help you find acceptable alternatives or an acceptable rule about when and how much they are allowed to eat of certain foods.

So, instead of insisting that the kids eat exactly what you eat, why not think about what they would like and include some of that if it isn't too much trouble? For an example, when planning your dinner, don't neglect the possibility of fruit or think that it has to be a dessert. For a young child it can be a major—sometimes *the* major—component of dinner. Fruit is often crunchy and almost always sweet. And it's full of all the vitamins and minerals you get in vegetables at a fraction of the emotional effort for you and the child.

Sweet and bland vegetables that have a pleasant or at least unremarkable consistency are another good possibility. This is why mashed potatoes are a nearly universal favorite. Sweet potatoes can also be a good option for the same reason; where mashed potatoes are safely bland, sweet potatoes are sweet. Cooked, cooled a bit and pureed or cut into small cubes, and eaten with toothpicks, they are a potential favorite.

Enlist fats sparingly (if you child doesn't have a weight or cholesterol problem) to help get more protein into your child's diet: provide nuts or sunflower seeds or pumpkin seeds as part of dinner.

Kids often really like them, and together with any grain-based starch, they boost your child's total protein intake. They are also the kind of healthy snack kids will eat without argument and may help to stave off terminal hunger while you are throwing the rest of dinner together.

As for salt, far be it from me in this salt-loaded culture to encourage you to let your children eat salt. But don't be surprised if, contrary to your own style of cooking, your children's tastes do include salt. Just try to keep them from learning about it as long as you can. Then let them use it; sparingly, unless your doctor recommends otherwise.

Keep a Rough Nutrition Count

In feeding fussy eaters we often worry if they're getting enough of all the essential nutrients. Earlier chapters discussed children's needs and good sources of nutrients. When it's time to cook dinner, do a rough tally of what your kid has eaten so far that day. Once you're familiar with the source and standby foods listed in Chapter Three, this arithmetic will come easily. What does your child still need to eat today? Did he get a lot of protein at lunch? If so, maybe you don't need to worry about that at dinner. Are you having a vegetable your daughter doesn't like? Perhaps an apple or carrot sticks would do as well. Think about whether she *really* needs that spinach before you go to war for it or even mention it. Perhaps you should offer some Prune-Grape Drink (see recipe in Part II) or apricot juice with dinner instead. Be flexible. Remember too that sometimes appetites vary from day to day. If they're really not hungry, fine—it may balance out tomorrow. Just don't let dessert and snacks replace real food.

Fix Ahead, Feed Ahead

For your own sanity, if it's practical, fix foods ahead of time, during a part of the day when you and your child are still in a good mood, if you're at home together, or the night before, if both parents are working. This can involve such chores as cleaning and cutting up foods, assembling casseroles (and, if necessary, setting aside the parts the child will eat), setting out necessary pots, dishes, equipment and ingredients (obviously this will work with very small children only if the children can't reach them), and even cooking anything that can reasonably be fixed in advance. (Don't forget freezing foods and using a microwave to defrost and heat them—a microwave oven is an incredible time-saver for parents who both work.)

Divide up preparation chores with other family members. If you're preparing things the night before, and there's more than one adult available to help, let one person do postdinner cleanup and bedtime duty while the other does meals for the next day. Coming home from the office to a bag of salad fixings that are already cleaned and cut up is a great boost at the end of the day—anything that gets you to dinner in a more pleasant frame of mind.

Also, do consider feeding the kids while you are fixing dinner for yourselves at the end of a long day. Kids often fuss because they are tired and crabby—and if you're tired and crabby, they'll pick up on it and act worse.

Set the Table with Standby Alternatives

These don't have to be fancy, and I don't mean you should encourage your children to think you are running a catering service. But dishes of things like carrot sticks or other raw vegetables, cottage cheese, fruit, applesauce—whatever your family likes that is reasonably nutritious and easy to fix—can be regular or occasional side dishes on your table.

Get the Kids Involved

We looked at this aspect of feeding kids in the preceding chapter, but it has special application to the fussy child. To have some idea of how the food got to the table in its final form, and to feel that he or she helped, is a great incentive for a child to participate in the eating process. This includes sprinkling on Parmesan cheese, cinnamon, sesame seeds, or other condiments on the food. Gomasio (see recipe in Part II) in a saltshaker is a kind of compromise if you're looking for ways to limit salt but not eliminate it altogether. You can also put wheat germ in a shaker that has large enough holes and let the child sprinkle that on foods. Just keep it refrigerated so it stays fresh.

Know Your Rules and Stick to Them

Rules are especially important for the fussy eater, because if you left it up to the child, he would fill up on snacks and then genuinely not be hungry (as well as already being picky) when mealtime comes. The clearer the rules are, the sooner and more often you mention them, the better off you'll be.

We have a rule in our house about dessert. (Yes, I know they tell you not to bribe your children, but do they have children?) Owen for one is old enough to understand negotiation and be good at it. But he also knows we have a few rules that are virtually inflexible, and one of those rules is that if you don't eat dinner you don't get dessert. What constitutes dinner is open to some negotiation, but the adults are the ultimate arbiters of that one.

We also have a rule about sweets at other times of the day. In general we don't eat sweets or snacks in the morning. That's simply a rule. What it means is that we get up to and through lunch without much argument about what we're going to eat.

We also have a sort of unspoken, floating rule that enough is enough—enough sweets or junk food—and the adults get to decide what is enough, whether it's enough for now or enough for the whole day.

Keep Portions Small

Especially if you're going to have rules about eating everything served or the like, you must be careful not to give your child too much. If you watch little children eat, you will soon realize that for them a whole sandwich or six tablespoons of a food may be too much. Don't back yourself into a corner, demanding that they eat something they don't want and—more important—don't need.

Respect Your Child

You can't always do so, but respect your child's wishes whenever possible. Also respect your child's instincts. I can't count the number of times Owen has opted for fruit for dinner and not wanted to eat anything else. Then, when I humor him, or at most insist that he just eat two spoonfuls of whatever else he's supposed to eat, I see a day or so later that everyone around him is sick, and he's not. Sometimes—not always (this rule doesn't apply to ice cream for obvious reasons)—I really think he knows better than anybody what he needs to eat. Isn't that what we would wish for our children—that they will instinctively know what to eat to nourish themselves and ward off infections? Of course they have all the food temptations of our culture to deal with. But let's give them credit. Sometimes they really do know best.

Don't Talk Negatively About Your Child's Eating Habits

Especially don't do so in front of them. When your daughter hears you say she's such a fussy eater, that's what she becomes. When your son hears you say he doesn't like or won't eat peas, he likes them even less. You risk programming yourselves and your children for more rejection this way. View the fussiness as a event, rather than as an ongoing problem, and things will go better. Instead of verbally confirming that your son doesn't like peas, say simply, "Oh. No peas tonight. Another time." Here is where your knowledge of standby foods comes in handy. Again, this doesn't mean that you run a catering service, but if the standby carrot strips, apple, melon, or other alternative is already on the table, your child can always help himself.

EIGHT

◇

Living in
the Material World

I f we are conscientious (some might say, compulsive) parents, we
approach our children's school years with a mixture of excitement and dread. We're about to start letting go—really. Will it work?
Will they know how to fly? Will they remember all we taught them?
(Of course not. Silly us.) Our hovering in the wings continues at a
perhaps diminished rate—as we and they become more confident—
for years, until they finally leave home.

During these years they continue to eat, of course, though we may
vociferously grumble about what they eat. What should be our
strategies for coping, as they go to eat at other folks' houses? When
we pack their school lunches? When as teenagers they need more
iron than ever, more protein, more calories, more, more, more, and
they want to go on a crash diet, or eat junk food all the time? Ah,
junk food. Welcome to the material world.

Well, on the one hand, we can't dictate to them. On the other
hand, we can try to keep lines of communication open. Starting at
the age that is just pre-school, we look ahead to the coming years,
and we know that in the long run, the kids will learn to keep their

elbows off the table, and they will have some idea about good nutrition, because we're going to keep at it. But of course we're not living in the long run—we're living day to day. Sometimes it seems as if there will never be an uninterrupted conversation or a clean plate at the table again. So, in the hope of easing the transition into the world for us and them, let's explore some ideas on table manners, eating out, school meals and after-school snacks, talking about food with the kids, making rules stick, and the care and feeding of teenagers.

Table Manners

Now that Owen's four, we've gotten this far: foods that are messy are not finger foods (applesauce with a spoon, please); there's no dessert unless he eats enough dinner (as defined by us, his parents); he eats sitting down; it's not polite to interrupt; he may not play with his food; and he doesn't (usually) eat dessert until everyone's ready. For the time being, we think our child's manners are pretty good, and this may be partly because we include him frequently in the conversation (sometimes telling him to wait until we finish this thought and then he'll have a turn), don't bug him too much about his eating style, and excuse him from the table when his attention starts to fade.

Other possible rules include the one that says "If you can't say something nice, don't say anything at all." That means no gagging motions, kamikaze dives, or cries of "Yecchh" over the Swiss chard. Among rules for children around age five is an at-least-one-bite (or two or three, as you prefer) rule. A little further down the road come proper use of utensils and elbows off the table.

I suggest that you treat the issue of manners on a sort of sliding scale. For instance, there's how we behave at home versus how we behave when we're out. And there's what we normally eat at home versus what we eat elsewhere. And then there are special occasions.

On the home front we may generally be more relaxed about manners, but stricter about what is eaten. At the same time, this doesn't mean manners aren't important. While children are still developing the motor skills that enable coordinated hand movements, there's no use getting mad at them if they spill things, eat with their fingers, and can't wield a knife and fork. At the same time, they can be encouraged to use a spoon (or a fork if they're feeling ambitious). (At our house, we try to minimize spills by using a place mat that has the spot for the cup or glass clearly marked. That way, if we find it perched precariously near the edge of the table, we can remind Owen, "Where does the glass go?")

By age five, children often want to cut up their own food. You can let them try with soft foods like pancakes, though it may take the entire meal. (At least it keeps them busy.) Girls typically are more advanced than boys in the fine motor skills and may get to this sooner. By age six they should be able on occasion to sit still for most of dinner, not interrupt, try at least a bite of everything, not lean all over the table, ask to be excused, and take their dishes with them. I say "on occasion." And I didn't mention breakfast or lunch. Take it slowly. This is a good age to begin dealing with preparing them to eat out. Eating at friends' houses, unaccompanied by you, will be one of the exciting adventures of their elementary school years. Somewhere along the line, perhaps as an adjunct to their table-setting duties, you'll hit them with the information that there are different utensils for different uses, so that when they grow up and have to dine at the White House, they won't eat the consommé with a coffee spoon.

Family Dinners

In these hectic two-career family days, dinners together don't always happen naturally. I think family dinners are important, and I suggest that you select one evening a week when you know everyone can be there and make that your regular night for a leisurely, sit-down-at-the-table family dinner. Pick a menu you know everyone likes and expect them all to be there. For parents of teenagers, or even middle-school children, I know the night may not be the same one every week, although it's nice if it can be. You can always find out every week which night will be a good one and plan the family meal for that night.

Try to start the tradition when the children start school (by then they're old enough to handle it) and continue it throughout their school years, to counteract the increasing tendency of everyone to go off in all directions. The meal doesn't have to be fancy, but save the more pick-up-and-go fare, like tacos and pizza, for less leisurely nights. One parent-chef I know says, "It's not always easy to find something everyone likes, but when they do sit down together, it seems like they like a big meal. If I haven't fixed a big meal, they look at it and say, 'Is this all?'" Your family will have developed its tastes over the years so that you know what meal will have appeal on a night when everyone's there. For many families, those favorite meals are comfort foods familiar from childhood. For others it might be a meal that takes too long to fix on most nights. Whatever it is, the ingredients should be as fresh as possible—save the frozen foods for meals on the run.

For other nights in the week, your schedules will govern your dinners. One family with four children lets each child have one night a week where he or she helps plan the menu and gets to pick what goes on it. This helps enlist their cooperation in eating the other dinners they didn't help plan.

The Child as Guest

With table manners just beginning to be established, you may wonder what your until-now fussy eater is going to do for the first time he or she goes to eat at someone else's house without you. Certainly one of the big adventures in the early school grades is staying to dinner at a playmate's house. So if you're wondering how that particular transition will be accomplished, you might be encouraged to know that many parents notice that appetite patterns change as children grow. Around six and seven there's a spurt of interest in eating, perhaps from the stress and energy expended in a full day of school. Try to expand your child's eating habits in the good foods before they get too firmly settled in their peer groups and "teen eating" sets in. The early contact with their peer group can actually work to your advantage, even with fussy eaters. When children see other kids eating things, they're suddenly willing to try them too. Dinner at someone else's house can work wonders. "You won't believe how surprised I was to find out that my Mary ate *green beans* at one house and *coleslaw* at another," says a mother of four. "She's never eaten anything green in her life." This particular mom had sent her children off with some general hints about being polite and trying a little of everything. "I didn't say they had to, but I encouraged it." Children, especially between the ages of four and about eight or so, are eager to please adults and impressed to the hilt by what their peers (and older children) do.

This may be a good time to read *Bread and Jam for Frances* (see Appendix A) with your fussy eater. Kids quickly see the humor in the story of the little skunk who turns up her nose at everything but bread and jam—until she starts getting it for breakfast, lunch and dinner.

And if you institute a firm at-least-try-one-bite rule at this time, the kids won't arrive at the age of sixteen and not know what spinach is. The other thing you want to do is to get *them* to help you make up a policy of what's eaten at home—and away from home.

Food at School

The first four or five years of your children's lives are a period of slow socialization, with you, the parents, still at the center of their world. Most nursery schools are pretty conscientious about the food they provide as snacks for the children in their care. If you do send your child to preschool, that's one of the items you want to discuss with the school before enrolling. It's also an item you want to look for in visiting the school; try to make your preenrollment visit while school is actually in session and include a question about the snack of the day on your list of things to find out about.

Once your child starts elementary school, you have progressively less say over what he or she eats. This is as it should be, but it doesn't mean you stop having input. Two areas where you can continue to influence your child are the school lunch and the school snack.

It's important for you to know, especially with grade-school children, whether any snack foods are sold on the premises of the school your child is attending and, if so, what they are. Lobby, if you need to, to assure that no junk food is available during school hours and that, if snacks are sold, they are healthy ones. This concern can extend to high school too, although by then you should allow your child more latitude in choices, since the real world—unsupervised by you—is looming directly ahead.

A number of school systems have rules about snacks, and these are an excellent idea. If your system doesn't, here are two existing rules in school systems that you might want to lobby for:

1. No trades. What this means is that children bringing their lunches eat what they brought. They can't trade their apple (or sandwich) for a cookie. This is a good rule for the beginning grades. By middle school, they'll be more independent in their choices, and may be buying lunch instead of bringing it.

2. Snacks are brought from home and must be nutritious (crackers with cheese or peanut butter, fruit, fruit rollups, and granola bars all pass muster here). This is a good area to enlist your child's help in planning—and while you're planning is a good time to talk about the concept of nutrition.

3. Snacks sold in the school include ice cream and Popsicles. You control the purchase power of children when they are first in school. Why not also make sure that the frozen treats offered include pure fruit varieties?

On to lunch. The key to good nutrition for children from age six up is involvement, whether you're considering snacks or something more substantial. If you send a lunch to school with your child, of course you can pack only healthy food. But can you be sure it will be eaten?

If your school has a no-trades policy about lunches, you're in luck. If not, try to get one. Meanwhile, what else can you do to make sure that what you're sending along doesn't end up in the trash can? The best thing you can do is listen. As one mother told me, "I started the year giving her the things I thought she ought to have. Then she began requesting other things, after she'd compared with what the other kids had." The results: Lunch went from a whole sandwich (too much for this six-year-old) to a half, plus fruit, juice, and a snack. "She'd want bologna or a BLT instead of peanut butter." The mother listened and agreed—sometimes. By agreeing sometimes, you can win your child's cooperation. Strike a bargain that once a week he or she can have the BLT; two or three times a week lunch will be simpler fare; and once or twice a week your child may buy lunch at school, if there's something on the menu she especially likes. Pizza is not a bad nutritional option, for instance, especially if you can strike a deal where that day's school snack is an apple brought from home.

For youngsters just starting the world of school, lunch can be an exciting event. From about age six and seven on, they are going to be increasingly sensitive to what their peers are eating—and not eating. So you do need to listen, and sometimes compromise. For the days you get to say what goes to school in the lunch box or brown bag, you have certain parameters to work with: you want to avoid foods that will spoil or lose their freshness and appeal after four hours at room temperature. You want to provide some semblance of variety, even though your main goals are to get everyone out of the house on time and make sure they have something reasonably nourishing to keep them from starvation.

It's true that what his or her peers are doing can sometimes be of paramount importance to your child. But try to play on the glamour of what's different, too: Jazz up a peanut butter sandwich with crunchy apple slices. Try to make sandwiches without bread for a whole week; get the kids to help think up alternatives, like Lettuce Rollups or Turkey Rollups (see recipes in Part II). Send along soup in a wide-mouth Thermos with packaged crackers like the ones you'd get in a restaurant. Praise fruit conserves as being better than jelly because they contain less sugar.

Talk About It

The best thing you can do is listen to what your child says about food at school, and then talk about it. Let your child know that you're not going to be angry if the answer is "No, I didn't eat my sandwich." Enlist the child's input into what makes a good lunch and bargain where necessary. Present the problems (variety, spoilage, nutrition value) and see what your child comes up with as solutions. You won't win any food wars by being too tough, because ultimately children will eat what they want when you're not around. What you want to do is make them *want* foods that are good.

They don't have to want foods that are good because those are necessarily the foods that taste best at the moment. There are lots of times when we probably all think a chocolate shake sounds like more fun than a pear. But your children's minds are your best allies in the food wars, and you can convince them to eat good food for the good things it does—especially if they know you don't expect them to eat it all the time.

Making Rules Stick
When the Going Gets Tough

My rule, "Not in Our House," is really the cornerstone of a larger eating philosophy that we as parents are all trying to implement: the idea that there are things we eat all the time, things we eat occasionally or in small quantities, and things we try to avoid.

I'm not saying there's necessarily going to be consistency in all of this. I let Owen have things at parties that don't appear on the dinner table. I sometimes let him have a soft drink, but we very rarely have them in our own refrigerator, and I absolutely draw the line at diet drinks, which as far as I can see are nothing but a collection of additives. I let him have candy, but we don't keep a supply of it in the house—I may buy him three or four gumdrops at the supermarket once a week or let him have a lollipop at the bank. Usually what he gets to take home from the supermarket, if anything, is sugarless gum. And as for sweets in general, we try to keep him from assuming he's entitled to them.

For a two-year-old, four animal crackers can be a big treat. As children get older, they get wiser in the ways of the world. By the time they are entering school—and especially if there are any hereditary health problems in the family—it's time to sit down and start to spell out the rules.

Let your school-age kids know that everybody likes a treat, even the grown-ups. Discuss objectives like healthy teeth, a healthy weight, and the importance of things that help us grow. Then map out a family strategy that includes what is eaten for breakfast, lunch, dinner, and in between.

It's good to involve children with their own nutrition in the early grades because the schools will probably help. The idea of nutrition is often introduced in first grade by the school nurse or a teacher; coming from a new source it often captures their interest. "Angie's not a breakfast eater," says one friend of mine. "I'd be happy if I could get half a slice of toast into her in the morning. Then one day she came home from school, and she said, I need to eat this and this and this for breakfast, because it will help me do better in school. I know I told her she'd have more energy if she'd eat breakfast. But sometimes they listen better to another adult."

Here are some things to discuss in formulating the rules:

Candy and Other Sweets

Of course your children know sweets are bad for their teeth—ho hum. Older children might be more convinced by the fact that many experts regard sugar as a drug that is habit-forming. According to Dr. Andrew Weil, a graduate of Harvard Medical School whose specialty is addiction studies, "The combination of sugar and caffeine seems to be especially habit-forming." In his book with Winifred

Rosen, *Chocolate to Morphine,* he reminds us that colas and choco-late are two major sources of caffeine. He also mentions that some soft-drink manufacturers put caffeine in drinks that are not ob-viously colas (another good reason to read the labels and look for "caffeine free" on the drinks you do buy).

Dyes and Additives

Explain to younger children that the pretty colors in some foods are not their real colors, but artificial, and that they haven't been around long enough for us to be sure they are really good for us. Add that in fact we know some of them aren't good for us and can actually make people and animals very sick.

Labels

Explain to school-age children how to read the labels. Tell them that everything won't always be listed on the label and that if they're confused they can bring the label home and you'll talk about it. Explain how a label works and that words like *fructose* and *glucose* really mean sugar. Teaching them to read labels will help protect them from bad choices when you're not around, especially when it's coupled with—

What They Learn in School

Many schools have helpful nutrition classes even in the lower grades. Encourage them to discuss what is taught about nutrition and add what you know. One mother says she thinks age seven really is the age of reason, because at that point her daughter really began to evaluate what she was eating: "I actually see her preferring the better snacks. She'll take fruit or cheese and crackers. Our younger one is still at the age where she wants the bright colors and the marshmallows."

Calories

Explain *fast* calories vs. *slow* calories—how the candy bar may give the child a great taste and a rush, but it uses up half the day's supply of calories and doesn't even begin to fill the child's stomach, where a half a sandwich or a piece of fruit has fewer calories but stays with him or her a lot longer and doesn't leave the child hungry.

Compromise

Tell the children you understand that everyone wants a candy bar once in a while, even though we know an apple is better for us, and that you'll play fair with them if they'll play fair with you. It's important to "let 'em eat junk" once in a while. It encourages them not to do it behind your back. Agree as a family on limits. You'll allow them one day a week when they can buy the snack of their choice right after school (you can tell them you'd rather it be an ice-cream sandwich than a candy bar) or when they can eat junk food at a friend's house, and you'll have a sweet treat at home for them once a week, if they'll cooperate and eat healthy snacks on the other five days.

It's good to get them to snack right after school, so they do minimal damage to their appetite for dinner. Encourage them to come home for their snack—or send something along with them, whether it's crackers and cheese, an apple and a cookie, or a couple of fruit rollups. Remember alternatives. Yes, they can even exist in the realm of junk food. Do let your children know that sometimes is okay, but not all the time; that some kinds of junk food are worse than others; and that you are all working on diet as a family, and won't ask anything of them that you aren't doing yourself.

One family I know makes it a point to talk about food at dinner when the whole family is together. They have had an ongoing discussion over the years about food and nutrition—not at every meal, but off and on. Children are allowed to say what they like or don't like, and why, but it's against the rules to say "because it's yucky." Their parents say you'd be surprised sometimes to find out why children don't like foods. Sometimes textures can be adjusted, or a sauce or dip may make a food palatable.

If you've talked about food enough without driving it into the ground, you may be able to enlist their minds to help you navigate these years when they prefer what one mother grimly refers to as

---

SOME NEWS ON FAST FOODS AND SNACK FOODS

Fast-food chains and snack manufacturers appear to be beginning to realize they must respond to consumers' concerns about food quality. Hardee's—one of the largest fast-food chains in the U.S.—has shifted from saturated to unsaturated cooking fat for all of its fried foods. The chain now uses a blend of soybean and peanut oils. According to a report in *Environmental Nutrition* (Oct. 1988), McDonald's and Burger King were still cooking french fries in a mixture of saturated beef fat and cottonseed oil.

The Sunshine Company, manufacturer of various cookies and crackers, has reported that it is changing from saturated to polyunsaturated vegetable shortening to its product line, and adjusting its recipes to work with the replacement oils to produce an acceptable result.

"teen food." Sure, you understand that they like to hang out at McDonald's, and that's okay sometimes. But tennis stars, runners, and gymnasts have shown that a high-carbohydrate, reasonably low-fat, junk-free diet is what really works. Of course, your children don't have to follow that all the time, as long as they're not planning to be in the Olympics. But you can strike a balance. You may be able to enlist your teenager's interest by designing *with* them an eating program that spells out the RDAs and the reasons for them; the

GLUTEN-FREE FAST FOODS

For those allergic to wheat and other glutinous flours, eating out can be difficult. The Greater Philadelphia Area Celiac-Sprue Support Group has surveyed several major fast-food chains and reports the following foods are gluten free (but cautions that recipes do change from time to time):

♦ Burger King: hamburger (minus bun and condiments), ham and eggs, french fries (but ask if any batter-dipped foods shared the fryer). Check condiment labels. Safe beverages include orange juice, Pepsi and diet Pepsi.

♦ McDonald's: quarter pounder and regular hamburger (minus bun, etc.), french fries (see above caution), Canadian bacon, sausage, scrambled eggs. Read condiment labels. Bring own salad dressing. Safe beverages include vanilla or strawberry shake and hot chocolate.

♦ Wendy's: kid's burger and regular burger (minus bun, etc.), hot stuffed baked potato (plain), french fries (as above), eggs fried or scrambled, sausage patty, bacon, oil and wine vinegar dressing. Safe beverages include orange juice, Slice, colas.

caloric needs for your child's height, weight, and age; and the nutrition options that will meet those needs.

Nutrition and Organized Sports

Coaches and parents, both of whom should know better, sometimes allow and even encourage shocking (in terms of health) practices in the name of competitive sports. These include things like having wrestlers virtually starve themselves to make weight or feeding young athletes excess protein (tough on the kidneys and a potential gout causer) in the mistaken belief that it's muscle food. If your child is involved in competitive sports, be sure you're involved too, to be sure that your child doesn't get so involved in competing that he or she loses out on nutrition. Try to single out athletes who have a responsible attitude toward nutrition as potential role models.

Making a Good Diet Work for Teens

I've been talking about making nutrition work for your kids with a diet that *is* in the mainstream of American eating, but with a little thought added to trimming the calories and the fat, and throwing in extra vitamins and minerals, with fiber and protein where appropriate. I suggest a life-style that's realistic, in terms of what's out there and in terms of what we have the time and energy for. But I also believe in a diet that gives our kids the edge on a lifetime of health.

The teen years are the final hurdle. After that, you've done all you can. In fact, many parents of teenagers will tell you you've done all you could before then. One mother, talking about her son's high school courses in advanced nutrition, said, "Of course none of that matters when they're teenagers. They're so—hedonistic. And they think they're immortal anyway."

And yet those final years of childhood are the years of a major growth spurt unequaled since infancy. In girls the growth spurt usually happens earlier than in boys, but a teen-age boy in full form can inhale more than 4,000 calories a day, and teenagers' needs for certain vital nutrients are unsurpassed by those of any group except pregnant and nursing women. Iron-deficiency anemia, for example, is a disturbingly common deficiency in this country, and it is not uncommon in teenagers.

So all of your foundation in nutrition culminates in these exciting, obstreperous years, where behavior is sometimes reminiscent of that earlier rebellion, the terrible twos. How do you handle this challenge?

Keep up the education in the nutrition basics and the compromise on popular items, and most of all, make the most of all the good foods you feed your family. The best way to get everyone to eat these foods is to start young, not give up trying at discreet intervals, and keep your cool. In addition, don't make the job too hard for yourself. If you're a working parent, you are not going to come up with four-star dinners seven days a week. Remember that little things can sometimes make a big difference and fill in nutritional gaps wherever the chance occurs.

This means that if you're trying to keep body and soul together on Thursday night, when your daughter has baseball practice, the adults worked late, and the cat has to go to the vet, you may be hauling out the frozen shrimp and fries. They're fast, everyone will eat them without complaint, and you're tired. Fine. Throw them in the oven, change your shoes—and put a container of cottage cheese, a plate of carrot sticks, and a dish of fruit on the table. Get those vitamins and minerals out there. It doesn't have to be a five-course meal.

Another place to target for the extra vitamins and minerals is soups, stews, chili and casseroles. These are excellent places to slip in those extra ingredients like nutritional yeast (B vitamins, iron), blackstrap molasses (ditto), and seaweeds (multiple minerals, including calcium and iron). We talked about these ingredients in Chapter Three. Now that you're thinking about feeding on-the-go older kids with their high nutritional needs, the alternative and standby foods are more important than ever. When incorporating them, you have to be a little careful not to upset the appearance or flavor of recipes, but anything that has a tomato or bean or pea base and is going to cook for any length of time will absorb any and all of these ingredients with no problem. The molasses is good in spaghetti sauce, baked beans, and chili, all of which need some sweetening anyway. Add one tablespoon and taste. Keep adding cautiously, and tasting, up to several tablespoons. Nutritional yeast goes into these dishes, too. Seaweeds can be added (and the seaweed kombu *should* be added) to any slow-cooking dried pea or bean dish.

Molasses can also be used in baking. One seaweed, kanten, can be used in jelled desserts.

During this growth period, protein and calcium are especially important. Send your kids off to school with a Cornell Triple-Rich Roll (see recipe in Part II), stuffed with cheese or just plain, for a snack, part of lunch, or even a grab-and-go breakfast. Use cultured dairy products and sesame seeds for extra calcium. Some teenagers might turn up their noses at yogurt or buttermilk as such, but people of most any age will eat Banana Yogurt Popsicles, Buttermilk Biscuits, or Creamy Yogurt Dressing (see recipes in Part II).

Teenagers and Dieting

A side issue, but a very important one with teenagers, can be dieting. Teens of both sexes can become totally preoccupied with the idea. And it is reaching, like so many other major issues that once affected only high-school-age kids, into younger and younger age groups. So what do you do to make sure that the good foods you're pushing aren't spurned? You need to have one of those talk sessions, armed with the facts about where the nutrients are versus where the calories are. If your child is determined to lose weight, put yourself, your spouse, and the child in question on a fitness-and-diet regimen. Don't let the child go it alone.

Keeping Older Children Involved

The last thing you need to remember in regard to teenagers is to keep them involved. If you can keep your children interested in cooking through the grade school years and into high school, you're way ahead of the game. A mother who started her son on the family egg-noodle recipe at three says he's still making it, and loving it, at sixteen. Another family has two boys whose specialties are cranberry sauce and corn muffins (kids will surprise you).

In another family the teen-age daughters weren't the best eaters until their enterprising parents got them involved in fixing healthy meals for the younger siblings (and then of course setting a good example by eating what they'd fixed). In yet another the exasperated mother says her son will eat pizza three times a day four days in a row. But she also knows he's had his courses in nutrition, and will come back to good eating when his pizza marathon is over. And he'll make his own pancakes. And if you make the batter out of good-quality ingredients, and put it in the fridge where they can find it . . .

Alternatives. And involvement. For the rest of it, you just have to trust your children. And keep those carrot sticks—and frozen yogurt bars and soy pancakes—coming.

Here are some specific thoughts on keeping teenagers involved in good eating:

- **Being there.** Once again, we all know how fragmented our schedules are. Try to keep a certain number of meals as family meals. Establish a bulletin board or bulletin-board section dedicated to foods. On it post needed grocery items, but also whatever schedules you can manage to pull together that pinpoint *when* you'll all be eating together and *who's* in charge of *what*.

- **Chores.** One way of keeping them involved may be to hold them responsible for a minimum of food-related chores. These can include menu planning, helping preparation, even shopping. Don't laugh. Recent polls have shown that in 1987, for example, America's 28 million teenagers spent more than $40 *billion* on products for their families. More than *half* of that went for groceries. One poll, the Rand Youth Poll, estimated that teenagers spent more than $27 billion in that year on food for their families, an increase of 20 percent over the preceding year. One reason for increased teen spending on family items—at a time when the teen population is declining—is that in many homes both parents work. Shopping falls to the teenagers. If chores are part of your

ploy, rotate the less creative ones, like cleaning up; and balance
chores with . . .

* **Rewards.** Rewards can include letting your teenager choose a
place and time to dine out, and perhaps bringing a friend along.
You might do this as a family, or perhaps you feel your teenager
can handle dining out with a friend on his or her own. Perhaps
you'll do it one way one time and one way another. Other rewards
can include favorite meals, snacks, or desserts, or allowing teenagers to plan entertainment, with food as part of it, for their
friends at your home.

* **News flashes.** Use part of your food bulletin-board space for
clippings that point out items of interest about nutrition. A short
item on a family health problem or on a good nutrition tip can
catch the eye of the person who's getting the grocery list off the
board. Encourage the family to post items.

* **Designer diets.** If your teenager is interested in dieting, or uses
the idea of it as an excuse for not eating some foods, marshal your
energy and sit down with the RDA chart and the facts. Facts like:
iron-deficiency anemia is especially common in teenage girls
(with the onset of menstruation not many years behind them,
they shouldn't have too much trouble seeing why) and excess
sugar intake decreases the body's ability to absorb iron (remember the box on Getting Enough Iron in Chapter Three? Time
for a review . . .); diet sodas are loaded with sodium, and sodium
is a factor in heart disease (to say nothing of its role as a water-
retainer, which counteracts the good effects of dieting). Try to hit
them with the most dramatic facts you can think of.

* **An ounce of prevention.** Try to be the one who engineers what
foods are available when there are alternatives—like having good
quality or homemade pancake mix available, like keeping cut-up
raw vegetables handy to add to a meal, like keeping a bowl of
fresh fruit or jar of nuts and dried fruit out on the kitchen counter,
perhaps with an article about athletes and complex carbohydrates taped to it.

• **Do it early.** Whatever your strategy, you'll have a better chance of success if you try to make it a habit starting at age 12 than if you start at age 17. Good luck, and start now!

Process, Not Problem

Remember that eating is a lifelong process. You can give your children the best information about food and put good food on the table without getting too judgmental about what happens next.

If you think of your children's eating habits as simply a process instead of a problem, you can take the long view. They are in the process of learning about food and learning about themselves and their relationships to the world at the same time. Food is just part of that relationship. As they grow older, it is essential that children have a sense that what they eat is increasingly their choice—and their responsibility. Because in fact it is their choice, and you have to respect that. You can't be with them twenty-four hours a day or for the rest of their lives.

For all ages the best you can do is try to teach them what you know about the connection between nutrition and a healthy body and mind and then follow your own good advice, because whatever you offer will have more effect if you practice what you preach.

But don't let this business of teaching nutrition and assigning responsibility get too serious. It's a wonderful world of food you have to choose from, and in the last analysis, eating should be a pleasure and an occasion for the delightful human habit of sharing things. To sit down to a meal together is a feast for the spirit as well as the body. If you keep food in perspective—as nutrition, as social occasion, as family health and family fun—so will your children.

Eating Right:
Putting It All on
the Table

B esides chapters on the three main meals of the day, this section offers recipes for first baby foods, breads, sweets, party foods, beverages, comfort foods, and foods for those with allergies.

Don't hesitate to mix up the recipes in the breakfast, lunch, and dinner chapters. There's no reason why dinner can't be soup and a sandwich, and for breakfast you *could* take a tip from the Japanese and try Basic Miso Soup. Closer to home, breakfast for kids in a hurry can be a Triple-Rich Roll or a muffin (both in the breads chapter), while the Fruit Platter in the salads section of the dinner chapter could be a dessert.

Most of these recipes can be made in an hour or less. That's about as much time as any of us has to spend in the kitchen. Recipes that take longer, such as soup stocks or beans, are things that can cook while you're around but doing something else or that you can cook in stages (for instance, part tonight and part tomorrow).

Kitchen Tools and Techniques

Useful tools for preparing good-quality meals for children include cooking pots of cast iron or stainless steel or with a heavy enamel coating; a good-quality carbon-steel knife (these are the knives that rust when wet) for cutting vegetables; a blender or food processor; muffin pans, cookie sheets, loaf pans, a stainless-steel steamer; a hand-operated baby food mill; extra ice trays.

Other things that are useful but not necessary include a microwave oven, a small mortar and pestle, a salad spinner, Popsicle molds, a waffle iron, and a juicer.

Among techniques that are frequently referred to in recipes are ways of cutting up vegetables. Besides chopping, mincing, and slicing, some recipes call for slicing vegetables into fine matchstick-sized pieces (also known as *julienne* or *nituke* from the Japanese). I also call for cutting onions into half-moon pieces—this means to slice the onion in half vertically and then keep slicing vertically into thin slices. (The time-honored way of chopping an onion is to peel it, slice off the top, and then cross-hatch the onion with a knife. Then, when it's sliced horizontally, each slice falls into small pieces.)

Ingredients

Most ingredients used in the recipes can be found in supermarkets. For soup stocks and bean recipes, seaweeds and shiitake mushrooms are often mentioned. These less common ingredients are used for their mineral content, to boost the nutritional value of the meal. You should be able to find them in any health food store. Fresh shiitake mushrooms are now commonly available in some supermarkets. For families with special problems such as allergies, there is a wealth of alternatives out there, at the health food store and also in mail order (see Sources, Appendix A).

Also available in health food stores are sugarless cookies like Barbara's Carob (or Vanilla) Animal Cookies, a favorite travel snack in their colorful box; Oatios, the health-food equivalent of Cheerios and another good snack; tamari soy sauce, miso, azuki beans, sesame seeds, amasake and amasake pudding, and prepared soy burgers of various kinds (tempeh in tempeh burgers is a good nonmeat source of vitamin B_{12}), roast bancha twig tea and kanten or agar-agar flakes; various nonwheat flours for making allergy-free recipes; wheat-free breads and other baked goods; liquid vitamin C without additives; good-quality vegetable oil and mild rice vinegar for salads. In fact, if the health food store isn't on your list of regular or occasional places to shop, you should consider taking a tour of one or two. Beware of the ones that sell primarily vitamins; vitamins and various nutritional supplements shouldn't occupy more than a quarter of the store if you're going to use it for your alternative foods grocery.

Other places to find some of these ingredients include Oriental, Middle Eastern, and other ethnic markets. Those are good places to visit occasionally anyway, for the ideas they'll give you. Don't be shy about asking if things aren't labeled in English.

Things you can get in your supermarket these days include tofu, ginger, ready-made hummus (chick-pea spread, great for pita sandwiches), egg roll wrappers, rice cakes, sugar- and salt-free peanut butter, and fruit juice and jam without added sweeteners. Remember to read the labels.

At this point, if you have a special nutritional need or desire, the product to answer it is probably out there, whether it's wheat-free flour or a hand-operated ice cream maker. All you have to do is find it. For baby products, look at the ads in the baby magazines, call a diaper service, ask your acquaintances. For food products, shop your supermarket, ethnic markets, neighborhood specialty shops, and the health food store. For cooking utensils, including interesting cookie cutters or other hand tools your child can use (nut choppers, egg slicers, vegetable scrapers), browse in a hardware store, a five-and-dime, a kitchen specialty shop, or a discount department store. You can make this part of an excursion with your child for a rainy Saturday morning. And get your hands on a copy of the Williams-Sonoma kitchen catalog so you can do some of it by phone (see Appendix A).

Make use of the alternatives. They are out there waiting for us—and for the kids.

NINE

First Things First: Baby Foods

When first feeding solid food to your baby, try Steve and Nancy Doyne's First Rice Cereal if the idea of commercial cereals doesn't appeal. First Rice Cereal can then be made with other nonwheat grains, such as oatmeal or barley, after you're sure your baby tolerates it.

Remember, give each new food at least a week by itself when first introducing it. Also, with baby food, any serving that has touched your baby's mouth, directly or via spoon or fingers, is considered to have been used (or "contaminated," as pediatricians more sternly put it) and should not be reused. This applies to jars, dishes, bottles—whatever. So if you're using commercial baby food, don't feed the baby straight from a jar unless you intend to throw the unused portion away. Serve from the jar to a dish, then feed the baby from the dish and save what's leftover in the jar for another meal. For homemade baby food, it's to your advantage to have small portions of things readily available, so you don't waste the food you've prepared.

FIRST RICE CEREAL

Nancy and Steve Doyne provided this basic First Rice Cereal recipe. Feel free to add breast milk to the cereal for a first food. Nancy says older babies sometimes like a little maple syrup cooked into the cereal. For older babies, a little amasake can also go into it (amasake is naturally sweet, though, so don't add another sweetener).

Cook good-quality long- or short-grained brown rice in a ratio of 1 part rice to 8 parts water. Start by rinsing the rice thoroughly; then put it and the water in a large pot with a small strip of kombu (or a few pinches of arame or hijiki seaweed, all available at health food stores, tied up in cheesecloth or one of those small fabric infusion bags that look like a teabag, can be reused, and are very handy). Bring to a boil, cover, and turn down the heat. Simmer for 1 hour, checking periodically to make sure liquid still covers the rice; if not, add water. When done, the rice should be *very* soft, and there should be some liquid left covering it.

This liquid is your first feeding of "solid" food for your baby, and you should have enough for a few feedings. After several days, if there's no adverse reaction, puree some of the liquid with a little of the rice in an electric blender. The consistency should be really still almost liquid. Proceed over a period of a week or more. If the cereal is well accepted, you may try the same process (skipping the pure liquid and going straight to the puree) with rolled oats, barley, and millet. Rotate these as first foods and staples of your baby's diet up to age one and beyond, allowing a coarser consistency as your baby grows. There's no reason these cereals can't stay with your child through toddlerhood.

A batch of the cereal keeps, refrigerated, for several days. It may also be frozen in cubes.

ALMOST-INSTANT BABY FOOD CUBES

Frozen cubes of homemade baby food are extremely handy for quick meals, meals away from home, meals anytime. Unthawed, they're also great for teething babies.

Cook until very soft any of the milder vegetables by themselves (or with a little onion, once your child has tested it out) in just enough water to cover the vegetables so the vitamins and minerals in the cooking liquid don't get lost. Drain the vegetables, reserving the cooking water. Puree the vegetables with some of the liquid to a very smooth consistency and spoon it into the sections of ice trays. Freeze, pop the cubes out, and store them in a clean plastic bag, sealed and dated, in your freezer. To use, remove the desired number of cubes, thaw them at room temperature or in a microwave or a little hot water, and serve.

Before serving microwaved food to very young children, test its temperature. Stir it well, then test or taste it to be sure it's not too hot.

You can also steam, bake, or microwave the vegetables to cook them, but you may not have enough liquid to puree them with. Add water, breast milk, formula, or other safe (for babies) liquid of your choice.

OTHER BABY FOODS

Up to nine months:
avocado
banana
cooked apples or pears

applesauce (sugarless—read the label; the individual-serving containers are handy for travel or just for single servings)

cooked pureed yellow, orange, or dark green vegetables (carrot, sweet potato, squash, leafy greens)

small amount of cooked onion as a seasoning (steamed or boiled or microwaved with other vegetables)

mashed potato (a good way to serve the leafy greens is to puree them with mashed potato and a little onion)

Oatios (from a health food store)

bread, lightly toasted

cottage cheese

yogurt

Nine to twelve months:
all of the above, plus—

amasake

arrowroot cookies

egg yolk

pasta

pieces of cooked vegetables from list above

soft cooked meat (mild meatballs, shreds of chicken or beef, boneless fish)

steamed tofu

Rice Dream or vanilla ice cream (during summer)

One year and up:
all of the above, plus—

whole eggs

beans, peas, other legumes (including peanut butter)

any cooked grain

low-sugar baked goods

soft cheeses

cucumbers and melons

berries

mild citrus fruit

SUGGESTIONS FOR TEETHING BABIES:

Frozen pureed food cubes, a frozen banana, or toast may be helpful, as well as whatever commercial teething biscuits you have tried. Try to avoid products with sugar, salt, and saturated fat, here as elsewhere. If buying teething biscuits, check the label. You may want to go to the health food store for them. Frozen Juicesicles and Yogurt Bars (see recipes) can also be good choices.

YOUR OWN YOGURT
Makes about 1 quart

You can of course buy plain yogurt at a supermarket (Dannon is a reliable brand) or a health food store. All you need to know is that it has active cultures (as stated on the label). But if you want to make your own, it's relatively easy to do, and there are advantages, such as quality control. You can choose to use goat's milk, for instance; add your own conserves or other sweetener while the yogurt is still warm; control the texture and sharpness by how long you ferment it (experiment).

1 *quart whole milk (cow or goat)*

2 *tablespoons plain yogurt with active cultures*

Heat the milk to a boil to kill off any possible culture-inhibiting substances. Cool it until tepid (so you don't kill off the active cultures). Add the yogurt, which is your starter (be sure it's a fairly fresh batch; buy it and check the date on the label), and stir it in well. Put the mixture in a container that will stay warm for 4 hours or so. A wide-mouthed Thermos has always seemed easiest to me, though many people swear by a bowl wrapped in a sweater or a covered bowl in an oven with a pilot light. If you're going to make yogurt often, you might invest in a yogurt maker, so you have the handy little storage cups. Otherwise, invest in a batch of small Mason jelly jars. Dishwasher-sterialized, they'll be ready for your next batch. After making the first home batch, you can use your own yogurt for a starter.

YOUR OWN SUGARLESS APPLESAUCE

Makes 3 to 4 cups of applesauce

6 *Granny Smith apples,*
  peeled and cored

½ *cup raisins*

3 *cups water, to start*

pinch salt
¼ *teaspoon cinnamon*

Put all the ingredients in a five-quart pot and bring to a boil. Turn down and simmer for at least half an hour, checking the water level and adding more if it seems to be boiling away. When apples are very soft, and most of the cooking liquid appears to have been boiled away or absorbed, puree in a food processor, blender, or hand food grinder.

HIMMEL AND ERDE

Makes 6 or more servings

This dish with its German name, which means "Heaven and Earth," is a nice accompaniment for any roast poultry, or for fish. For little people it may be a meal in itself.

1 *cup applesauce*

3 *cups mashed potatoes*

1 *tablespoon unsalted*
  butter (optional)

Both potatoes and applesauce should be very hot. Turn into a 2-quart baking dish, swirl together, dot with butter, and let sit in a preheated 350-degree oven until potatoes are lightly browned.

T E N

◇

Breakfast

Of course the word *breakfast* comes from the idea of breaking the fast that the night provides. But to some of us, as the kids thunder through the kitchen on their way to school, it may seem more like the fast break, and the question is how to get some nourishment into them before they disappear for the day.

There are various philosophies on early-morning nourishment. But for children, who are expending an enormous amount of energy in that first half of the day, some protein, some good slow-burning carbohydrates, and—yes—some fat seem in order. The protein is for their ever-growing bodies. The carbohydrates are for the slow release of energy over the morning. The fat is a help because, measure for measure, it provides twice the calories of protein or carbohydrates, and is necessary to the metabolism of protein. It is the "stick to your ribs" factor.

Obviously you must tailor your meals to your own child's needs. If you have a child who is overweight, perhaps no fat is in order. If the child has allergies, you must adapt the high-carbohydrate, grain-based recipes (see Chapter Eighteen). If it's Saturday, and everyone is at home, maybe you would like to have a morning meal of just fruit and let the body rest. (Or perhaps that's your day to emphasize togetherness with homemade waffles.) The breakfast recipes given here lean mostly to the high-carbohydrate side, but they are also high in complementary protein. You can vary the fat content through your choice of skim or whole milk, full-fat or low-fat soy powder and dried milk and by whether you add cheese, butter, or other fat sources to the recipes.

CINNAMON FRENCH TOAST

Makes 3 small servings or 1 large serving

This is one of the quickest things to fix in the mornings, and kids of all ages seem to love it. Toddlers will sometimes eat it even without syrup. It's an excellent source of protein, carbohydrates, and (cooked in butter or oil) some fat. (The protein comes from the milk, eggs, and the grain in the bread, which "piggybacks" its protein onto the complete protein in the milk and eggs.)

1 *large egg, beaten*

¼ *cup milk*

1 *teaspoon vanilla extract*

¼ *teaspoon ground cinnamon*

3 *slices bread*

unsalted butter or light sesame oil (available at health food stores)

Beat the egg, milk, vanilla, and cinnamon together in a fairly flat dish, such as a soup plate or pie pan, that will accommodate the bread and make it easy to remove the bread once it's wet. Add 1 slice of bread at a time, turning so that both sides are coated and absorb some of the liquid. Remove the bread, slice by slice, to a plate. Heat the butter or oil on a large griddle or skillet, reduce the heat, and brown the bread briefly on each side. Serve with syrup, honey, cooked or raw fruit, other topping of your choice, or plain. The cinnamon and vanilla give this version an especially nice flavor.

> The best-quality syrup is pure maple. It costs more than the name-brand syrups that are actually mostly corn syrup, but you use less of it, and it is another way to avoid loading your child's system with excess corn-based products. Remember, corn is one of the foods people are most apt to be allergic to.

Allergy Note: For those trying to avoid wheat, milk, and eggs, try a nonwheat bread (from a health food store) and soak it in amasake (also from a health food store). You may add the cinnamon and vanilla if you like. Cook in sesame oil.

PROTEIN PANCAKES

Makes at least 12 pancakes

The addition of soy flour or powder to these homemade pancakes boosts the protein content; you now have the milk, the eggs, and the soy plus grains. If you're trying to work extra oats into your child's diet, buy oat bran at a health food store and substitute it for the regular bran.

1½ *cups unbleached (wheat) flour*

½ *cup bran*

¼ *cup rolled oats, ground in blender, or ¼ cup cornmeal*

¼ *cup soy flour or soy powder* (not *granules*) (*available at health food stores*)

1 *teaspoon baking powder*

¼ *teaspoon baking soda*

1½ *cups (or more) milk*

2 *eggs*

3 *tablespoons plain yogurt*

2 *tablespoons light sesame oil*

unsalted butter or extra oil for the pan

Mix the dry ingredients in a bowl. Beat the liquid ingredients (including 2 tablespoons of oil) together and add them to the dry ingredients. Stir to mix well, mashing out the lumps with a wooden spoon. Add more liquid if necessary; the batter should pour off the spoon slowly but smoothly. You can use water instead of milk after you've added the first 1½ cups of milk. Mix to the right consistency.

Brush a hot skillet or griddle with oil or butter. The skillet should be well greased; I get the desired effect by heating a couple of tablespoons of oil or butter and then wiping the skillet clean with a paper towel, which I save for regreasing. I also use 2 cast-iron skillets for cooking the pancakes, which I make rather large (about ¼ cup batter per cake). With two good pans, the cooking goes faster. Heat the skillet and cook the pancakes on the first side over medium-high heat until the surface bubbles; turn and cook briefly on the second side. Transfer the pancakes to a warm plate.

Note: In a hurry? Mix the dry ingredients in advance; keep them in a jar on the counter. Omit the yogurt if you don't have it and add more milk. Let older children make their own (tape instructions on the jar of premixed flour). *Really* in a hurry? Use a commercial mix, replacing a couple of tablespoons per cup of the mix with soy powder and/ or oat bran to give your children extra nutrition. The soy adds protein; the oat bran is a cholesterol fighter.

WHEAT-FREE PANCAKES

Allergy prone? Buy oat flour or (in the case of celiac disease) a nongluten flour at a health food store. Proceed as for Protein Pancakes, using substitute flour instead of wheat flour. Omit cornmeal. Instead of soy flour/powder, use amaranth flour (also available at health food stores and an excellent source of protein, iron, and calcium). Use amasake diluted half and half with water for the liquid instead of milk; add a tablespoon of arrowroot powder (from a health food store or supermarket) instead of egg.

NonGluten Buttermilk Pancakes

4 Servings

With thanks to Phyllis Brogden of the Greater Philadelphia Area C-S Support Group.

1 *egg*	¾ *level cup pure rice flour*
1½ *teaspoons baking soda*	
1 *teaspoon baking powder*	1 *tablespoon oil*
	1 *cup buttermilk*
¼ *level cup tapioca flour*	

Beat egg in bowl with fork. Sift together baking soda, baking powder and tapioca flour. Mix all ingredients together. Let sit for 5 minutes. Fry on 375 degree skillet until done. Flip only once.

Note: To replace buttermilk and eggs:

Ener-G egg replacer

¾ *cup water*   1 *teaspoon lemon juice*

Hearty Winter Oatmeal

Oatmeal should be cooked with enough liquid so that it has a creamy consistency when done. Sometimes you may need to taste it to see if the oats are soft, then add a little more cooking water if needed. Don't add too much, or you could end up with watery oatmeal. You'll know how much to use after you've done it once, and this recipe then becomes a very easy winter morning meal. Serve with milk or amasake (a delicious nondairy way of topping off and cooling the oatmeal).

Oatmeal in this country is made with rolled oats. In the British Isles it's often made with less processed oats, which you can buy here in the gourmet section of the supermarket or in a health food store. It takes longer but is delicious.

2 *cups (or more) water*	*a handful of raisins*
1 *cup rolled oats*	½ *sliced apple*
¼ *cup oat bran or wheat germ (optional)*	¼ *teaspoon salt*
a handful of nuts	

Bring the water to boil in a saucepan and add the remaining ingredients. Cook over very low heat until the oatmeal reaches a nice creamy consistency, adding water as necessary—cook for at least 5 minutes. Cover, turn off the heat, and let stand 1 minute or more. Top with a teaspoon of maple syrup per bowl; then add milk or amasake if desired. (With the raisins, apples, and amasake, you can skip the syrup.)

GEORGE WASHINGTON'S CORN CAKES

Makes about 8 small cakes

If you avoid the corn syrup and other corn additives that are so prevalent in prepared foods, you can afford to eat the real thing once in a while.

These old-fashioned corn cakes are the real thing. They are corn cakes as the early American colonists would have made them, and they are very plain and a little heavy (no leavening), but kids like them with maple syrup. They are inspired by a wonderful little book called *George Washington's Breakfast* (see Appendix A) in which a little boy sets out to find out just what the great man did eat for breakfast. Once we'd read it at our house, there was nothing to do but go ahead and make the corn cakes, which in George's day were known as "Indian hoecakes."

1 *cup cornmeal*	*light sesame oil for the pan*
½ *teaspoon salt*	
water	

Mix the cornmeal and salt together in a bowl. Add enough water to moisten thoroughly. Form small, fairly flat cakes by hand and put them immediately into a hot skillet to which 2 tablespoons of oil have been added. The cakes will tend to fall apart around the edges, so turn them only once, when you can see the bottom edge getting browned. It's important to keep enough oil in the pan to prevent the cakes from sticking. Add it as needed. Serve with maple syrup.

WAFFLES

Makes 6 to 8 waffles

The secret to good waffles is extra oil and separated eggs. A non-electric waffle iron (to be used on the stove) is available through the Williams-Sonoma catalog (see Appendix A).

2 *cups unbleached flour*	1¼ *cups milk*
1 *tablespoon baking powder*	2 *eggs, separated*
½ *teaspoon salt*	⅓ *cup light sesame oil or melted unsalted butter*

Mix the dry ingredients in a bowl. Blend the milk, egg yolks, and oil or butter together in another bowl. Beat the egg whites until fluffy, almost stiff. Mix the dry and liquid (except whites) ingredients together. Mash out any lumps. If the batter seems dry or doughy, add more milk or some water. Fold in the egg whites with a wooden spoon. The batter should be a little thicker than pancake batter. Spoon it onto a hot greased waffle iron and cook until both sides are crisp. (Don't check for at least 1 minute after the cooking starts, or you'll tear the waffle apart.)

CREAMY SCRAMBLED EGGS

Makes 3 servings

We hardly ever eat eggs as eggs in our house. But these are nice once in a while for a leisurely breakfast, perhaps with Home Fries or a Grilled Tomato (recipes follow).

4   *eggs*

1   *tablespoon cream cheese*

2   *tablespoons milk*

1   *tablespoon unsalted butter*

¼   *teaspoon salt*

coarsely ground pepper (optional)

Beat the eggs in a bowl. Add the cream cheese in little pieces. Add the milk and stir. Heat the butter, but don't brown it, in a skillet add the eggs, and cook, over moderate low heat, stirring with a wooden spoon as curds form. Add the salt after the eggs are cooked, and pepper if the family likes it.

CLOWN FACES

Makes 1 serving

A large breakfast for weekend mornings when you have time and want to feed your family a meal that will stick with them.

1   *large pancake (see Protein Pancakes or other pancake recipes)*

2   *poached or fried eggs, trimmed (see note)*

3   *orange slices*

½   *cherry tomato*

Make the pancakes in advance and set them in the oven to keep them warm. Poach or fry the eggs. To assemble the faces, place the pancakes on a plate, with eggs for eyes, orange slices for ears and mouth, and a tomato half for the nose.

Note: For a lighter meal, omit the eggs and make this a pancake breakfast with 2 pancakes on each plate. Use apricot or peach halves for eyes and half a fresh cherry for a nose. For another variation, omit the pancakes and use the plate as the face. Set the eggs or rounds of toast on the plate as eyes. Arrange the orange slices and tomato as ears and nose. Make a smile of home fries (recipe follows).

HOME FRIES

Makes 2 to 3 servings

2 *small leftover baked potatoes, sliced*

1 *onion, chopped*

2 *tablespoons light sesame or olive oil*

¼ *teaspoon salt*

paprika

Sauté the potatoes and onion in heated oil in a skillet, turning them and adding salt as they brown. Sprinkle with paprika before serving.

GRILLED TOMATOES

Makes 4 servings

2 *medium to large tomatoes, cut in half horizontally*

4 *tablespoons fresh bread crumbs*

4 *teaspoons freshly grated Parmesan cheese*

1 *tablespoon olive oil*

1 *teaspoon dried oregano or basil*

Preheat the broiler. Top the tomatoes with a mixture of the bread crumbs, cheese, oil, and herbs. Grill under the broiler until the topping is browned and the skin of the tomatoes is wrinkled, about 7 minutes.

TOFU SAUSAGES

Makes 4 servings

I discovered that, as a sausage fancier who no longer eats pork sausage, these tofu sausages offer much the same texture and flavor. I made them one morning for a friend who had her eight-year-old along. The boy looked at them with polite suspicion and asked, "What's that?" "Tofu," I said. "Toad food?" he replied with no malice but some incredulity. Try them.

½ *pound firm tofu, cut into strips 2 inches long and ½ inch wide and thick*

1 *garlic clove, chopped*

4 *tablespoons olive or sesame oil*

1 *teaspoon crumbled dried sage*

¼ *teaspoon cayenne pepper*

1 *tablespoon tamari soy sauce (available at health food stores)*

1 *tablespoon water*

Sauté the tofu and garlic in the heated oil in a skillet. Turn the tofu as it cooks (it will be pale gold and crisp on the cooked sides), adding oil if necessary. Add the sage and cayenne while cooking. When the tofu is golden, add the tamari and water, cover at once, and turn off the heat. Tilt the pan to distribute the liquid and let sit 2 minutes. Serve with pancakes and eggs.

HOMEMADE GRANOLA

These days you can buy granola at the health food store and get the low-sodium variety or any kind you want. Beware of what's in the supermarket; it probably is made with saturated fat to retard spoilage. If you want to make your own, here's my sister Jeanne's recipe, tried and true. The peanuts or soybeans plus oats and seeds add up to complete protein.

4 *cups rolled oats*	1 *teaspoon ground cinnamon*
½ *cup wheat germ*	½ *teaspoon freshly grated nutmeg or ground cardamon*
¼ *cup sesame seeds*	
¼ *cup shelled peanuts or dry-roasted soybeans*	*raisins, grated coconut, nuts, or dried fruit (optional)*
2 *tablespoons light sesame oil*	
¼ *cup honey*	

Preheat the oven to 350 degrees. Toast the oats, wheat germ, seeds, and legumes lightly on baking sheet for 5 to 10 minutes, until slightly browned. Remove and cool. Heat the honey and oil together in a small pot; drizzle it over the dry mixture. Sprinkle with cinnamon and nutmeg or cardamon. Return the mixture to the baking sheet and heat in the oven for 5 minutes. Stir or turn. Bake for a few minutes more, until crispy but not too browned. Remove and cool. Add raisins, nuts, or dried fruit if desired.

Other Breakfasts

In the cereal aisle, read the labels for saturated fat, salt, and sugar. You may have to bargain with your children as they get older, watch TV, and see what other people are eating. Make a rule that they can have junk cereal only once every three days or so. Intersperse it with your own breakfasts.

For mornings when time is short, here are some ideas for high-protein, high-carb breakfasts:

leftover Cornell Triple-Rich Rolls (see recipe), with or without cheese
toast with peanut butter
Wheatena or oatmeal for hot cereal, shredded wheat for cold
leftover muffins with a cup of cocoa (commercial, Ovaltine, or caffeine-free CaroCoa from a health food store)
leftover frozen pancakes or french toast popped into the toaster

And a final thought: when I was growing up, I loved leftover pizza or chili for breakfast. I think it was my way of rebelling against Mom and cornflakes. If your kids want to eat pizza or even pumpkin pie for breakfast, think about the nutritional value of what they're clamoring for. If you don't have it earmarked for a later meal, let 'em. A piece of homemade pie and a glass of milk . . . well, you could do a lot worse.

ELEVEN

Lunch

Lunch is lunch is lunch, right? At least when we're talking about taking lunch to school. It has certain requirements: it must be edible, be socially acceptable to a jury of your kids' peers, and be sturdy enough so that it doesn't melt, fall apart, or get soggy while it's waiting to be eaten. That's why we're all grateful for peanut butter. Here are some new wrinkles—on that old sandwich plus some others—to help you get the lunch box packed. And remember that the kids should be helping too, by suggesting menus, making sandwiches, and remembering to take the lunch box with them.

Lunches to Go

High-Protein Sandwiches

The following suggestions actually contain a balance of protein, fat, and complex carbohydrates—sandwiches that will stick to the ribs and provide energy for active minds during the afternoon at school.

PEANUT-BUTTER APPLE

Peanut butter and banana sandwiches are a favorite with lots of kids. At our house, we like peanut butter and apple.

Spread 2 slices of whole-wheat bread thinly with peanut butter. Slice half of a peeled medium apple and sprinkle lightly with lemon juice. Arrange apple slices to cover half of the sandwich and top with the other half. Cut into halves or quarters.

SESAME CHICK-PEA SPREAD

Rich in protein and calcium, this variation on hummus makes a tasty lunch.

1 *cup cooked (or canned) chick-peas, mashed*

3 *tablespoons sesame butter (available at health food stores)*

½ *small onion, minced finely, or 1 clove garlic, minced finely (optional)*

2 *teaspoons extra-virgin olive oil*

2 *tablespoons fresh lemon juice*

slices of bread or pita pockets

grated carrots (optional)

alfalfa sprouts (optional)

Combine the mashed chick-peas, sesame butter, onion or garlic, oil and lemon juice in a bowl and mix well. Refrigerate the extra for another day. Spread on bread or in a pita pocket and add grated carrots and alfalfa sprouts (more calcium) if the kids like them.

Variation: Omit onion or garlic and add raisins and/or nuts instead.

CHEESE-VEGEMITE SANDWICH

Vegemite is the trade name of a spread that is popular in Australia, and I am indebted to Chris Burger for introducing it to us. There are a couple of nice things about Vegemite, which is made by Kraft Foods. It is made from yeast, which means it has some nutritional value. It won't spoil, so you don't have to worry about sending it unrefrigerated to school. And it has a nice tangy taste that goes great with cheese. (A similar spread, Marmite, made in England and Canada, is sometimes found in U.S. grocery stores.)

Spread 2 slices of bread of your choice with Vegemite. Add favorite cheese—have the kids tried Muenster? It's nice and mild. Top with sprouts, grated carrot, or sturdy lettuce (such as romaine) or escarole.

Variations: For kids with allergies, remember that feta cheese isn't made from cow's milk. Also, a slice of tofu, steamed, can be substituted for the cheese. No one (except you and your kid) even needs to know.

CREAM CHEESE-VEGGIE SPREAD

¼ *cup grated carrot*

¼ *cup chopped nuts*

2 *radishes, chopped fine*

1 *tablespoon chopped onion*

1 *tablespoon chopped green pepper*

4 *ounces cream cheese*

Mix all ingredients and spread on bread or use as a filling in Nonbread Sandwiches (below).

Variations: Use other vegetables of your choice, or pineapple and raisins, or raisins and nuts.

NONBREAD SANDWICHES

For variety, try these "rollups" instead of bread as a way of making lunch:

* *Lettuce Rollups:* Use romaine, iceberg, or escarole. You can even use spinach leaves if you have the patience. Spread them with cream cheese, ricotta, Sesame Chick-pea Spread, or any other filling. Or roll lettuce around pieces of cheese and chicken or turkey, perhaps with a pineapple chunk if the kids like to mix tastes.

* *Turkey Rollups:* Use turkey instead of lettuce and fill with the spread or filling of your choice. Cream Cheese-Veggie Spread and alfalfa sprouts make a nice filling.

* *Variations:* Use other wrappings for your rollups. These could include cheese slices or low-fat sliced lunch meats if you use them.

HARD-COOKED TREATS
Makes 4 servings

Since the yolks contain the cholesterol and the whites contain the protein, you may want to skip the yolks. This recipe lets you do that. Many children don't like one part of the egg but do like the other. If you have a whites-lover, here's your recipe. (If you have a yolks-lover, add them to egg salad described under Minus Mayo Sandwiches.)

8 *halves of hard-cooked eggs, whites only*

FILLING SUGGESTIONS:

pieces of melon, banana, berries, or olives dabs of peanut butter,

Sesame Chick-pea Spread (see recipe), pudding, or preserves

Fill the egg halves with any favorite food.

Note: A number of all-fruit preserves are now available in grocery stores.

TIPS ON PACKAGING

* The rollups need to be packed in a plastic sandwich box with a lid so they won't get smashed in transit. Sandwiches also travel well in these boxes.

* Don't overlook the possibility when packing lunch that you can now keep things chilled with a plastic cold pack. One type, made by Coleman, is available in supermarkets. It's plastic; you just fill it with water and freeze. It will stay frozen and keep things cool for several hours in a lunch box. When its ice melts, the water is contained for refreezing—and no spills. Coleman makes a small size that is perfect for lunch boxes.

* The plastic Thermoses that come in many lunch boxes don't really seal well. My own experience has been that unless you keep them upright all the time, they slowly leak all the juice or whatever all over the rest of the lunch box. So we use juice boxes instead. This also allows more room in the lunch box for a cold pack.

* If you send raw veggies, pack them in a plastic bag and sprinkle with water or add one ice cube before sealing to help keep them moist (the ice cube will melt but they'll absorb the water). If you send slices of apple instead of an apple with its skin on, sprinkle with a mixture of water and lemon juice in equal amounts. This helps keep the apple from turning brown. Lemon juice also works this way with avocados, pears, or any other fruit that will discolor when exposed to air.

MINUS-MAYO SANDWICHES

Use cottage cheese instead of mayonnaise if you're worried about spoilage. This works well with both tuna and egg salad.

Mash 1 6½-ounce can of tuna *or* 4 hard-cooked eggs in a bowl. Add 4 ounces of the smallest curd cottage cheese. Add chopped vegetables (onion, celery, carrot, pepper, or radish) if desired. Spread your tuna or egg salad thinly on 2 slices of bread; put lettuce or sprouts in the middle if desired and press together.

FINGER SANDWICHES

Sometimes a little variety can give the same old sandwich new appeal. Try finger sandwiches, any sandwich with the crusts trimmed off and the sandwich then cut into smaller pieces. These can be rectangles, squares, or triangles. Use a small round biscuit or cookie cutter for rounds.

Other Lunches

Don't forget possibilities like peanut butter crackers, hard-cooked eggs, Deviled Eggs, or leftover Little Pies, Cheese Rolls (see Basic Rolls recipe), or Cheese Puffles (see recipes). If you think your child can remember to keep the lunch box upright, you can send along hot soup in a Thermos on chilly days.

Snacks

Be sure to find out what your school's policy is regarding snacks so that you can pack something appropriate if there is a snack break. Schools often encourage something wholesome for a snack, like crackers or whole fruit. For dessert, Fruit Leather or Fruit Brittle (see recipes) or homemade cookies are nice options if you have them. You can also buy sugarless cookies and other treats, including trail mix, at a health food store. (Just because they're sugarless doesn't mean they are totally good for the kids, but you can tell by trying them that they are more wholesome than the average store-bought cookie.)

Lunch at Home

Some things are just too messy to take to school, but are fun to make with the kids and their friends on a day when you're home.

PEANUT-BUTTER TURTLES

Slice an apple in half. Make several slits in each half. Fill with peanut butter or sesame butter. Attach seedless grapes with toothpicks for the head and legs and stick a carrot shaving on for a tail (tuck it into one of the slits).

PEANUT-BUTTER CATERPILLARS

Peel and slice a banana. Spread slices with peanut or sesame butter and connect the slices with toothpicks. Add a grape up front for a head, with toothpicks for antennas if you like.

CUTOUTS

Spread any sandwich filling between 2 slices of bread. Then let your child use cookie cutters to make shapes to eat. Dinosaur cookie cutters are especially popular for this, if you can find them. Another good activity to do with friends.

HOAGIES

Hoagies are also known as poor boys, heroes, and submarines, though these are not 100 percent identical. Hoagies traditionally are made with cheese, ham, and salami.

Slice in half horizontally torpedo rolls or a long loaf of French or Italian bread. Line with slices of cheese (we like provolone). Top with thinly sliced tomatoes and onions. Add shredded lettuce. Sprinkle with oregano (and cayenne pepper or hot pickled pepper relish if desired). Drizzle with oil and vinegar.

Variations: A favorite variation is to add egg salad after the cheese. You can also use tuna salad or turkey.

TWELVE

Dinner

H ere we are at dinner, the main meal of the day in our culture, but not necessarily for little people who have had a long day and are tired. Here are entrees that can be fixed fairly easily and quickly (or that can be made in advance when you have time), that include ingredients kids generally like, and that round out the nutrition picture for the day. With that said, don't be distressed if dinner isn't the big meal of the day for toddlers. Just try to see that there is something nutritious on the table for them.

Soups

Soups can be a meal in themselves—and for small appetites they often are. So why not make sure they're as chock-full of good nutrition as they can be? Hearty soups are a good place to hide the nutritional goodies. Many hearty soups are made of dried beans, peas, or lentils, so be sure to include a piece of the *kombu* seaweed that makes beans and peas more digestible. It will dissolve in the cooking and adds valuable minerals.

Blend or puree the hearty soups to make them easy for kids to eat. They can even help you with a hand food mill, large or small. For soups that are more brothy, you can put the broth in a cup and the solid ingredients on a plate or dish, if that makes the soup easier for very young children (thin broth can go flying off a spoon).

Add a good bread or a salad for bigger appetites, and soup becomes a meal that's fixed in advance and quick to serve.

Broths are the basis for other soups; they are also good fare for kids who have a cold or a touch of flu. Feed them Basic Chicken Stock or Easy Chicken Rice Soup or a simple Miso Soup. The hot broth with its easy-to-digest nutrients, plus the rice or noodles, will have them feeling better in no time. A study done in the early 1980s concluded that chicken soup really does make people feel better. So does miso.

BASIC CHICKEN STOCK

Makes about two quarts

Use a cooked chicken carcass if you have one or start with fresh chicken breasts.

3 *quarts water*

1 *cooked chicken carcass* or 2 *whole chicken breasts, lightly sautéed*

1 *bay leaf*

1 *carrot, cut into chunks*

1 *small onion, peeled*

3 *peppercorns*

   salt to taste (optional)

Bring the water to a boil in a stockpot and drop the chicken into the water. Add the remaining ingredients except salt and simmer until the chicken comes easily off the bones. Add more water as necessary to keep the chicken covered and provide a good amount of stock. If you have time to let it cook all day, so much the better (but you will have to keep adding water). It should cook for at least several hours, until the broth has a good flavor. You may wish to add salt to taste at this point. Strain out the bones and meat and discard the bones.

The meat and broth may be stored separately or together. If you used the chicken breasts, you won't need all the meat for soup. Reserve some for other chicken recipes; freeze it or use at once. Freeze the stock by the quart or by the cube, in ice trays; freeze it with or without meat chunks; or make some of it into chicken soup (see recipes in this section) at once.

BASIC VEGETABLE BROTH

Makes about 1 quart

Use this instead of meat broth or as the basis for a court bouillon. Make it in large quantities and freeze for convenience.

1 *large carrot, sliced thin*

1 *small onion, quartered*

1 *rib celery, sliced*

5 *fresh or dried shiitake mushrooms*

5 *cultivated mushrooms, sliced*

¼ *cup shredded cabbage*

1 *leaf wakame seaweed, crumbled (optional; available at health food stores)*

2 *quarts water*

1 *tablespoon tamari soy sauce (available at health food stores)*

Simmer the vegetables and mushrooms in water in a stockpot for 30 minutes; add tamari and cook for 30 minutes longer. Taste to correct seasoning. Strain and store in the freezer by the quart or in ice cube form or both. Use as a base for any vegetable, bean, or miso soup or for court bouillon in poaching fish.

BASIC FISH STOCK
Makes about 2 quarts

Ask at a fish store for heads, tails, and skeletons. Try to get the less oily fish—flounder, haddock, halibut, tilefish, monkfish, cod—for a less "fishy" stock. Use this as a base for fish or vegetable soups, or to poach any flounder-like (white) fish.

3–4 *quarts water*

3–4 *fish carcasses (head, skeleton, tail)*

½ *carrot*

1 *rib celery*

3 *peppercorns*

1 *small onion, halved*

1 *teaspoon salt*

Bring the water to a boil in a stockpot and add the remaining ingredients. Return the mixture to a boil, then simmer for 2 to 3 hours, until the liquid volume is reduced by at least one third and the stock has some substance when tasted. Freeze by the quart or as cubes in ice trays.

BASIC MISO SOUP
Makes 4 servings

Miso is rich in B vitamins and has a high proportion of usable protein. It is comforting and nourishing as a broth or served with the vegetables and with Japanese udon noodles in it.

½ *small onion, sliced into half-moons*

1 *small carrot, sliced thin*

wakame seaweed (available in health food stores)

1 *tablespoon tamari soy sauce (available in health food stores)*

3 *cups water*

1–2 *tablespoons miso paste*   *chopped scallions*
    (available in health   *(optional)*
    food stores), dissolved
    in ¼ cup warm water

   1 *cup cooked udon*
    noodles (optional;
    available at health
    food stores)

Simmer onion, carrot, wakame, and tamari in 3 cups water until the carrot is soft, about 20 minutes. (The wakame comes in dried pieces that expand a lot in water; start with no more than three the first time you try it.) The udon noodles take a while to cook; you can cook them separately at the same time while the vegetables are cooking. (You may want to add some or all of the water that the noodles were cooked in to the soup; if so, add more tamari or miso for flavor is necessary.) When the carrots are soft, turn the heat down as low as possible and slowly add the miso mixture to the pot. (If the heat is too high, the miso will curdle; like yogurt and fresh cream, it shouldn't really be cooked, just heated.) Start with 1 tablespoon and taste. If it tastes too bland, add more miso, again blending first with warm water. Serve just the broth or serve the broth with vegetables and noodles, garnished with chopped scallions.

Notes: Thin lemon slices make a nice garnish too, though not a traditional one. Basic miso soup may also contain daikon radish (available in health food stores and some supermarkets), shiitake mushrooms, leafy greens, or other vegetables. Keep it simple, though; alternate your ingredients, but limit the vegetables down to 3 or 4 at a time. Miso soup is a traditional breakfast dish in Japan. For us it may make a complete lunch or a first course at dinner. With the lemon slices it is quite an elegant dish.

MISO CONSOMMÉ

Makes 4 servings

This is good for really hot days.

Use the broth from Basic Miso Soup. Add ½ stick kanten *or* 2 tablespoons agar-agar (both available in health food stores). Stir over very low heat until the kanten or agar-agar is thoroughly dissolved. Chill in individual bowls until set, at least 1 hour. Stir to break up the surface; garnish with thin slices of lemon and serve at once.

AVGOLEMONO

Makes 4 to 6 servings

Greek egg-lemon soup is the Mediterranean answer to egg-drop.

1 *quart Basic Chicken Stock (see recipe), with or without meat*

1 *cup cooked rice*

2 *eggs*

juice of 1 lemon

salt and freshly ground white pepper to taste (optional)

chopped fresh parsley (optional)

Bring stock to a boil in a saucepan; add the rice. Beat the eggs well in a ceramic bowl; add the lemon juice and beat well. Add about ½ cup hot stock to the egg-lemon mixture, beating well so that the eggs don't curdle. Turn off the heat under the stock with rice and add the egg mixture, stirring to blend it in. Season with salt and pepper and garnish with parsley if desired.

QUICK EGG-DROP SOUP

Makes 4 servings

Start 'em on it young. It's a good source of protein and nice on cold nights. Serve it with Basic Stir-Fry for a homemade "Chinese" meal.

3 *cups Basic Chicken Stock (see recipe)*

1–2 *scallions, chopped*

3–4 *leaves fresh spinach* or 1 *leaf escarole, cut into ribbons (optional)*

1 *egg, beaten*

Heat the stock to a boil in a saucepan and add scallion and greens if available. Cook for 3 minutes and lower the heat. Pour in the egg and stir over very low heat with a circular motion so that it breaks into threads.

ACORN SQUASH SOUP

Makes 3 servings

A wheat-free, dairy-free, egg-free soup that is hearty and sweet. Children love the taste of winter squashes. In soup their texture is easy to like, too. Adults will also love this mildly spicy soup.

1 *acorn squash*

2 *tablespoons nut or seed oil*

1 *tablespoon soy flour (available at health food stores)*

2 *cups boiling water*

2 *teaspoons tamari soy sauce (available at health food stores)*

¼ *teaspoon ground cinnamon*

¼ *teaspoon curry powder*

Preheat the oven to 350 degrees. Split the squash and clean out the seeds. Bake it face down on a greased cookie sheet until you can pierce it easily with a fork—30 to 45 minutes. Peel and set aside. Heat the oil in a saucepan and blend in the soy flour as to make a *roux* (as for a white sauce). Slowly add the boiling water, blending until smooth. Put the liquid and squash in a blender or food processor and blend until smooth. Season to taste with tamari, cinnamon, and curry powder.

SPLIT-PEA SOUP

Makes 4 to 6 servings

This is another soup to start kids on early—babies seem instinctively to appreciate the taste, and it is a good complementary protein for them, coupled with some kind of grain, such as corn bread or some other good bread (or for older kids, a grilled cheese sandwich).

1   *cup split peas*

1½ *quarts water or Basic Vegetable Broth (see recipe)*

1   *strip kombu (available at health food stores)*

1   *bay leaf*

3   *peppercorns*

1   *medium carrot, sliced thin*

1   *small onion with a clove inserted at each end*

½   *rib celery, sliced*

1   *tablespoon tamari soy sauce (available at health food stores)*

salt to taste (optional)

Combine all the ingredients except salt in a large pot and bring to a boil. Skim off foam and reduce the heat. Simmer for 1 to 2 hours, until the peas are soft. Puree in a food processor or blender and add salt if needed.

Note: For added flavor, you can crumble a slice of cooked bacon on top of the soup for the meat-eaters in the family and sprinkle the soup with Gomasio (see recipe) or roasted sesame seeds for the non-meat eaters. This has to be done on a bowl-by-bowl basis, obviously.

Kids in the Kitchen: Let older toddlers help by making their own soup. Put some of the peas and the liquid in your (retired) infant food mill and hold the base *firmly* so the liquid doesn't spill. Let them crank the handle and watch the soup appear magically through the strainer plate.

LENTIL SOUP

Makes 4 to 6 servings

Lentil soup offers the same good nutrition as pea soup, and children can puree it through the hand blender in the same way. Combine it with a grain of some kind for complete protein. Again, bread by itself or in a sandwich is easy.

1 *cup lentils*

1½ *quarts water or stock*

1 *strip kombu (available at health food stores)*

1 *bay leaf*

½ *teaspoon dried thyme*

1 *chopped tomato (optional)*

1 *carrot, sliced*

1 *small onion, chopped*

1 *garlic clove, minced*

1 *tablespoon tamari soy sauce (or to taste; available at health food stores)*

Combine all the ingredients in a pot and simmer for about 2 hours, adding more water or stock if necessary. Lentil soup doesn't need to be pureed except for very young children, but toddlers may want the fun of doing it anyway.

Note: In cooking bean, pea, or lentil soups, do not add salt until after the beans or peas are tender, or they won't get tender. Miso, as well as salt or tamari, may be used in all of these soups for flavor. Add it by the teaspoon, stir well, and taste.

About Bean Soups

Beans are usually soaked overnight before cooking. You can take a shortcut by putting rinsed beans in cold water, bringing it to a boil, boiling for 2 minutes, and then letting the beans stand, covered, for 1 hour. Be sure the liquid is more than enough to cover them; they'll be absorbing liquid while they sit, and you want to allow enough (that's how they get soft).

LIMA BEAN SOUP

Makes 6 servings

A nice way to eat limas. Serve it with grated cheddar cheese for complete protein.

1½ *cups dried lima beans, soaked overnight*

1 *quart water*

1 *16-ounce can tomatoes, with liquid*

1 *strip kombu (available at health food stores)*

1 *rib celery, chopped*

1 *medium onion, chopped*

1 *teaspoon dried basil*

1 *bay leaf*

2–3 *peppercorns*

salt or tamari soy sauce (available at health food stores)

1 *cup grated cheddar cheese*

chopped fresh parsley

Cook the drained beans with the remaining ingredients except salt, cheese, and parsley, until the soup thickens—at least 2 hours. Add extra water if necessary. Remember, don't add salt until the beans are thoroughly soft. Garnish with cheese and parsley.

SEVEN-BEAN SOUP

Makes about 3 quarts

This soup is colorful and zesty.

DRY INGREDIENTS:

½ *cup dried black beans*

1 *cup dried navy beans*

½ *cup dried kidney beans*

½ *cup dried lima beans*

½ *cup dried pinto beans*

½ *cup split peas*

½ *cup lentils*

½ *teaspoon hot red pepper flakes*

1 *bay leaf*

2 *teaspoons dried oregano*

1 *teaspoon garlic powder*

1 *strip kombu (available at health food stores)*

FRESH INGREDIENTS:

1 *medium carrot, sliced*

1 *rib celery, chopped*

1 *medium onion, chopped*

3 *quarts water or Basic Vegetable Broth (see recipe)*

salt or tamari soy sauce (available at health food stores) to taste

Soak the black, navy, kidney, lima, and pinto beans overnight (lentils and split peas don't need to be soaked). Drain and discard the cooking water. Simmer all the ingredients except salt in a large stockpot until the beans are tender—2 to 3 hours. Season to taste with salt or tamari.

Kids in the Kitchen: Get kids involved by letting them help you prepare a large batch of the dried beans for it, mixed in the proper proportions, to be stored in glass jars (a big mayonnaise jar or several peanut butter jars will do). Children will enjoy naming the beans and peas and playing with the different colors and textures. You and they can also make colorful and inexpensive holiday gifts for favorite teachers or neighbors by mixing up jars of the dry ingredients and covering the lid with a piece of bright fabric, secured around the neck of the jar with a ribbon.

POTATO SOUP
Makes 6 to 8 servings

The best flavor for this soup comes from leeks, but you can use onions instead.

6 medium potatoes, peeled and sliced thin

2 cups sliced, cleaned leeks or 1 cup sliced onions

1 quart water or stock

1 tablespoon unsalted butter

1 teaspoon salt

freshly ground white pepper to taste

1 cup plain yogurt or buttermilk

chopped fresh chives

Combine the potatoes, onions or leeks, water or stock, butter, and salt in a large pot and simmer until very tender, about 30 minutes. Puree in a food processor fitted with the steel blade or a blender and return it to the pot. Stir in additional salt if needed and pepper to taste over very low heat. Turn off heat and stir in yogurt or buttermilk. Serve hot or cold, garnish with chives.

BROCCOLI VICHYSSOISE
Makes 6 to 8 servings

To 1 recipe Potato Soup (preceding recipe), add 1 cup chopped fresh or frozen broccoli when the potatoes are tender. Cook until the broccoli is tender but still bright green. Then proceed as for Potato Soup. Chill for 2 to 3 hours before serving and garnishing.

PURPLE SOUP

Makes about 6 servings

Thanks to Sally Mann for introducing us to her version of this wonderful soup. My theory about beets is the less said, the better. That's why we call it Purple Soup.

1 *cup sliced cooked or canned beets*

½ *small onion, sliced*

½ *teaspoon salt*

large pinch freshly ground black pepper

2 *teaspoons fresh lemon juice*

⅔ *cup leftover mashed potatoes or 1 boiled potato, sliced*

1 *cup Basic Chicken Stock (see recipe)*

2 *tablespoons mayonnaise*

¼ *cup sour cream*

½ *cup plain yogurt*

1 *cup cracked ice*

chopped fresh chives or dill

Combine beets, onion, salt, pepper, lemon juice, and potato in a blender. Blend at high speed to puree. In a separate container (preferably a pint-size or larger measuring cup), combine all other ingredients except ice. Add this mixture slowly to the blender, blending until smooth. Add ice and blend for 1 minute. Chill; serve with a garnish of chopped chives or fresh dill.

Note: For finicky eaters, omit the garnish.

PUMPKIN EATER SOUP

Makes 4 servings

You probably know that the canned pumpkin you buy in stores isn't really pumpkin at all; it's a cousin, one of the squashes. Real pumpkin, the kind you make jack-o'-lanterns out of, has a different texture from the "pumpkin" sold for pies. But either works equally well, we find, in making pies or soup. The advantages in using real pumpkins is that they are plentiful and cheap in the fall and the children often enjoy the idea of cooking the pumpkin you bought on a farmstand excursion. You can even cook your jack-o'-lantern if you don't let it sit too long after Halloween. Just slice off the face and use the rest.

1 *small onion, chopped*

2 *tablespoons unsalted butter*

2 *cups raw peeled pumpkin chunks or canned pumpkin*

1 *cup water*

1 *tablespoon unbleached flour*

1 *cup milk, heated*

salt or tamari soy sauce (available at health food stores) to taste

pinch cayenne pepper (optional)

ground cinnamon

Sauté onion in 1 tablespoon of the butter in a saucepan. Add the pumpkin if you're using fresh and water and simmer until the pumpkin is very tender (test with a fork). Meanwhile, melt the remaining butter, blend in the flour, and gradually add the milk. Puree the pumpkin and milk mixture in a food processor fitted with the steel blade. Return the puree to the heat, add salt or tamari to taste and cayenne pepper if desired. Garnish with cinnamon.

Note: For a festive serving when pumpkins are in season, buy an extra one, small to medium size. Slice off the top and clean out the seeds and strings. Use as a soup tureen to hold a double recipe of Pumpkin Eater Soup. (You may embellish the tureen, before filling it, by cutting its rim into a zigzag pattern.)

Kids in the Kitchen: Your child can help puree the pumpkin with the small hand food mill, and his or her portion can go right to the table, to cool and be garnished.

BARLEY SOUP
Makes 6 servings

Rich in protein, carbohydrates, and fiber, this is also a comforting hot soup for winter nights.

2 *quarts Basic Chicken Stock (see recipe)*

1 *cup bite-sized cooked chicken meat*

1 *small onion, sliced into half-moons*

1 *rib celery, chopped*

1 *small parsnip, sliced thin*

1 *cup pearl barley*

1 *small strip kombu (available at health food stores)*

1 *teaspoon dried basil*

¼ *teaspoon freshly ground white pepper*

salt to taste (optional)

shredded carrot (optional)

Combine all the ingredients except salt and carrot and simmer until the barley is cooked, about 45 minutes. Season to taste with salt if needed and garnish with shredded carrot if desired.

Note: Barley soup can be a soothing and digestible meal for convalescents. Omit the chicken meat to make it easier to eat.

CHICKEN NOODLE SOUP

Makes 6 servings

A superquick soup, if you keep stock on hand, that pleases every-body. This is one of those soups whose ingredients may be separated to make them more palatable for the fussy eater—a bowl of noodles, a cup of broth, and chicken on a plate.

- 1 *quart Basic Chicken Stock (see recipe)*
- 1 *cup bite-sized cooked chicken meat*
- 1 *medium carrot, sliced thin*
- 1 *small onion, chopped*
- 1 *rib celery, chopped*
- ½ *green bell pepper, chopped (optional)*
- ½ *cup dry egg noodles or Homemade Noodles (recipe follows)*

Combine all the ingredients and cook for 15 minutes.

Note: If you don't have Basic Chicken Stock on hand, this can still be an easy dinner to prepare. Just make the stock recipe using chicken breasts. Remove bones and extra meat and add noodles.

HOMEMADE NOODLES

Recipes with flour are always potentially messy, especially with a child around, but my sister swears by this one. Her son has been making these noodles, which are from his grandmother Richards's recipe, since he was about three. So let the kids help and never mind the mess.

Mash ½ stick (4 tablespoons) unsalted butter together with 2 large eggs until the butter is in little pieces. Add enough unbleached flour to make a dough that holds together and doesn't stick to your hands. Take a little dough at a time and roll it out very thin on a well-floured board, using a rolling pin that has been greased and floured. Cut into noodles of the desired width. Drop noodles into boiling broth as soon as each little batch is made.

CHICKEN OATMEAL SOUP

Makes 4 to 6 servings

This soup was inspired by some reading I was doing about allergies. Chicken, carrots, and oatmeal were listed as three of the seven or eight foods people are least likely to be allergic to. I was looking for a way to make this rather limited selection of foods into a meal when I hit on Chicken Oatmeal Soup. It has a mild yet pleasing flavor and a creamy texture. It's soothing for kids who are under the weather or good anytime for lunch or supper.

2   *whole chicken breasts, skinned and halved*

2   *quarts water*

1   *carrot, cut into thin matchsticks*

½   *cup rolled oats*

salt to taste

Simmer the chicken breasts, uncovered, in the water in a saucepan until the liquid is reduced by half (at least 45 minutes). Remove chicken. Reserve 3 halves of breasts for another use (freeze them whole or in stir-fry-sized pieces). Cut the remaining half into small pieces, and return it to broth with the carrot and oatmeal. Cook until the oatmeal is soft and gives the broth a slightly creamy consistency. Add salt to taste.

CHICKEN GUMBO

Makes 8 servings

A traditional Louisiana dish, *gumbo* refers to the okra that is essential to this soup. Children like the mildly spicy flavor, the mixture of textures, and the way the okra cross sections look like little flowers.

2½ quarts Basic Chicken Stock (see recipe)

1 cup cooked chicken meat in chunks

1 cup chopped fresh or drained canned tomatoes

1 bay leaf

2 teaspoons filé powder (see Note)

1 cup whole fresh okra

½ cup raw rice

½ teaspoon salt

Bring the stock to a boil in a stockpot. Add the remaining ingredients and simmer until the rice is tender, about 45 minutes. Remove okra, cut up, and return. Taste and correct seasonings.

Note: If you can't get gumbo filé powder (available in supermarkets or gourmet stores), here's how to improvise: Substitute 1 teaspoon sassafras powder *or* 1 tablespoon sassafras tea (from a health food store) tied up in cheesecloth (the sassafras tea needs to be tied up to keep the bark from getting into the soup) plus ½ teaspoon cayenne pepper, ¼ teaspoon ground coriander, and ¼ teaspoon ground cardamon. If you used sassafras tea, remove it when the soup is done.

SEAFOOD GUMBO

Follow the preceding Chicken Gumbo recipe, substituting ½ pound fillet of any white fish plus ½ pound peeled and deveined shrimp for the chicken and Basic Fish Stock for Basic Chicken Stock. Add the fish and shrimp about 10 minutes before the soup is done.

CREAM OF TOMATO SOUP

Makes 4 to 6 servings

A nice lunch or dinner with grilled cheese sandwiches.

4 tablespoons (½ stick) unsalted butter	1 tablespoon unbleached flour
1 garlic clove, chopped	½ cup milk, heated
1 medium onion, chopped	chopped fresh parsley or chives (optional)
3 cups fresh or drained canned whole tomatoes	4–6 teaspoons plain yogurt
3 cups Basic Vegetable Broth (see recipes)	

Melt 2 tablespoons of the butter in a heavy saucepan. Add the garlic and onion and sauté until tender. Add the tomatoes and cut them up as they simmer, about 15 minutes. Add the broth and simmer for 1 hour. Force the mixture through a sieve (or puree in a blender or a food processor fitted with the steel blade if you don't mind leaving in the skin and seeds).

Add the remaining butter to a saucepan, blend in the flour over low heat, and add the milk slowly to form a sort of thin white sauce. Combine this with the tomato mixture and stir well over low heat. Garnish with parsley or chives and a teaspoon of yogurt per bowl.

Note: For a one-bowl meal, top with croutons and shredded cheddar cheese.

COLD GREEN PEA SOUP

Makes 4 servings

Great for hot days, this pretty moss-green soup was inspired by a favorite recipe from Marian Carlsson.

1 *10-ounce package frozen peas, cooked*

1 *cup cold Basic Chicken Stock (see recipe)*

2 *teaspoons curry powder*

1 *cup plain yogurt*

salt to taste (optional)

chopped fresh chives

Blend the peas, stock, curry, and yogurt in a blender or a food processor fitted with the steel blade. Chill for at least 1 hour. Add salt if needed. Garnish with chives.

"WOLF" SOUP

Makes 8 to 10 servings

My grandmother Kilbourne's invention, this was supposed to be the soup that was cooking in the Three Little Pigs' house when the wolf came down the chimney. I guess my grandmother knew a few things about getting children to eat their soup. We loved it.

1 *pound beef pot roast, with bone(s)*

2 *tablespoons olive oil*

3 *quarts boiling water*

1 *16-ounce can tomatoes, with liquid*

1 *bay leaf*

4–5 *peppercorns*

1 *large carrot, sliced*

2 *medium onions, sliced into half-moons*

1 *rib celery, chopped*

1 *cup peeled sliced potatoes*

1 *cup fresh green beans*

½ *cup fresh corn kernels*

1 *cup shredded cabbage*

Brown the meat in the oil in a heavy skillet. Remove from the skillet, discarding all rendered fat, and transfer the meat to a stockpot. Pour over the boiling water and add the tomatoes, bay leaf, peppercorns, carrot, onions, and celery. Simmer for 2 to 3 hours, until the meat is falling into shreds. Add the rest of the vegetables and cook for 20 to 30 minutes.

Note: Soup may be chilled and skimmed to remove additional fat, then reheated.

Salads

Salads can be a meal or a nice light side dish that complements your main dish, gives you a bundle of good nutrients, and eliminates the need to cook a vegetable. Toss a simple one together in a minute on a night when you're in a hurry. Or make a hearty one ahead of time to avoid cooking on hot nights.

For washing and drying lettuce and other greens, you'll find a plastic salad spinner, available in department stores and kitchen-ware stores, indispensable. If you don't have one, dry greens as well as you can in a colander and then pat dry with a towel or wrap them firmly in a towel and shake rapidly.

As for ingredients, it's really important to use good-quality oil and vinegar. I recommend any extra-virgin olive oil, available at supermarkets, or cold-pressed nut oils from a health food store. Brown rice vinegar, available in health food stores, is a nice mild vinegar that is easy to digest. For flavor, a regular rice vinegar or a white wine vinegar from the supermarket is equally good.

Impeccably fresh, well-drained salad greens and good-quality oil and vinegar are really all you need for a good green salad. You can, however, add a little garlic or honey to make a fancier dressing to try one of the dressing recipes in this section. Add enough oil to coat the dry greens lightly. Then add a bit of salt or Gomasio (see recipe). Add vinegar, equal in amount to the oil or slightly less, and season with a little freshly ground pepper.

SIMPLE SALAD

For a side dish, keep it simple. Use one salad green—whatever you have, though I suggest romaine is more interesting than iceberg. Add one vegetable (grated carrot is easy; so is a handful of cabbage shreds—just slice across the cabbage head and you've got them). Hardy vegetables that keep in your fridge for days or even weeks (see sidebar) are handy everyday choices. Add scallions or chopped onions if you like them. Add a handful of nuts (crumble them if they're larger than peanuts). Toss with oil and vinegar and salt and freshly ground pepper to taste, as explained in the introduction to salads. (Caution: don't feed nuts or chunks of raw vegetable to infants young enough to choke on them. You can offer them lettuce if they'll eat it.)

HARDY VEGETABLES

Here are some good vegetables to keep on hand for salads.

+ Carrots last for weeks.

+ Cabbage lasts for weeks; if it develops black specks, just peel off and discard the outer leaves.

+ Radishes will keep for weeks, but leaves may wilt or even turn black and mushy; just rinse them away. The radishes will still be fine.

+ Peppers will keep for about a week.

+ Celery keeps for weeks; just cut off any brown parts.

THREE-GREEN SALAD

Makes 6 to 8 servings

This salad combines iceberg, romaine, and escarole for a refreshing effect. Again, the salad is simple; just throw all the greens in a dishpan, fill to rinse, then drain, dry and tear them up by the handful. Use oil and vinegar (see introduction to salads) or Easy Mustard Dressing or Creamy Dressing (see recipes)

½ head iceberg lettuce

6–8 romaine leaves

¼ head escarole (discard tough outer leaves first)

1 garlic clove (optional)

oil and vinegar or other dressing

Wash and dry the greens. Rub a salad bowl with the peeled, split garlic clove if desired. Combine the leaves in the bowl and toss with dressing immediately before serving.

OK CORRAL SALAD

Makes 6 to 8 servings

This pasta salad is good as a whole meal on hot days. It gets its name from the wheel-shaped pasta we use in it, but you can substitute shells or rotini and rename it Seashell Salad or Drill Salad. Look for the three-colored (white, green, and orange) pasta shapes in Italian specialty shops or a health food store. Some of the pastas from health food stores have even more colors. The multicolored pasta is part of the appeal of this salad to kids.

4 cups cooked pasta wheels

1 raw carrot, scrubbed and sliced into thin matchsticks

1 medium onion, chopped

1 rib celery, sliced thin

½ green bell pepper, chopped

5–6 radishes, sliced thin

1 6½-ounce can solid white water-packed tuna, drained

½–1 cup Easy Mustard Dressing (see recipe)

Toss all the ingredients in a large salad bowl and chill. The salad can be made the night before and refrigerated.

Note: If you really want to take it easy, just slice all the vegetables with a food processor into whatever shapes and textures are easiest.

Dovetail: Younger kids sometimes will eat many or all of the ingredients, but not combined. Save out some pasta wheels, some bits of tuna if they like it, some carrot slices, radishes, and any other ingredients. Set aside in a separate dish in the refrigerator.

BEET AND BEAN SALAD
Makes 6 to 8 servings

Beets and Beans? I'm drawing on personal experience for this one. As a child I categorically hated all vegetables except corn and tomatoes (neither one a true vegetable, of course). But for some reason my mother's Beet and Bean Salad was delectable. I think the dressing makes the vegetables taste completely different.

2 *cups cooked green beans*

1 *cup cooked beets, sliced into thin matchsticks*

½ *cup Paprika Dressing (see recipe)*

lettuce leaves

Combine the beans, beets, and dressing in a bowl and chill for several hours before serving. Garnish the serving bowl with lettuce leaves or serve on individual plates on lettuce leaves.

Note: Use frozen beans and pickled beets for quicker preparation.

POTATO-VEGETABLE SALAD

Makes 4 to 6 servings

A nice almost-meal for hot days. Round it out with something cooked on the grill (be it just hot dogs or some fish or chicken), or with a dish of cottage cheese, or with some cheese chunks on toothpicks. Or top the salad with 2 or 3 sliced hard-cooked eggs for a full meal.

4 *medium boiling potatoes, peeled and sliced*

¼ *head lettuce, torn into pieces*

1 *medium onion, sliced thin*

1 *cup cooked snap beans*

2 *large tomatoes, cut into wedges*

½ *cup Basil Dressing (see recipe)*

Boil the potatoes until you can pierce them easily with a fork, about 15 minutes. Let cool for 10 minutes. Arrange in a salad bowl on top of lettuce and add the other vegetables in layers. Drizzle with dressing and refrigerate for at least 2 hours.

Dovetail: For kids who won't eat salad, save a potato and mash it. Serve with a hard-cooked egg, hot dog, bit of chicken, or whatever else is making the rest of the meal.

KALE-CORN SALAD

Makes 6 servings

A nice mild salad that's especially appealing in the spring. The trick is to just barely cook the kale. With the vinegar dressing, even greens haters may learn to like this one, and it's worth trying, because kale is rich in minerals.

3 cups kale, washed and sliced into thin ribbons

1 cup fresh or thawed frozen corn kernels

1 large carrot, scrubbed and sliced into thin matchsticks

1 tablespoon toasted sesame seeds

¼–½ cup rice vinegar

½ teaspoon Gomasio (see recipe)

Blanch the kale in boiling water for about 30 seconds. Rinse immediately in a colander under cold water to stop the cooking. Set aside. Steam the corn and carrot together for 3 minutes. Toss all the vegetables with the remaining ingredients. Serve at room temperature.

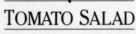

TOMATO SALAD

Makes 4 to 6 servings

A nice side dish for summer days.

3 ripe fresh tomatoes, sliced

1 medium onion, sliced

1 tablespoon fresh basil or 1 teaspoon dried

3 tablespoons extra-virgin olive oil

2 tablespoons wine or rice vinegar

Marinate the tomato and onion slices for at least 1 hour before serving.

BULGUR WITH CHICK-PEAS

Makes 6 servings

Bulgur wheat is a partially processed wheat product used in Middle Eastern cooking. Also called *cracked wheat,* it has a nice nutty taste and texture. This salad combines it with chick-peas (aka garbanzo beans) for complete protein and a complete meal, good in summer.

1½ cups bulgur wheat (available in supermarkets or health food stores)

1 medium onion, chopped

10–12 cherry tomatoes, halved

½ cup chopped fresh parsley

1 cup cooked (or canned) chick-peas

¼ cup extra-virgin olive oil

juice of 1 lemon

salt or Gomasio (see recipe) to taste

freshly ground pepper to taste

lettuce or escarole leaves

Soak the bulgur for 45 minutes in cold water to cover. Drain off any remaining liquid. Add the onion, tomatoes, parsley, and chick-peas. Toss. Add the oil, lemon juice, salt or Gomasio, and pepper. Serve on lettuce leaves.

RICE AND LENTIL SALAD

Makes 6 to 8 servings

A delicious and colorful salad—and a meal in itself. For heartier meal, serve with grilled chicken or fish.

3 cups cooked rice

1 cup Basic Lentils (see recipe)

1 medium onion, sliced thin

1 rib celery, sliced thin

1 carrot, sliced into thin matchsticks

2 medium tomatoes, chopped

½ teaspoon dried thyme

¼ cup olive oil

¼ cup brown rice vinegar

salt to taste

paprika

Toss the rice, lentils, vegetables, and thyme together gently in a bowl. Add oil, vinegar, and salt. Sprinkle with paprika.

PARSLEY RICE SALAD WITH WALNUTS

Makes 8 servings

Good as a side or main dish.

- 4 *cups cooked rice*
- ½ *cup walnuts*
- 3 *scallions, chopped*
- 1 *small carrot, sliced thin*
  1-inch chunk of daikon radish, sliced into thin matchsticks
- 3 *red radishes, sliced thin*

- ½ *cup chopped parsley*
- ¼ *cup olive oil*
- ¼ *cup brown rice vinegar*
- 1 *teaspoon Gomasio (see recipe)*
  cayenne pepper to taste

Mix the rice, nuts, vegetables, and parsley in a large bowl. Toss with oil, then vinegar, Gomasio, and a sprinkling of cayenne.

MILLET RAISIN SALAD

Makes 6 servings

Millet is the most alkaline of the grains, and this is why it is so digestible. It is a grain used widely in the Middle East. With the nuts the salad provides complete protein and is nearly a meal in itself. Serve it with any mild white fish, or with Grilled Eggplant (see recipe), or with a Fruit Platter (see recipe) or a light salad.

- 3 *cups cooked millet (see Note)*
- 1 *cup raisins*

- ½ *cup pine nuts or chopped pecans*
- 1 *medium carrot, grated*

¼ cup light sesame oil

juice of 1 lemon

salt to taste (optional)

1 teaspoon (or more)
ground cinnamon

Toss the millet, raisins, nuts, and carrot together gently in a bowl. Add the oil, then add the lemon juice gradually, tasting to see if all of it is needed. Add salt to taste if desired and cinnamon to taste.

Note: To cook millet, boil it as you would rice, in 2 to 3 parts water to 1 part millet, for at least 30 minutes, until tender.

GRAIN SALAD DOVETAILS

Kids usually like grains of all kinds. If your kids aren't currently delighted by various things mixed together, as in salad, remember to save out some of the cooked rice, millet, bulgur, or whatever for them. Also save any vegetables they might like, or raisins, nuts, and the like. Round out a meal for a summer night with a piece of fruit or a hard-boiled egg. Don't expect them to eat too much if it's really hot.

PRESSED SALAD
Makes 4 servings

Refreshing for hot days, this salad can be served as a side dish with cold soup or with something from the grill, or with a grain salad.

1 large cucumber, peeled and sliced (see Notes)

4 red radishes, sliced thin

a 1-inch chunk of daikon, sliced thin

1 medium onion, sliced thin

2 tablespoons light sesame oil

2 tablespoons rice vinegar

1 teaspoon Gomasio (see recipe)

Arrange the vegetables in layers in a bowl with straight sides. Drizzle with oil and vinegar. Sprinkle with Gomasio. On top of the salad, place a saucer or plate that fits inside the bowl. On top of the plate, set a half-gallon container filled with water. Allow to sit for at least 1 hour. Serve at room temperature.

Notes: To make the cucumber sweeter, cut off both ends, salt one of the small end pieces, and rub the ends of the main part of the cucumber with it. Then rinse off the cucumber, peel, and slice.

Instead of using the plate-and-weight method, you can use a salad press, available at Oriental groceries, health food stores, and some department stores.

POCKET SALAD

For a quick and easy summer meal when everyone's rushing off to ball games or swim team practice, stuff pita pockets with Simple Salad (see recipe) or Three-Green Salad (see recipe) topped with one of these:

tuna
cottage cheese
feta cheese
chopped hard-cooked egg
hummus
yogurt

Serve with the dressing of your choice and a plate of carrot sticks, celery, and whole cherry tomatoes.

FRUIT PLATTER WITH JUICESICLES

Makes 6 to 8 servings

For days when it's so hot that you can't even bear to think of eating, let alone cooking, try this.

½ *cantaloupe, peeled and cut into chunks*

1 *cup strawberries, washed, hulled, and halved*

½ *cup fresh (or chilled canned) pineapple chunks*

½ *cup pitted cherries or white grapes, halved*

sliced fresh peaches or plums

iceberg lettuce

Juicesicles (see recipe)

Arrange fruit on a bed of iceberg lettuce on a large chilled platter. Just as you serve it, add an ice tray full of plain Juicesicles (made with toothpicks or sectioned straws for easy handling). Eat quickly! *Note:* Substitute summer fruits of your choice as desired.

COLESLAW WITH BUTTERMILK

Makes 4 to 6 servings

A delicious slaw with low-calorie, low-cholesterol protein from the buttermilk.

½ *head cabbage*

1 *medium onion*

½ *cup (or more) buttermilk*

2 *tablespoons mayonnaise*

freshly ground black pepper

Shred the cabbage and onion in a food processor. Toss with the buttermilk and mayonnaise. Add more buttermilk if the slaw is not moist enough. Season with pepper to taste.

DINOSAUR SALAD

Basically just fresh sliced veggies of your choice, to go with a dip. Peel the vegetables if you are worried about what might be in or on the skins (as in chemical residues) or if your kids don't like to eat the skins. If you have an organic carrot you're really sure about, on the other hand, you might just scrub it and serve it. Dinosaur Salad was an invention of Margaret Brossy's family.

carrots, celery, cucumbers, or zucchini, sliced lengthwise ("logs")
zucchini or cucumber slices ("lily pads")
broccoli flowerets ("trees")
sprouts ("vines")
cherry tomatoes ("dinosaur fruit")
sliced fresh mushrooms ("umbrella plants")
lettuce, spinach leaves, or cabbage. sliced thin ("grass")
Dinosaur Dips (recipe follows)

Add your own favorites and let everyone help invent names to go with them. Serve Dinosaur Salad with a dip; let the kids help themselves to salad, and dip from a central dish or from their own little cups if that's more fun.

DINOSAUR DIPS

To ¼ cup of any of the dressings (Creamy, Basil—see Basic Dressing recipe), add 2 tablespoons mayonnaise and 2 tablespoons small-curd cottage cheese. Blend and serve.

Note: One mother tells me her kids love a good-quality commercial bleu cheese dressing for a dip. Just be sure to read the label to avoid saturated fats. Or make your own by blending 2 tablespoons of crumbled bleu cheese into this dip recipe.

Allergy Note: For kids with allergies, omit cottage cheese and add chèvre or feta cheese; omit mayonnaise and add 1 teaspoon honey and ½ teaspoon paprika or dry mustard.

WATERCRESS-GRAPE-ORANGE SALAD

Makes 6 to 8 servings

3 *cups cleaned watercress leaves*

1 *cup orange slices*

1 *cup halved seedless grapes*

¼ *cup sliced scallions*

¼ *cup chopped walnuts or sunflower seeds*

Toss all the ingredients together. Dress with oil and vinegar or Basic Dressing (see recipe).

Dovetail meal: Reserve some of the orange slices and grape halves for the kids' dinners. Give them nuts or seeds too if they like them.

SURPRISE SALAD

A glass or clear plastic bowl really makes this work well. What's surprising about this salad is the combinations kids like. You would think they would like only fruit with fruit or vegetables with vegetables, but they like the strangest things together. One parent I know even puts Jell-O cubes in the bottom of the bowl. Whatever you come up with, part of the fun is in getting to the next layer. Make it a deep-sea diving expedition or an archaeological dig. Try any of the following together.

sliced cucumbers
sliced celery
shredded lettuce, cabbage, spinach, or escarole
shredded carrots
nuts
raisins
sliced apples
hard-cooked egg slices

crumbled cheese
orange slices
strawberries
white seedless grapes

Dress with Creamy Dressing (see Basic Dressing recipe) by dribbling ½ cup or more slowly over the layered salad. Do not toss.

Salad Dressings

---◆---

BASIC DRESSING

Makes a little less than 2 cups

1 *cup extra-virgin olive oil*

⅔ *cup brown rice vinegar (available at health food stores)*

1 *teaspoon salt*

2 *teaspoons honey*

freshly ground black or cayenne pepper (optional)

1 *garlic clove, mashed*

Combine all the ingredients and shake well or blend. Refrigerate and use as needed for large or individual salads. Keeps for up to a week in the refrigerator.

VARIATIONS

Basil Dressing: Add 1 teaspoon chopped fresh *or* ½ teaspoon dried basil to Basic Dressing. If possible, blend.

Easy Mustard Dressing: Add 2 teaspoons dry mustard.

Paprika Dressing: Add 2 teaspoons paprika.

Creamy Dressing: Add 2 tablespoons plain yogurt and ½ teaspoon dried oregano; omit salt and add 2 teaspoons Gomasio (recipe follows).

GOMASIO

*Makes about ⅓ cup, enough to season your salad and
soup for a couple of weeks*

1 *teaspoon salt
   (traditional recipes use
   sea salt)*

4 *tablespoons sesame
   seeds*

Heat the salt in a heavy iron skillet until you can smell chlorine. Add
the seeds and stir over low heat until the seeds begin to brown and
pop. Remove from heat and grind in a spice grinder or in a mortar
and pestle. (The traditional Japanese method uses a mortar called a
suribachi, which you may be able to buy at a health food or Oriental
grocery, if you want to be authentic. The results of grinding in a
spice or coffee grinder or even a blender will be about the same for
all except purists.) Store, covered, in a cupboard away from the
stove.

Entrees

With entrees the idea of "dovetail meals" comes into play. A child
who won't eat Shepherd's Pie as is may eat the mashed potatoes, the
meat or lentils, and perhaps some raw carrots on the side. If your
child hates spaghetti sauce, the plain spaghetti is fine, again with
some kind of vegetable or fruit. If your child is not a big meat eater,
concentrate on putting grain foods together with legumes or with
some kind of dairy product or eggs, so that complete protein is still
part of the meal. Throughout the Entrees section, I will remind you
about dovetail possibilities as we go along.

Because we live in the mainstream, you'll find some meat recipes
among the entrees. But for vegetarians and quasi-vegetarians, there
is always a companion recipe—so that Shepherd's Pie, for instance,
is paired with Lentil Shepherd's Pie, and Shish Kebab comes in a tofu
variety as well as with meat. In our family's cooking these recipes
often do end up on the table together; since all the ingredients but

one are basically the same, it really isn't any extra work for the chef. And it offers you and the children alternatives in eating well.

Note: Chicken recipes found here will often call for breast meat only, because of its lower fat content. If you wish to use a whole chicken or dark meat pieces, by all means do so. Remember! Dark meat does mean more iron.

SHEPHERD'S PIE

Makes 4 servings

Definitely a comfort food in winter, easy to fix and easy to eat.

- 1 *tablespoon extra-virgin olive oil*
- 1 *pound lean ground beef*
- 1 *medium onion, chopped*
- 2 *carrots sliced into thin matchsticks*

- ½ *teaspoon dried thyme*
- ½ *cup baby peas, canned or frozen*
- 3 *cups Basic Mashed Potatoes (recipe follows)*
- 1 *tablespoon unsalted butter or oil*

Preheat the oven to 350 degrees. In an all-iron skillet, heat the olive oil and sauté the beef, onion, carrots, and thyme together. Drain off excess fat. Add the peas to the mixture and stir. Spread the potatoes on top. Dot with butter or brush with oil. Bake until the crests of the potatoes are lightly browned, about 20 to 30 minutes.

Note: The skillet should have an iron handle so that it can go straight into the oven. Otherwise you must transfer the meat mixture to a baking pan before adding the potato layer.

Dovetail meal: Reserve some mashed potatoes and meat mixture separate from the main meal. Serve with carrot sticks or fruit.

BASIC MASHED POTATOES

Makes 4 servings

A side dish for us, a meal for the kids. Made with dairy product, mashed potatoes are a meal in themselves, with good amounts of protein, calcium, vitamins, minerals, and fiber.

> 1 *pound potatoes (about*   *salt to taste (optional)*
>   *4 large), peeled and*
>   *sliced*
>
> 1 *tablespoon unsalted*
>   *butter and ½ cup milk*
>   *or ½ cup buttermilk or*
>   *plain yogurt*

Boil or steam the potatoes until tender. Drain. Mash with butter and add milk; mash until smooth. Or, mash the potatoes until fluffy, add buttermilk or yogurt, and mash until smooth. Season with salt if desired.

Note: To be fluffy and not gummy, potatoes are best mashed by hand, using a masher, a fork, or a wooden spoon. They must be mashed while very hot, immediately after cooking and draining.

LENTIL SHEPHERD'S PIE

Makes 4 servings

> 2 *cups Basic Lentils*   *unsalted butter or*
>   *(recipe follows)*   *extra-virgin olive oil*
>
> 2 *cups Basic Mashed*   ½ *cup baby peas, canned*
>   *Potatoes (see*   *or frozen*
>   *preceding recipe)*

Preheat the oven to 350 degrees. Spread the lentil recipe in the bottom of a well-oiled all-iron skillet. Spread a layer of mashed potatoes on top and dot with butter or brush with oil. Bake until the potatoes are dotted with golden brown, about 20 to 30 minutes.

BASIC LENTILS

Makes enough for one recipe Shepherd's Pie or
1 Lentil Beet Loaf, about 2 cups

1 tablespoon extra-virgin olive oil

1 medium onion, chopped

1 small carrot, sliced into thin matchsticks

1 garlic clove (optional), minced

1–2 dried shiitake mushrooms, soaked in warm water for 5 minutes and sliced

1 small strip kombu (available at health food stores)

2 cups lentils, washed and drained

2 cups water

1 bay leaf

2 peppercorns

1 tablespoon tamari soy sauce (available at health food stores)

Heat oil in a saucepan. Sauté the onion and carrot (and garlic if desired) in the oil until tender. Add the mushrooms, kombu, lentils, water, and seasonings, and cook over low heat until the lentils are tender, at least 30 minutes, adding water if necessary. When finished, the mixture should have some liquid but not be runny.

Note: Remove the mushrooms after cooking if you don't like their texture.

MEAT LOAF WITH APPLESAUCE

Makes 6 to 8 servings

Meat loaf is a place where many unexpected ingredients come together, as the next few recipes attest. For non-meat eaters, a meatless loaf follows the meat loaf recipes. Served cold, these recipes are the American equivalent of pâtés or terrines.

LOAF:

- 1 *pound lean ground beef*
- 1 *cup finely chopped onions*
- 1 *cup applesauce*

- 1 *cup coarse fresh bread crumbs*
- 1 *cup small chunks cheddar cheese*
- 1 *egg, beaten*

GLAZE:

- ½ *cup Dijon mustard*
- ½ *cup Hain's ketchup (available at health food stores)*

- 2 *tablespoons tamari soy sauce (available at health food stores)*
- 4 *tablespoons water*

Preheat the oven to 375 degrees. Mix all loaf ingredients together and shape into 1 large or 2 small loaves. Mix the glaze ingredients and spread half over the top of loaf or loaves. Bake for about 1 hour, reglazing once or twice. Allow to sit for 10 minutes before slicing.

MEAT LOAF WITH LIVERS

Makes 6 to 8 servings

Liver is high in cholesterol, but also in iron. Meat loaf with chicken livers is a sneaky way to get that iron into your diet. Chicken livers are higher in iron than beef liver. This also provides a truly pâtélike loaf.

Omit the applesauce and cheddar from the preceding recipe; add 1 cup mashed cooked chicken livers, 1 garlic clove, chopped, and 2 teaspoons dried thyme. Omit ketchup from the glaze and add ¼ cup dry sherry.

SOUTH-OF-THE-BORDER MEAT LOAF
Makes 6 to 8 servings

Omit the applesauce, bread crumbs, and cheddar from Meat Loaf with Applesauce. Add 1 cup shredded raw spinach, ½ cup shredded Monterey Jack cheese, and 1 2-oz. bag low-salt corn chips, crumbled. Add 2 tablespoons mild salsa to the glaze. (El Paso is a brand of salsa often available in supermarkets.)

LENTIL BEET LOAF
Makes 8 to 12 slices

If you want your kids to like lentils and beets, start serving recipe early and serve it often. Thanks to Margaret Mary Carroll and Larry Stoiaken for this one.

½ *cup chopped onion*

1 *garlic clove, chopped*

1 *cup peeled and grated beets (use food processor if possible)*

¼ *cup grated lemon zest*

¼ *cup chopped fresh parsley*

1½ *cups cooked lentils (see Basic Lentils recipe)*

2 *eggs, beaten*

2 *teaspoons melted unsalted butter*

½ *cup bread crumbs or ground oatmeal*

2 *tablespoons melted unsalted butter*

Combine all the ingredients except the 2 tablespoons butter and pack the mixture into a 9-inch loaf pan. Preheat the oven to 350 degrees. Brush the loaf with 2 tablespoons melted butter. Bake for 30 minutes.

Note: For nicely seasoned lentils, cook them with a little salt, a pinch of thyme, and a bay leaf.

TACOS FOR ALL

Makes 4 servings

Another recipe that can be made with or without meat. With a heaping platter of add-your-own veggies and the basic recipe multiplied to meet your needs, this can be a festive party dish for children. Serve with Quick Beans and Rice (see recipe) for a heartier meal.

1 *cup Basic Beef Mixture and 1 cup Basic Tofu Crumbs or 2 cups of Basic Meat Mixture or Basic Tofu Crumbs (recipes follow)*

8 *taco shells*

½ *small head Romaine or iceberg lettuce, shredded*

4 *tomatoes, chopped*

2 *onions, chopped*

other chopped vegetables such as bell peppers, avocados, cucumbers, radishes (optional)

2 *cups shredded sharp cheese*

Tabasco sauce or mild salsa (El Paso or available brand) and/or Green Dressing (recipe follows)

Preheat the oven to 350 degrees. Fill each taco shell with ¼ cup of beef or tofu mixture. Heat in the oven for 5 to 7 minutes. Serve at the table with add-your-own toppings, including veggies, cheese, and hot sauce or dressing.

BASIC BEEF MIXTURE

Makes enough to fill 4 tacos

1 tablespoon extra-
virgin olive oil

1 garlic clove, chopped

1 medium onion,
chopped

1 teaspoon ground
cumin

½ pound lean ground
beef

Heat the oil in a skillet and sauté the garlic and onion until the onions are translucent. Add the cumin and beef and sauté over low heat until cooked through. Drain.

BASIC TOFU CRUMBS

Makes enough to fill 4 tacos

Follow the Basic Beef Mixture recipe, substituting 1 pound crumbled firm tofu for the beef. Add 1 tablespoon tamari soy sauce with the tofu.

GREEN DRESSING

Makes about 1 cup

¼ cup extra-virgin olive
oil

1 garlic clove, mashed

juice of 1 lemon

¼ cup plain yogurt

1 avocado

1 teaspoon honey

½ teaspoon salt

pinch cayenne pepper

Blend all the ingredients in a blender or food processor fitted with the steel blade until smooth. Serve with any tossed salad or with Tacos for All or (Pita) Pocket Salad (see recipes).

Note: This dressing by itself is almost a meal for a toddler. Let kids use it as a vegetable dip, perhaps with some low-salt corn chips on the side.

BEEF AND PEPPERS

Makes 4 servings

Both this recipe and Tofu with Peppers (recipe follows) make a wonderful pseudo-Chinese meal over rice—delicious and filling. For an easily prepared meal that feeds meat eaters and vegetarians alike, just use two skillets and divide the peppers, tomatoes, and onions between the two recipes. (If you are preparing the two recipes together, double the amounts of vegetables given in this recipe to make enough for both.) For a fuller meal, serve with Egg-Drop Soup (see recipe).

½ *pound sirloin or chuck steak, sliced*

1 *tablespoon light sesame oil*

1 *cup green bell pepper chunks*

½ *cup red bell pepper chunks (optional)*

½ *cup onion in half-moons*

¾ *cup halved cherry tomatoes*

1 *tablespoon tamari soy sauce (available at health food stores)*

1 *tablespoon mirin (see Note)*

Sauté the meat in the oil in the skillet, turning, for 1 minute; add the peppers and onions and sauté until the onions are slightly browned. Add the tomatoes and cook over medium heat until they are soft. Add tamari (and mirin, if available) and cook for 1 minute, stirring gently. Serve over rice.

Note: Mirin is a winelike condiment used in Oriental cooking; it is available at health food stores and some supermarkets. Sherry can be substituted.

TOFU AND PEPPERS

Makes 4 servings

Follow the recipe for Beef with Peppers, using ½ pound tofu, cut into chunks, instead of beef. Use 3 tablespoons oil for the sautéing. Be sure that the oil is very hot and that the tofu is patted dry; if it's wet, the oil will spit and burn, and if the oil isn't really hot, the tofu will stick. Let the tofu turn slightly golden on one side before turning it. The less you have to handle it, the less it will fall apart. You may want to add extra tamari to the tofu. Serve over rice.

SHISH KEBAB

Makes 4 servings

Nice because it can be prepared a day in advance, then cooked quickly.

1 *pound beef, chicken, shrimp, or tofu, cut into bite-sized pieces*

2 *cups Basic Marinade (recipe follows)*

1 *pint cherry tomatoes*

2 *green bell peppers, cut into squares*

2 *medium onions, quartered and separated*

1 *pound mushrooms, cleaned and stems removed*

Marinate the beef; chicken, shrimp, or tofu in Basic Marinade for at least 3 hours or overnight. Thread 12-inch skewers with alternating items. Cook over hot coals on a grill or under a preheated broiler until the meat (or substitute) is done and the vegetables are browned, basting with marinade and turning carefully at least once. Serve over rice for a fuller meal.

Note: Rice for the meal can also be prepared a day in advance and reheated in about 2 minutes over the intense heat an ordinary steamer provides.

BASIC MARINADE
Makes about 1 cup

1 *cup extra-virgin olive oil*

juice of 1 lemon or ½ cup wine or rice vinegar

½ *cup white wine, water, or Basic Vegetable Broth (see recipe)*

1 *garlic clove, mashed*

1 *bay leaf*

1 *teaspoon honey (optional)*

1 *tablespoon tamari soy sauce (available at health food stores)*

½ *teaspoon coarsely ground black pepper*

oregano, thyme, or other herbs (optional)

Shake up all the ingredients in a 2-quart jar and add whatever is to be marinated. Marinate for at least 3 hours and overnight if convenient.

TOFU BARBECUE
Makes 4 servings

A handy standby for the non-meat eaters when everyone else is having hamburgers and hot dogs.

1 *pound tofu, cut into strips*

2 *cups Spicy Peanut Marinade (recipe follows)*

Marinate the tofu for several hours. Thread on bamboo skewers (available in Oriental or kitchen specialty stores) and broil or place carefully in a hinged grill and cook over charcoal, turning just often enough to keep the tofu from sticking.

SPICY PEANUT MARINADE

Makes about 1 cup

½ cup light sesame oil

juice of 1 lemon

2 tablespoons peanut butter

2 teaspoons honey

1 teaspoon cayenne pepper

Blend all the ingredients well and use for Tofu Barbecue.

BRUNSWICK STEW

Makes 6 to 8 servings

A standard dish in the Old South, Brunswick Stew was traditionally made with squirrel meat. Chicken is the base of this one, which is included here with fond memories of a stew that a dear friend's grandmother once brought on a picnic. We were all about 10 years old, and we loved it.

Although squirrels no longer find their way into Brunswick Stew, I suppose to approximate the taste of the original stew you could include rabbit meat with the chicken or in place of it. Fresh lima beans and corn give the stew its distinctive flavor and texture. Serve with corn bread or other hearty bread for a one-pot meal.

1 3- to 5-pound stewing or frying chicken, cut up

extra-virgin olive oil

1 garlic clove, chopped

1 large onion, chopped

2 cups quartered tomatoes

2 cups fresh or frozen lima beans

2 cups boiling water

pinch cayenne pepper

pinch ground allspice

1 tablespoon tamari soy sauce (available at health food stores)

¼ *cup mirin or dry*   2–3 *cups fresh or frozen*
   sherry (optional)   *corn kernels*

Heat the oil in a skillet, add the garlic and onion, and sauté until
lightly browned. Remove to a stewing pot. Add the chicken pieces to
the skillet and brown them. Transfer the chicken to the pot and add
the tomatoes, beans, boiling water, and seasonings. Simmer, covered, until the chicken is tender, at least 1 hour. Add the corn and
cook, covered, for 15 minutes. Remove the bones before serving if
desired.

CHICKEN YELLOW RICE

Makes 4 servings

Children like the idea of yellow rice (saffron gives it its color)
because it's pretty novel. An easy one-dish meal inspired by a recipe
from our friend Barbara Sievers.

2 *whole chicken breasts,*   1 *cup raw rice*
   halved
                                 3 *cups water*
1 *tablespoon extra-*
   virgin olive oil   1 *large pinch saffron*
                                    threads or powder
1 *garlic clove, chopped*
                                 1 *cup chopped fresh or*
1 *small onion, chopped*   *frozen broccoli*
   fine

Sauté the chicken in the oil with the garlic and onions until lightly
browned. Remove the chicken to a large pot, leaving excess oil in
the pan. Add the rice, water, and saffron to the pot and bring to a
boil. Reduce the heat and simmer, tightly covered, until the rice is
tender (at least half an hour), adding extra water if necessary. When
the rice is nearly tender, add the broccoli to the top of the pot and
cover. Cook for five minutes more. Broccoli should be bright green
and tender when the meal is cooked. If the rice is done before the
broccoli, simply turn off the heat, cover the pot again, and let the
broccoli finish cooking by steaming.

CHICKEN VALENCIENNE

Makes 4 to 6 servings

A recipe we loved as children, with thanks to my mom.

½ onion, chopped and sautéed until tender

1 onion, chopped

1 16-ounce can tomatoes, drained

2 carrots, sliced thin

1 green bell pepper, chopped

1 2½- to 3-pound frying chicken, cut up and browned in 1 tablespoon oil

1 cup raw rice

1 teaspoon salt

1 quart Basic Chicken Stock (see recipe)

1 12-ounce can or 1 10-ounce package frozen baby peas

Preheat the oven to 375 degrees. In a greased casserole dish, put cooked and raw onion, tomatoes, carrots, peppers, and chicken. Add rice, salt, and stock. Bake, covered, for 50 minutes or until rice is tender, adding stock if necessary. Add peas; return dish to the oven for 5 minutes.

CHICKEN CACCIATORE

Makes 3 to 4 servings

A quick and easy meal if you have cooked chicken meat on hand—perhaps the product of Basic Chicken Stock! Serve over the pasta of your choice with a Watercress Salad (see recipe).

- 2 *teaspoons oil*
- 1 *large garlic clove, chopped*
- ¼ *green bell pepper*
- ¼ *cup fresh shiitake or other mushrooms, sliced (optional)*
- 2 *large ripe tomatoes*
- 1 *cup bite-sized cooked chicken*
- ½ *cup water, white wine, Basic Chicken Stock, or Basic Vegetable Broth (see recipes)*
- 2 *tablespoons plain yogurt*

Heat the oil in a skillet and sauté garlic, peppers, and mushrooms lightly. Reduce the heat and add the tomatoes. Simmer until they disintegrate. Add the chicken and the water, wine, or stock. Simmer over very low heat for 5 to 7 minutes. Turn off the heat. Add the yogurt and stir in.

Dovetail meal: Younger children may prefer just the chicken, the pasta, and some grapes and oranges from the salad, although the liquid of this stew, with the shiitake mushrooms and yogurt, will add nutrients if you can persuade them to try some.

CHILI CHICKEN BARBECUE

Makes 4 servings

For a good summer meal, serve this with a Parsley Rice Salad with Walnuts (see recipe) made in advance.

1 *cup Hain's ketchup (available at health food stores)*

juice of 1 lemon

1 *bay leaf*

1 *teaspoon ground cumin*

1 *teaspoon dried thyme*

½ *teaspoon cayenne pepper*

2 *whole chicken breasts, halved*

Mix the ketchup, lemon juice, and seasonings to make a marinade for the chicken. Marinate, refrigerated, for several hours or overnight. Use the marinade to baste the chicken as it cooks. Grill until thoroughly done—45 minutes to 1 hour if you're using an open charcoal fire. Chicken cooks slowly; test for doneness by cutting one piece to the bone; there should be no pink or translucent meat. The cooked white meat looks fluffy and white when done.

RISOTTO

Makes 6 to 8 servings

Because it's cooked in chicken broth, risotto is a good protein source for those little eaters who prefer grains to chunks of meat. You can serve it with Braised Chicken Livers (see recipe) for those in the family who will eat them—or make the Risotto itself a meal for those with smaller appetites.

3 *tablespoons light sesame (available in health food stores) or extra-virgin olive oil*

1 *medium onion, minced*

2 *cups raw rice*

2 *tablespoons mirin (optional)*

1½ *quarts Basic Chicken Stock (see recipe), heated*

Heat the oil in a saucepan and sauté the onion until translucent. Stir in the rice and continue stirring, over low heat, until the rice is coated with oil. Add marin, if desired, and the chicken stock, 1 cup at a time. After each cup of stock, cover the pot and let the rice cook until liquid is absorbed. Continue adding stock, *without stirring,* until the rice is tender (taste a grain) but not too soft.

BRAISED CHICKEN LIVERS

Makes 4 to 6 servings

For those who will eat them, chicken livers are a good source of iron. Liver is an acquired taste, but chicken livers seem more acceptable to many people—including kids—than beef liver.

2–3 tablespoons unsalted butter or extra-virgin olive oil

1 small onion, chopped

½ cup chopped fresh parsley

1 teaspoon dried sage

½ pound mushrooms, sliced

1 pound chicken livers

½ cup Basic Chicken Stock (see recipe) water, or white wine

coarsely ground black pepper (optional)

Heat the butter or oil in a skillet and sauté the onion until translucent. Add the parsley, sage, and mushrooms. Sauté until the mushrooms are limp. Add the chicken livers and the stock, water, or wine. Cook for about 15 minutes over low heat, until the livers are done. Garnish with black pepper if desired. Serve with risotto or plain rice.

Dovetail meal: Plain risotto for those who aren't of the liver persuasion.

KEDGEREE

We are indebted to Chris Burger for this version of a traditional Australian recipe. It can be tailored to the family's tastes (and pocketbook), since it may be made with different sorts of seafood ranging from tuna and salmon to lobster and crab. Remember, salmon as a cold-water fish offers a higher percentage of monoun-saturated fat; canned salmon is also regarded as a fair calcium source.

3	*tablespoons extra-virgin olive oil or unsalted butter*	pinch	*salt and freshly ground pepper*
1	*medium onion, chopped*	1	*cup cooked rice (best if cooked a day before)*
1	*green bell pepper, chopped*	1	*pound canned salmon, tuna, shrimp, crab or lobster, drained*
1	*large garlic clove, chopped*	2	*hard-cooked eggs, sliced*
2	*teaspoons ground turmeric*		*fresh parsley chopped (optional)*
	juice of 1 lemon		
½	*teaspoon ground ginger*		

Preheat the oven to 350 degrees. Heat the butter or oil in a skillet; add the onion, green pepper, and garlic and sauté until soft. Add the turmeric, lemon juice, ginger, salt, and pepper. Lightly stir in the rice and fish; when thoroughly mixed, turn into a lightly greased cas-serole dish and heat in oven before serving. Garnish with sliced eggs and parsley.

Dovetail meal: Reserve some rice and fish separately; save some of the egg too or cook an extra one for the children to peel and slice themselves.

STEAMED BLUEFISH

Makes 4 to 6 servings

This cooking method may be used with any of the darker-fleshed or oilier fish. It is a way of getting rid of the extra oil, thereby producing a milder taste and also removing toxins that have been passed up the food chain to these predatory fish. In the steaming process the oil drips into the pan below and is discarded with the cooking water. Accompany the dish with rice and steamed vegetables.

1 *pound bluefish fillets*	1 *tablespoon chopped fresh parsley*
1–2 *lemons, sliced thin*	
2–3 *garlic cloves, sliced thin*	1 *teaspoon dried basil, thyme, or marjoram*

Lay the fish fillets on a lightly greased upturned vegetable steamer (or use a fish steamer or poacher with a rack) in a large skillet with about ½ inch of water in it. Bring water to a boil while covering the top of the fillets with a row of lemon slices, garlic, and herbs. Steam, covered, for 7 to 10 minutes, until the fish is very tender when pierced with a fork.

POACHED SALMON

Makes 3 to 4 servings

Again, this cold-water fish should be a regular on your menu, in one form or another. Given a chance, children generally seem to like fish, and salmon is a good choice not only because of its nutritive value but also because its bones are usually pretty large and easy to find. Still, always check bits of fish carefully before giving them to young children. This recipe is delicious with Steamed Parsleyed Potatoes and Carrots (see recipe).

1 *pound salmon fillets*	1 *bay leaf*
2 *cups Basic Fish Stock* *(see recipe)*	2 *peppercorns*

Preheat the oven to 350 degrees. Put the salmon in a large baking dish and add the stock, bay leaf, and peppercorns. Cover and bake for 10 minutes. Remove, still covered, and allow to stand until the liquid is just warm. The fish will be moist and tender.

"GRIZZLY BEAR" SALMON

Makes 4 servings

Mary Kahn Tutwiler plays the name game with her children with this recipe, the game in this case being "What do bears like to eat?" Children for some reason seem to love bears (as they do dinosaurs, too), and the author of this recipe explains to her kids how the bears fish with their paws for the salmon in a stream. Bears of course also love berries; hence the blueberries that make this salmon platter festive. If you want to continue the game, serve bread and honey with the meal. Adults may want their "Grizzly Bear" Salmon with baked potatoes and a salad.

4 *salmon steaks*	1 *pint fresh or thawed frozen blueberries*
1 *tablespoon unsalted butter*	
juice of 2 lemons	*sprigs of fresh mint or parsley*

Preheat the broiler or light a grill. Grill the salmon under the broiler for about 7 minutes on each side or over charcoal for 7 to 10 minutes per side. Dot with butter and sprinkle with lemon juice while cooking. Serve on a platter, surrounded by fresh blueberries and garnished with mint sprigs or parsley.

SOUFFLÉ-STUFFED PEPPERS

Makes 4 to 8 servings

4 *large or 8 small green bell (or sweet red or yellow) peppers*

2 *tablespoons unsalted butter or light sesame oil*

2 *tablespoons unbleached flour*

1 *cup milk, heated*

¼ *teaspoon salt*

pinch *cayenne pepper*

1 *cup grated cheddar or Monterey Jack cheese*

4 *eggs, separated*

Cut large peppers in half lengthwise or cut the tops off small peppers. Parboil for 3 minutes in salted water and drain.

Preheat the oven to 375 degrees. Prepare the soufflé filling by heating the butter or oil in a saucepan and stirring in the flour to form a roux for a white sauce. Add the heated milk and stir until thickened. Add the salt, pepper, and cheese; stir well and set aside.

Beat the egg whites until fluffy; little peaks should form in the surface of the whites when touched with a spoon. Beat the egg yolks into the cheese mixture; fold in the egg whites gently with a wooden spoon. Spoon the soufflé mixture into the peppers and transfer the peppers to a large pan. Pour a scant ¼ inch of water into the pan and bake for 20 to 30 minutes.

STUFFED RED PEPPERS

Makes 4 to 8 servings

Any easy dish that makes a meal when served with cooked grain and/or a salad. Rice, millet, bulgur, and kasha are all good alongside stuffed peppers. The red peppers and green filling make a pretty contrast.

4 *large red bell peppers*	½ *teaspoon salt*
10 *ounces fresh spinach, washed, cleaned, and shredded*	1 *pound ricotta cheese*
	2 *eggs, beaten*
1 *small onion, chopped*	
1 *tablespoon extra-virgin olive oil*	

Cut the peppers in half lengthwise. Parboil them for 3 minutes in salted water and drain. Preheat the oven to 350 degrees. Sauté the spinach and onion in the oil in a skillet. Add the salt. Mix with ricotta and eggs and stuff the peppers with the mixture. Transfer the peppers to a large pan and pour in a scant ¼ inch of water. Bake for 30 minutes or until the mixture is set.

BAKED EGGPLANT BOATS

Makes 4 servings

The worst thing about eggplant is its name. The vegetable is actually delicious, and older children often like it. The younger ones, say, age three, probably won't unless they've been raised on it. And regardless of their age, you may have better luck if you don't call it by name. You could always call it *aubergine,* as the British and French do. Serve these "boats" on a bed of rice or other grain or with a pasta salad, with wedges of fresh ripe tomatoes if available.

2 medium eggplants

salt

2 garlic cloves, minced

2 tablespoons olive oil

½ cup dry bread crumbs

¼ cup freshly grated Parmesan cheese

¼ cup chopped fresh parsley

Cut the eggplants in half lengthwise. Scoop out the flesh, leaving about ¼ inch for a firm shell. Salt the flesh lightly and let the shells drain flesh side down on paper towels for 10 minutes. Preheat the oven to 400 degrees. Meanwhile sauté the eggplant flesh with the garlic in the oil in a skillet for 5 to 7 minutes, stirring. Toss with the bread crumbs, cheese, and parsley. Fill the eggplant shells and bake in a shallow pan for 35 to 40 minutes, until the tops are browned and the sides are tender.

Note: The Baked Eggplant Boats can even be fitted with "sails," made from toothpicks with tomato wedges on them or skewers with leaves of lettuce. Skewers with tomato wedges can be oars as well.

GRILLED EGGPLANT

Makes 3 to 4 servings

A light summer meal that can be cooked on a grill. Also a discreet way to introduce eggplant, since each slice is thin. Serve with rice or a pasta salad.

1 garlic clove, split

¼ cup sesame or olive oil

juice of 1 lemon

¼ teaspoon cayenne pepper

¼ teaspoon ground cumin

¼ teaspoon dried thyme

½ cup plain yogurt

½ teaspoon salt

1 large eggplant, sliced thin lengthwise

¼ cup chopped fresh dill

Mix all the ingredients except the eggplant and dill. Marinate the eggplant slices in half of this mixture, reserving the rest, at room temperature for 3 hours or more. Light a grill. Grill eggplant over charcoal until lightly browned, turning once. Add the dill to the reserved yogurt mixture and serve this as a sauce for the eggplant.

RATATOUILLE RAREBIT

Makes 4 or more servings

While we're on the subject of summer vegetables, ratatouille is a delicious way to use them. The stewed vegetables in their tomato sauce are served in this version over toast with a cheese sauce—a one-dish meal that takes about an hour to prepare.

STEW:

salt	4 *large tomatoes, cut into wedges*
1 *small eggplant, sliced horizontally*	1 *medium zucchini, sliced into rounds*
½ *small onion, chopped*	1 *teaspoon dried basil* or 1 *tablespoon fresh*
2 *garlic cloves, chopped*	½ *teaspoon dried oregano*
1 *small green bell pepper, chopped*	
3 *tablespoons oil*	

SAUCE:

1 *tablespoon unsalted butter*	2 *tablespoons mirin or sherry*
1 *cup grated sharp cheddar cheese*	½ *cup milk*
pinch *cayenne pepper*	1 *egg yolk*

TOAST:

> 4 *(or more) slices bread
> of your choice, toasted*

Salt both sides of the eggplant slices and lay the slices on paper towels. Cover with paper towels and allow to drain for 10 minutes. Meanwhile, sauté the garlic, onion, and peppers in 1 tablespoon of oil in a large pot until tender. Add the eggplant, tomatoes, zucchini, and herbs; simmer over low heat until the vegetables are falling apart and the flavors are well blended, about 30 to 45 minutes.

Meanwhile, prepare the sauce. Melt the butter in a double boiler and add the cheese, stirring until the cheese is melted. Add the cayenne and mirin or sherry. Stir the milk in slowly, cover, and let sit until the ratatouille is ready. Just before serving, reheat the cheese sauce and stir in the egg yolk. Serve immediately on top of ratatouille over toast.

Dovetail meal: omit the ratatouille for small children and serve them just the rarebit sauce over toast from which the edges have been trimmed. Serve with raw vegetables, a slice of melon, or an apple.

TOFU ONION PIE

Makes about 8 servings

A quichelike dish that makes a meal when served with a salad. The secret of this pie is the large, sweet Vidalia onions.

> 1 *large Vidalia onion,
> sliced into very thin
> rings*
>
> 2 *tablespoons unsalted
> butter or oil*
>
> 12–16 *crushed low-salt
> crackers (Saltine size)*
>
> 1 *pound tofu, crumbled*

> 1 *tablespoon tamari soy
> sauce (available in
> health food stores)*
>
> 8 *ounces crumbled feta
> cheese*
>
> ½ *cup Basic Vegetable
> Broth (see recipe)*

In a skillet, sauté the onion rings in the butter or oil until soft. Preheat the oven to 350 degrees. Line the bottom of a greased 9-inch baking or pie pan with half the cracker crumbs. Cover with the onions, followed by the crumbled tofu. Sprinkle with tamari. Top with a mixture of the remaining cracker crumbs and the crumbled feta cheese. Moisten the top layer with vegetable broth. Bake in oven until golden, about 30 minutes.

Allergy note: This recipe contains no cow's milk products. For those trying to avoid common allergens, it may also be made with wheat-free crackers.

COTTAGE CHEESE BAKE

Makes 4 servings

With thanks to Chris Burger

1 *tablespoon light sesame oil*

1 *small onion, chopped*

1 *cup chopped raw vegetables (mushroom, peppers, zucchini, carrots, etc.)*

1 *cup cottage cheese*

3 *eggs*

1 *cup quick or regular rolled oats*

1 *tablespoon dried herbs (thyme, basil, oregano, or a mixture)*

2 *tablespoons tamari soy sauce (available in health food stores)*

salt and freshly ground pepper

chopped fresh parsley (optional)

Heat the oil in a skillet, add the onion, and sauté until golden. Add the vegetables and sauté for 2 to 3 minutes. Mix the cottage cheese and eggs in a bowl and add the oats. Add the sautéed mixture, herbs, soy sauce, and salt and pepper to taste. Preheat the oven to 400 degrees. Spread on a lightly oiled 9-inch square pan and bake for 20 minutes. Garnish with parsley if desired.

BASIC RED SAUCE

Makes about 1 quart

Useful for spaghetti dishes, pizzas, and as a base for chili. If you don't have time to make your own, I suggest Aunt Millie's and Classico as two brands that are not too salty and taste as close to homemade as you're likely to get.

1 *medium onion, chopped*

2 *garlic cloves, chopped*

3 *tablespoons extra-virgin olive oil*

2 *teaspoons dried oregano*

2 *teaspoons dried basil*

2–3 *fennel seeds, crushed*

1 *bay leaf*

3 *cups chopped fresh tomatoes or drained canned whole tomatoes*

1 *tablespoon tomato paste (optional)*

½ *teaspoon salt*

1 *teaspoon honey*

3 *tablespoons beer (optional)*

Sauté the onion and garlic in the olive oil in a heavy saucepan until soft. Add the herbs and tomatoes and simmer over low heat for 30 minutes. Add the tomato paste if desired (it makes a richer sauce but also adds sodium). Add the salt, honey, and beer, if desired (the beer seems to make the flavors blend better), and simmer until the sauce is smooth, about 15 minutes more. Add more liquid (vegetable broth, liquid from canned tomatoes, or water) if needed. Correct the seasoning. Use for spaghetti and other pasta.

SPAGHETTI WITH MEAT SAUCE
Makes 4 to 6 servings

Serve a red meat sauce over linguine, spaghettini, or other pasta. For non-meat eaters, Spaghetti Sauce with Tofu (recipe follows) can be made in minutes.

To make red meat sauce, combine 1 recipe Basic Beef Mixture (see recipe) with 1 recipe Basic Red Sauce (preceding recipe). If you are starting from scratch, begin by making the Basic Beef Mixture and then, as the meat finishes cooking, add the ingredients for Basic Red Sauce, starting with the oregano. Serve over pasta.

SPAGHETTI SAUCE WITH TOFU

An alternative to Spaghetti with Meat Sauce (for non-meat eaters)

To 1 recipe of Basic Red Sauce, add ½ pound firm tofu, cut into chunks and lightly sautéed in 2 tablespoons extra-virgin olive oil with 1 garlic clove, chopped, and 1 tablespoon tamari soy sauce (available at health food stores). When the tofu is heated through, the sauce is ready to serve.

Dovetail meal: This recipe dovetails well since toddlers often like tofu. Reserve some of the chunks and serve them alongside the plain pasta, with freshly grated Parmesan cheese if they like it. Add raw fruit or vegetables for a complete meal.

LINGUINE WITH RED CLAM SAUCE

Makes 4 or more servings

Who under the age of 21 eats clams? Not many, I suppose. See the dovetail meal suggestion at the end of the recipe.

1 large garlic clove, minced

1 tablespoon extra-virgin olive oil

1 cup canned clams, drained and liquid reserved

2 teaspoons unbleached flour

½ cup chopped fresh parsley

2 cups Basic Red Sauce (see recipe)

1 pound cooked linguine

2 teaspoons unsalted butter (optional)

freshly grated Parmesan cheese

Sauté the garlic in the oil in a saucepan over medium heat until soft. Add the drained clams and sauté for 30 minutes, stirring. Blend the flour into ½ cup of the reserved clam juice; add to the pan of clams, stirring. Add the parsley and red sauce and stir until well blended. Serve over linguine, tossed with the butter if desired, with grated Parmesan cheese passed separately.

Dovetail meal: We like to serve this with Watercress-Grape-Orange Salad (see recipe). Toddlers end up with a dish of pasta on which they can sprinkle their own cheese; they eat the seedless grapes and oranges reserved from the salad.

EASY TOFU LASAGNE

Makes 6 to 8 servings

The key to the quick preparation of this lasagne is the zucchini; as it cooks, it releases a lot of liquid, which cooks the lasagne noodles right in the pan. So you don't have to waste time boiling noodles. The tofu in this recipe also makes it a lower-fat, lower-cholesterol version of an old favorite. Make one pan to eat and freeze the other.

3 cups Basic Red Sauce (see recipe) or commercial spaghetti sauce

lasagne noodles (about 12)

3–4 small or 2–3 medium zucchini, sliced into rounds

1 teaspoon dried oregano

1 pound tofu, crumbled

1 pound ricotta cheese

1 cup grated mozzarella cheese

1 cup plain yogurt

2 eggs, beaten

freshly grated Parmesan cheese

Preheat the oven to 350 degrees. Coat the bottom of 1 9- by 13-inch pan or 2 9- by 9-inch pans with red sauce. Top with a layer of uncooked noodles. Add a layer of zucchini slices to completely cover the noodles. Sprinkle with oregano. Top with the tofu and ricotta, mixed together. Sprinkle with mozzarella. Pour the remaining red sauce over the mozzarella. Add the remaining noodles. Cover with the remaining zucchini and top with the egg and yogurt, beaten together. Sprinkle with Parmesan cheese and bake until you can easily pierce all layers of the lasagne with a sharp fork, at least 30 minutes.

TOFU-FETA PIZZA

Makes 4 servings

Here is a pizza for those who can't eat cow's milk products. To feed both those who can't and those who can, make your pizza half and half: tofu (and feta, if you like) on one side, cheese on the other—the feta adds flavor and is not made with cow's milk.

DOUGH:

1 ¼-ounce package dry yeast

1 cup lukewarm water

1 teaspoon salt

1 teaspoon sugar

1 tablespoon extra-virgin olive oil

2–3 cups unbleached (wheat) flour

cornmeal

TOPPING:

2 cups Basic Red Sauce (see recipe)

1 pound tofu, crumbled

½ pound feta cheese, crumbled (optional)

2 teaspoons dried herbs, such as oregano, basil, thyme

cooked vegetables, olives, or other toppings (optional)

Sprinkle the yeast in the bottom of a ceramic bowl and add the water, salt, and sugar. Let stand 5 minutes, until yeast begins to foam a little. Add the oil and 2 cups of the flour and mix thoroughly, adding more flour as needed to form a workable dough. Turn out onto a well-floured board and knead until dough is elastic—about 10 minutes. Shape into a ball and set in a clean ceramic bowl. Oil the surface of the dough lightly. Cover with a clean towel and let stand in a warm draft-free place until doubled in bulk.

Preheat the oven to 400 degrees. Punch down the dough, turn it onto a floured board, and knead 8 to 10 times. Roll it into a circle about 14 inches in diameter. Fold it carefully in half and unfold it on a lightly greased 14-inch pizza pan that has been sprinkled lightly with cornmeal. Cover the dough to within an inch of the edge with the sauce and tofu (plus feta, if desired), the herbs, and any other topping of your choice. Bake for 15 to 20 minutes or until the crust is done.

Note: For a half-cheese pizza, cut the amounts of tofu and feta in half and add an equal amount of combined shredded mozzarella and provolone cheeses.

LITTLE PIES

Makes 4 servings

Called *empanadas* in Spanish, little pies filled with meat, tofu, cheese, and vegetables, or whatever you like, are a good hand food for lunch or dinner.

DOUGH:

2 *cups unbleached flour*

1 *teaspoon salt*

½ *cup light sesame oil (available at health food stores)*

1 *cup milk*

FILLING SUGGESTIONS:

Basic Beef Mixture (see recipe)

Basic Tofu Crumbs (see recipe)

1 *part Basic Tofu Crumbs, 1 part cheese, and 2 parts cooked spinach*

leftover stir-fry

Preheat the oven to 400 degrees. Stir the flour and salt together in a bowl. Add the oil and blend well. Add milk and stir to form a dough.

Turn the dough out onto a well-floured board, form it into a ball, and roll it out to a thickness of about ¼ inch. Cut the dough into 4-inch squares, put several spoonfuls of filling in the center of each square, and fold dough over to make triangles. Pinch the dough to seal it around the edges, prick the top of the dough with a fork to let steam escape, and bake until the crust is light brown—about 20 minutes.

SPOON BREAD

This nearly is a meal in itself for small appetites, offering a good amount of protein. It is sort of a cooked pudding and a standard dish in the American South. Add cheese or corn kernels for interest and flavor. Serve with salad and/or soup. Or try it with maple syrup for lunch.

½ *cup cornmeal*

½ *cup unbleached flour*

1 *teaspoon baking powder*

¼ *teaspoon baking soda*

½ *teaspoon salt*

1 *cup buttermilk*

2 *tablespoons light sesame oil or melted unsalted butter*

2 *eggs, beaten*

Preheat the oven to 375 degrees. Mix the dry ingredients in a bowl. Beat the buttermilk, oil or butter, and eggs together in a separate bowl. Add the liquid to the dry ingredients and mix until smooth. Turn into a well-greased 2-quart soufflé dish or glass baking pan and bake until golden brown, at least 40 minutes. Spoon bread should be crusty on top and soft underneath.

Note: Add ½ cup sharp cheese or ½ cup corn kernels to the batter before baking for variety.

BASIC STIR-FRY

Makes 6 to 8 servings

A quickly made standby to serve over rice. We make it in two pans, one with sliced steak, the other with tofu, adding vegetables to both. Serve over long- or short-grain brown rice.

4   *tablespoons peanut oil*

¾   *cup uncooked sliced boneless steak or chicken, small whole shrimp, or tofu chunks*

1   *cup thinly sliced hardy vegetables, such as onion, carrot, broccoli, celery, cauliflower*

¼   *cup chopped nuts*

1   *cup thinly sliced soft-skinned vegetables, such as zucchini, yellow summer squash, mushrooms, red and green bell peppers*

1   *tablespoon minced fresh ginger*

2–3   *tablespoons tamari soy sauce (available at health food stores)*

hot red pepper flakes to taste (optional)

In a wok or large skillet, heat the oil until very hot. Add the meat, fish, chicken, or tofu and sear it over high heat, stirring. Add the hardy vegetables and nuts and fry, stirring, until the onions begin to brown. Add the soft vegetables and ginger; stir until they begin to soften. Add the tamari, reduce the heat, and cook, covered, for 2 minutes. Serve over rice with hot red pepper flakes for those who like them.

Note: Add other ingredients that your family likes, including cooked beans, fresh bean sprouts or daikon radish.

Dovetail meal: The rice at least is a meal for most little ones, plus vegetables, raw or cooked. If your kids like raw summer squash or other veggies, reserve some out. They may also like the meat, chicken, fish, or tofu better if it's separate.

◆

COOKED AZUKI BEANS
Makes 6 to 8 servings

Azuki beans are about half the size of most other dried beans, and they have a mild, earthy taste. They are easier to digest than most beans, too, and they have the added advantage of cooking pretty quickly. Even without soaking, they will cook in about 40 minutes. This makes them a handy bean for meals in a hurry. Serve them by themselves over grain, or mix in some canned beans with them for variety, on a night when you don't have time to cook larger beans from scratch.

2   *cups azuki beans*

1   *quart water*

2   *tablespoons tamari soy sauce (available in health food stores)*

1   *small onion, cut into half-moons*

1   *bay leaf*

1   *strip kombu (available in health food stores)*

3–4   *dried shiitake mushrooms*

1   *small carrot, sliced into thin matchsticks*

   salt to taste

Rinse and drain the beans. Put the beans and water in a deep pot and bring to a boil; reduce the heat and add the remaining ingredients except salt. Simmer until the beans are tender, at least 40 minutes. Add salt to taste. Serve over rice, or with any cooked grain and a salad.

Note: These beans are a very good dish to get your children used to early. The azukis are a mild and nourishing meal, and their small size appeals to the kids.

QUICK BEANS AND RICE

Makes 6 to 8 servings

With a salad, this is a meal in itself. If you use already cooked (or canned) beans, preparation takes only about 30 minutes.

1 *cup converted rice*	3 *scallions, chopped,* or
2–3 *cups water*	½ *cup chopped onion*
pinch *salt*	½ *cup chopped fresh parsley*
2–3 *cups cooked or canned beans, heated*	1 *cup grated cheddar or Monterey Jack cheese*

Cook rice over medium heat in water with salt, at least 20 minutes. When tender and fairly dry, stir in the cooked beans. Serve with dishes of scallions or onions, parsley, and cheese as garnishes.

Dovetail Meal: For kids, serve separate small dishes of rice and beans, cheese chunks if the kids like them, and small individual containers of unsugared applesauce (from the supermarket).

ONIGIRI

A classic Japanese lunch or snack. Also good as part of a dinner with a hearty soup. Thanks to Linda Wengerd, whose children dubbed their grandmother's traditional onigiri recipe "nigi-nigi."

⅓ *cup cooked short-grain rice per ball*	*Gomasio (see recipe) or tamari soy sauce (available at health food stores)*
nori seaweed (optional; available at health food stores)	*white or black sesame seeds*

The rice should be cooked until it's sticky—that's why short grain rice works well. Wet your hands and pat and roll each ⅓ cup rice into a ball. For a traditional rice ball sprinkle the ball with Gomasio, seeds, or tamari and then wrap in nori (see Note). Or dip the ball in tamari and then roll it in the sesame seeds.

Note: To use nori (square sheets of pressed seaweed), toast each sheet lightly over an open flame or burner until the edges are golden. Cut the nori sheet into quarters and use 2 quarters for each ball. Wrap so the corners of the 2 pieces match up, and you've got a rice ball.

The kids can help roll up the rice balls and do their own dipping or covering. Just be sure to put a big bowl of water on the work surface for rinsing hands in between steps.

QUICK CHILI
Makes 8 to 12 servings

A quick pot of chili can be assembled readily if you have the cooked components on hand. This is a point in favor of making things like Basic Red Sauce (see recipe) in double batches and freezing them. Serve your chili with some kind of grain—over rice, millet, or kasha or with corn bread or crackers on the side—and a big plate of carrot sticks.

1   *recipe Basic Red Sauce*

1   *recipe Basic Beef Mixture or Basic Tofu Crumbs (see recipes)*

2   *cups cooked beans such as 1 cup azuki beans and 1 cup kidney beans*

1   *tablespoon ground cumin*

1   *teaspoon (or less) cayenne pepper*

1   *teaspoon ground cardamon*

1   *teaspoon ground coriander*

2   *tablespoons rice vinegar*

Tabasco sauce to taste (optional)

In a large pot, combine the red sauce, meat or tofu, and beans. Add all the seasonings except Tabasco. Simmer for 15 minutes, taste, and correct the seasoning. Add Tabasco to taste if you like a hot chili. If you like a very mild chili, don't start with a teaspoon of cayenne; start with less and add to taste.

Note: You can divide the red sauce and beans into 2 pots if you want one with tofu and one with meat.

Dovetail meal: For children who don't like foods mixed up, reserve out some beans and some meat or tofu; serve separately with whatever grain you choose on the side, plus carrot sticks.

BAKED BEANS
Makes 12 servings

A good recipe to take to picnics. It takes time to prepare, but you can make it in advance and freeze it. Mustard greens really add to the flavor; buy them at ethnic markets if they are not available in your supermarket.

1 *pound navy beans, soaked overnight*

2 *quarts boiling water or Basic Vegetable Broth (see recipe)*

1 *strip kombu (available at health food stores)*

1 *bay leaf*

1 *16-ounce can tomatoes, drained and liquid reserved*

1 *medium onion, cut into half-moons*

2 *tablespoons tamari soy sauce (available at health food stores)*

a handful of mustard greens, chopped, or 1 *teaspoon dry mustard*

Simmer the soaked and drained beans in the boiling water with the kombu for 1 hour in a covered pot. Add the remaining ingredients and simmer until the beans are tender and the mixture is beginning to thicken. Add water, vegetable broth, or liquid from the tomatoes during cooking if needed.

CORN BREAD PIE

Makes 6 to 8 servings

An appealing and nourishing one-dish meal—sort of a south-of-the-border pot pie.

1 *garlic clove, chopped*

1 *medium onion, chopped*

2 *teaspoons extra-virgin olive oil*

1 *teaspoon dried oregano*

1 *cup canned whole tomatoes*

1 *whole acorn squash, baked and cut into chunks (see Note)*

2 *cups cooked or canned kidney beans*

1 *recipe Corn Bread (see recipe) batter*

In an all-iron skillet, sauté the garlic and onions in the olive oil until translucent. Add the oregano and tomatoes. Cook for 30 minutes, cutting up the tomatoes as they cook. Preheat the oven to 425 degrees. Add the squash and beans. Cover the mixture with Corn Bread batter, and bake until lightly browned, about 35 to 45 minutes. Cut the top of the pie into wedges; serve with any extra filling left in pan as sauce.

Note: Acorn squash may be baked whole at 350 degrees on a baking pan until the skin can be pierced easily with a fork—at least 30 minutes. Or split it in half, scrape out the seeds, and turn the halves flesh down on a well-greased baking pan and bake for 30 minutes.

Dovetail meal: Reserve some of the squash and beans and serve them with a little of the corn bread top on the side.

CRÊPES

Makes 12 to 16 crêpes, about 4 servings

Children are often fascinated by the idea that you can eat a *pancake*, with things *in* it, for crying out loud, for *dinner.* Popular fillings include chicken, seafood, or spinach (or broccoli) and ricotta, all with a basic white sauce. If you have time and your family likes all the fillings, make an assortment for a festive meal. Serve with a simple tossed salad or Watercress-Grape-Orange Salad (see recipe).

CRÊPES:

2 *cups unbleached flour*

2–3 *cups cold water*

2 *eggs, separated*

2 *tablespoons light
sesame oil*

¼ *teaspoon salt*

*unsalted butter or oil
for the pan*

WHITE SAUCE:

2 *tablespoons unsalted
butter or light sesame
oil*

2 *tablespoons
unbleached flour*

1½ *cups milk or stock
(chicken, fish, or
vegetable; see recipes),
heated*

1 *tablespoon white wine,
sherry, or mirin*

pinch *cayenne pepper*

¼ *teaspoon salt*

¼ *cup plain yogurt*

FILLING SUGGESTIONS:

4 cups chopped cooked
chicken or seafood
(shrimp, crab,
monkfish, lobster, etc.)
or 2 cups cooked
broccoli florets or
spinach mixed with 1
cup ricotta cheese and
½ cup crumbled tofu

1 teaspoon dried
tarragon

1 teaspoon freshly
grated nutmeg

½ cup chopped almonds
or other nuts
(optional)

Make the crepes: Mix the flour, water, egg yolks, oil, and salt in a bowl until smooth. In a separate bowl, beat the egg whites until stiff, then fold them into the batter. Stir with a wooden spoon. Heat a 6- to 8-inch pan (a crêpe pan or an omelet pan is ideal, but a regular skillet will do) and add a few drops of oil or a pat of butter. Wipe out the excess with a paper towel (save the towel). When the skillet is hot enough so that a drop of water "beads" on it, pour in about ⅓ cup of the batter. Tilt the pan to spread the batter evenly over the bottom, making it as thin as possible. If there's excess batter in the pan, tilt immediately to pour it back into bowl; the batter should just cover the bottom of the pan thinly. (If the whole bottom of the pan isn't covered, don't worry; you'll just have a small crêpe.) When the edges of the crêpe appear done, lift gently with a spatula or your fingers and turn over. Cook a minute or less.

Make the sauce: Heat the butter or oil in a saucepan and blend in the flour, stirring constantly. Slowly add the milk or stock, stirring. When the basic sauce is thickened, add the remaining ingredients except yogurt. Thin the sauce before serving, if necessary, with additional stock or milk. Add the yogurt just before serving. Correct the seasonings and add the filling.

Make the filling: Mix the chicken or seafood or vegetable/cheese/tofu mixture with the seasonings, plus half the nuts if desired. Add enough white sauce to moisten and make a smooth filling. Spread the filling on the crêpes, dividing evenly, and roll them up. Line the crêpes up on a serving platter or plates and pour the remaining white sauce over them. Garnish with remaining nuts if desired.

STUFFED POTATOES

Makes 4 servings

For little people these can be a meal in themselves. Adults might want to add fish or chicken or perhaps just a salad.

4 *medium potatoes, baked*

1 *tablespoon unsalted butter*

½ *cup milk*

½ *cup grated cheddar cheese*

¼ *teaspoon salt*

1 *cup broccoli florets, parboiled*

Preheat the oven to 350 degrees. Carefully spoon the potato out of the skins; save the skins. Mash the potatoes with butter until fluffy, then add the milk and mash smooth. Mix in the cheese, salt, and broccoli and scoop the mixture back into the potato skins. Bake in a shallow baking pan for 10 minutes or until the cheese is melted and the tops of the potatoes are lightly browned.

COLCANNON

Makes 4 to 6 servings

This is a traditional Irish dish, but it is also found in Holland and Germany. It is usually served at Halloween, and fortunes are told over it, but it is a wonderful dish for winter nights too. Serve it as a main dish or alongside Tofu Sausages (see recipe).

1 *pound potatoes, peeled and sliced*

3 *tablespoons unsalted butter*

1 *cup boiling milk*

6 *scallions, chopped*

2 *cups fresh kale, washed and cut into ribbons*

1 *tablespoon chopped fresh parsley*

salt and freshly ground white pepper to taste

Boil the potatoes until you can easily pierce them with a fork. Mash with half the butter until fluffy; add the milk and mash until well blended. Sauté the scallions in the remaining butter in a skillet for 1 minute; add the kale and cook briefly, until the kale is dark green and tender. Add the parsley. Mince the kale with a knife and fork in the pan. Drain. Toss gently with the potatoes and add salt and pepper to taste.

Vegetable Side Dish Ideas

Sturdy vegetables with hard outer skins should be baked. Sturdy vegetables like broccoli or string beans are best steamed (string beans are also good when boiled). Soft-skinned vegetables like zucchini are best sautéed in a little oil or butter, perhaps with an herb. Carrots can go either way. Sliced very thin, they sauté well; thicker, they are good steamed or in stews. Of course broccoli and string beans can be stir-fried, but I usually steam or parboil them a little first.

Work unusual vegetables like parsnips, daikon radish, or jícama into stews, soups, or stir-fries (slice them very thin for the last). Daikon is a mild white radish used in Japanese cooking, traditionally considered an aid to digestion, specifically the digestion of fats.

Don't overcook leafy greens. They can be sautéed briefly or parboiled by immersing them in boiling liquid for no more than 30 *seconds.* They should be bright green when cooked.

We don't eat winter squash or sweet potatoes a lot in this country. These sweet vegetables appeal to children from the earliest age. If you keep offering them regularly, the taste for them continues. They are also good sources of vitamins and minerals and are very easy to cook from scratch.

When boiling or steaming vegetables, save the cooking water for pureeing or freeze (by the cube or the batch) to use in soup or as the liquid in bread (instead of water); add to Basic Vegetable Broth (see recipe).

Here are a few specific side dish ideas.

STEAMED PARSLEYED POTATOES AND CARROTS

Makes 3 to 4 servings

Nice with fish or chicken

6–8 *new potatoes, scrubbed and halved*	2 *tablespoons chopped fresh parsley*
3–4 *small carrots, sliced on the diagonal*	*salt or Gomasio (see recipe) to taste*

Arrange the potatoes and carrots in a vegetable steamer set in a pot with a small amount of water in the bottom. Sprinkle with parsley. Steam until tender when tested with a fork. Season with salt or Gomasio to taste.

ACORN SQUASH

Preheat the oven to 350 degrees. Split acorn or other winter squash. Remove seeds. Brush well with oil and dust with ground cinnamon. Bake on a cookie sheet until you can easily pierce the outer skin with a fork—about 30 to 40 minutes.

SWEET POTATOES

Preheat the oven to 350 degrees. Scrub the potatoes and prick with a fork to allow steam to escape. Bake directly on the oven rack until you can easily pierce them with a sharp fork—about 30 minutes. Split open and serve with a little unsalted butter.

Two kinds of sweet potatoes, or yams, are found in supermarkets. Those marked "sweet potato" usually have orange flesh; the "yams" are more yellow. Both are sweet. For small children, winter squash and sweet potatoes, cut into chunks, make an ideal finger food. Older toddlers may enjoy grinding them through an infant food mill.

BROCCOLI OR CAULIFLOWER

Wash and cut the broccoli or cauliflower into chunks and florets. Peel the broccoli stems. Steam until tender—5 to 7 minutes. Rinse immediately in cold water to preserve color and flavor (but don't throw out the liquid the vegetables steamed over; use for purees, soups, or bread.

"ELEPHANT" VEGETABLES

Most kids love peanuts. Add a handful of chopped peanuts to any steamed or stir-fried vegetable—beans, broccoli, summer squash, etc.—as it is cooking.

CRANBERRY SAUCE

Makes 4 to 6 4- to 6-ounce jars

1 *pound fresh cranberries, washed and drained*

2 *cups water*

2 *tablespoons honey*

½ *bar kanten or 2 tablespoons agar-agar flakes (available at health food stores)*

1 *6-ounce can frozen orange juice concentrate*

½ *teaspoon ground cinnamon*

Boil the cranberries in the water in a saucepan until they begin to disintegrate, at least 10 minutes. Add the honey and kanten or agar-agar and cook over low heat, stirring, until the kanten or agar-agar is dissolved. Add the cinnamon and orange juice (undiluted) and chill for at least 3 hours.

Kids in the Kitchen: Kids can help stir in the orange juice, pour the cranberry sauce into the jars, and put on the fabric. Buy small preserve jars with screw-on lids at a hardware store. The ones with the two-part lid are best. Separate the outer ring of the lid from the flat top portion and insert colorful fabric. Tie with a ribbon. Use as holiday gifts in the winter. Be sure to attach a tag or label that indicates that sauce should be stored in the refrigerator.

◇

THIRTEEN

Bread

Here are recipes for breads you can make for the kids—and with the kids. Baking with yeast is probably something you'll want to do by yourself at first, so start kids with the quicker baking recipes. But when they're old enough to knead bread with you (and that is as soon as your patience can stand the relatively minor mess that flour and dough can make), they'll jump at the chance. After all, kneading bread is like playing with Play-Doh, modeling clay, or sand—only better, because in the end you have something good to eat, and your kids can say "I made this."

Another good thing about homemade baked goods is that your children will eat them. So make them nutritious and full of fiber. Serve a complete protein breakfast in a Cornell Triple-Rich Roll; add cheese for an even more delicious meal-in-itself. Make Zucchini Buns or Apple-Carrot Bran Muffins for extra fiber. Make homemade biscuits, corn bread, or rolls to round out dinner (making them is actually less of a hassle than running to the store for bread during evening rush hour, and it takes about the same amount of time).

Ingredients

Flour, unless otherwise stated, means *unbleached all-purpose flour.* Ceresota is a brand available in supermarkets, or buy your flour at the health food store. Substitute whole-wheat flour, if you prefer, for part of the flour called for, but keep in mind that using all whole-wheat flour makes a heavier bread (which may not be as appealing to kids, depending on what they're used to).

For leavenings, note that baking powder will raise any kind of flour all by itself, but baking soda needs a sour catalyst, like yogurt, buttermilk, or lemon juice. Yeast needs the gluten found mostly in wheat flour, so if you're avoiding wheat flour, you might want to stick with the quick breads, at least at first. There is gluten in some other flours, such as rye, but if you're avoiding wheat because of allergies, check with your doctor to be sure your child's allergy is not actually to gluten.

You can substitute fruit juice or honey or barley malt or maple syrup for sugar in virtually any recipe. Here's what will happen: You are adding more liquid to the recipe, which will make it heavier. It will need to cook longer, probably at a lower temperature. And you may have to get used to a slightly heavier, moister bread. This section offers recipes made with various sweeteners, according to what seems to yield the best texture. Feel free to alter them. The substitution is usually ½ cup of honey for 1 cup of sugar. If you're using fruit juice, decrease other sweeteners by about half and reduce the amount of other liquids in the recipe by an amount equal to or slightly less than the amount of juice you're adding. (For example, if a recipe calls for 1 cup of sugar and 1 cup of milk, and you want to use apple juice, just substitute the apple juice for the milk entirely and cut the sugar to ½ cup.) To help prevent burning in baked goods made with honey or fruit juice, add ¼ teapoon of baking *soda* per cup of juice or honey to neutralize the acid content of these sweeteners.

Quick Breads

BASIC BRAN MUFFINS
Makes 12 Muffins

Good for breakfast, tea, or anytime. Eat them with soup as a meal. Raisin Bran Muffins, a variation, make a delicious meal with Pumpkin Eater Soup (see recipe). An ideal recipe to use to start your baking adventures with a toddler.

¼ cup light sesame oil (available in health food stores) or cold-pressed corn oil

¼ cup brown sugar or 2 tablespoons honey

2 tablespoons maple syrup

⅔ cup milk

1 egg

1 cup flour

1 cup bran

1 tablespoon baking powder

¼ teaspoon salt

Preheat the oven to 400 degrees. Beat the oil and sweeteners together in a bowl until fluffy. Add the milk and egg; blend in. In a separate bowl, mix the dry ingredients. Add the liquid ingredients to the dry ingredients and mix just to moisten. Spoon the batter into 12 well-greased muffin cups, filling them one-half to two-thirds full. Bake for 15 minutes or until a toothpick inserted into the center of a muffin comes out clean.

VARIATIONS

Raisin Bran Muffins: To Basic Bran Muffins, add ½ cup raisins before baking.

Blueberry Bran Muffins: To Basic Bran Muffins, add ½ cup blueberries. You may want to add an extra tablespoon of sweetener.

Banana Bran Muffins: To Basic Bran Muffins, add ½ mashed banana and reduce the milk in recipe by half. Works with cooked fruit too.

Nut Muffins: To Basic Bran Muffins, add ¼ cup to ½ cup chopped walnuts or other nuts.

Oatmeal Muffins: A good way to use up leftover oatmeal. To Basic Bran Muffins, add ½ cup to 1 cup cooked oatmeal. Add 1 tablespoon maple syrup and ½ teaspoon baking powder for each ½ cup oatmeal. Add ½ cup raisins. Bake at 350 degrees.

Apple-Carrot Bran Muffins: Double the Basic Bran Muffins recipe. Instead of milk, use apple juice, and reduce the amount by one third. Add a cup of apple-carrot pulp from the juicer. If you're adding freshly grated apple and carrot from a food processor, start by reducing the amount of apple juice by half; add more if the batter seems too dry. Add ¼ teaspoon baking soda. These muffins can be very good with raisins or nuts too.

--------------- ✦ ---------------

MARY'S BANANA BREAD
Makes 1 8½- by 4½-inch loaf

Mary Flynn Day's banana bread is an institution among those who have tried it. Bake a double batch and freeze a loaf.

½ cup (1 stick) unsalted butter	1 teaspoon baking soda
	½ teaspoon salt
1 cup sugar	1 cup mashed bananas
2 eggs	(about 3)
2 cups flour	½–1 cup chopped nuts

Preheat the oven to 350 degrees. Cream the butter and sugar thoroughly in a mixing bowl. Add the eggs 1 at a time; beat well. Sift all dry ingredients together, then add them to the creamed ingredients alternately with the mashed bananas. Stir in the nuts. Pour the batter into an 8½- by 4½-inch loaf pan. Bake for 55 to 60 minutes. Cool thoroughly in the pan before slicing.

PEANUT BUTTER BREAD

Makes 1 8½- by 4½-inch loaf

Thanks to the Herron family for this favorite recipe, which has a lot of complete protein due to the flour (grain) plus peanut butter (legume) and the milk.

2 *cups flour*	⅔ *cup brown sugar*
2 *teaspoons baking powder*	1 *teaspoon vanilla extract*
¾ *teaspoon salt*	1½ *cups milk*
⅔ *cup smooth, good-quality (unhydrogenated) peanut butter*	

Preheat the oven to 350 degrees. Combine the dry ingredients in a mixing bowl. Blend the peanut butter, sugar, and vanilla in a separate bowl. Add the milk, beating until smooth. Add the wet ingredients to the dry ingredients and stir to moisten. Pour into an 8½- by 4½-inch loaf pan and bake for 1 hour or a little longer. Cool on a wire rack for 10 minutes. Store in the refrigerator for 1 day before slicing.

PUMPKIN BREAD

Makes 2 loaves

This basic quick bread can be adapted for various holidays.

1½	cups light brown sugar	½	teaspoon baking soda
½	cup light sesame oil	1	cup chopped nuts
1½	cups pureed cooked or canned pumpkin	½	teaspoon ground cinnamon
3	eggs, beaten	½	teaspoon freshly grated nutmeg
½	teaspoon salt		
4–5	cups unbleached flour	pinch	ground cloves or allspice (optional)
1½	tablespoons baking powder		

Preheat the oven to 350 degrees. Combine the sugar, oil, pumpkin, and egg. Sift the salt, flour, baking powder, baking soda, and spices together. Toss the nuts in the flour mixture. Combine the wet and dry ingredients and mix well. Pour into 2 8- or 9-inch loaf pans and bake for 45 minutes or until a toothpick inserted in the center comes out clean. Let cool for 10 minutes before removing from pans.

CRANBERRY BREAD

Using the preceding Pumpkin Bread Recipe, substitute 1½ cups orange juice for the pumpkin. Add 3 cups chopped cranberries and 2 teaspoons grated lemon zest after combining the wet and dry ingredients.

NUT BREAD

Using the preceding Pumpkin Bread Recipe, omit the pumpkin and add 1½ cups buttermilk. Omit the baking powder. Increase the nuts to 1 cup. Omit cinnamon and nutmeg.

BUTTERMILK BISCUITS
Makes 12 or more biscuits

A light and flaky bread, delicious with soups and stews.

1¾ cups flour	⅓ cup milk
½ teaspoon baking soda	⅓ cup buttermilk
½ teaspoon salt	
4 tablespoons unsalted butter	

Combine the dry ingredients in a large mixing bowl. Cut the butter into the flour mixture with a knife and fork, working them against each other until the butter is all cut up and the flour has a texture like coarse cornmeal. Add the liquid ingredients and mix quickly to form a moist dough.

Turn the dough onto a well-floured board, sprinkle with flour, and knead by folding over about 10 times. Dust the board with flour again and pat the dough down. Preheat the oven to 450 degrees. Roll out about ½ inch thick with a floured rolling pin and cut the dough into rounds with a biscuit or cookie cutter or with a can (a baking powder can is the ideal size) whose ends have been removed. Prick each biscuit with a fork. Bake on ungreased baking sheet for 10 minutes or until golden.

Note: Save scraps or even more of the dough to make Biscuit Cookies (see recipe) with your child.

CORN BREAD

Makes corn bread or 12 corn muffins

Grease 10-inch iron skillet, and heat it in the oven while you're making the batter to improve the texture of the bread (but be careful to keep the hot pan out of little hands). For corn muffins, use the same batter, spooned into a greased 12-cup muffin pan. This ideally would be heated, too, but not if your child is helping you.

1 *cup flour*

1 *tablespoon baking powder*

1 *cup yellow cornmeal*

½ *teaspoon salt*

1 *cup milk*

1 *tablespoon honey, barley malt (available at health food stores), or molasses*

1 *egg*

3 *tablespoons light sesame oil*

Preheat the oven to 425 degrees. Mix the dry ingredients in a mixing bowl. Beat the milk, sweetener, egg, and oil together in a separate wool. Add the wet ingredients to the dry ingredients and stir to moisten thoroughly. Pour into 10-inch skillet and bake for 30 minutes or until golden (15 minutes for muffins).

Note: For muffins, you may want to increase the amount of sweetener a little.

SCONES

Makes 12 or more scones

Pronounced "scahns" in Ireland, these cousins of biscuits are delectable as a tea-time treat.

2½ *cups flour*

1 *teaspoon baking soda*

1½ *teaspoons baking powder*

½ *teaspoon salt*

½ *cup (1 stick) unsalted butter*

¼ *cup sugar*

a *handful of raisins (optional)*

1 *egg*

1 *cup milk*

Preheat the oven to 400 degrees. Mix the dry ingredients except sugar in a mixing bowl and cut the butter into the flour until the butter is in small flakes. Add the sugar and a handful of raisins if desired. Beat the egg and milk together and add to make a moist dough (use more milk if necessary). Turn onto a floured board, dust with flour, pat into a thick round slab, and roll out ½ to 1 inch thick. Cut into rounds and bake on ungreased baking sheet until golden, about 15 minutes.

IRISH BROWN BREAD

This wonderful bread is a staple at mealtimes in Ireland, and although it's a soda bread (and therefore quick), it is not sweet at all. It serves very well, in fact, as a meal in itself if you're pressed at breakfast or as a hearty snack. Serve with soup for lunch or dinner. If you slice it carefully, it might even make a sandwich.

The secret ingredient, whole-meal flour, is not obtainable in this country but can be approximated by using a half-and-half mixture of bran and flour.

1½ *cups bran*	1½ *teaspoons baking soda*
2½ *cups flour*	1–1½ *cups buttermilk*
1 *teaspoon salt*	

Preheat the oven to 400 degrees. Combine the dry ingredients in a mixing bowl. Make a well in the center and gradually add the buttermilk, stirring with a wooden spoon. The dough should be soft but not so sticky that you can't handle it. Form the dough, still in the bowl, into a ball. Set on a greased and floured baking sheet and pat down into a slab about 2 inches thick. Cut a cross in the top of the dough so that it will break into the traditional quarters, or "farls," when done. Bake for 30 minutes. Reduce the heat to 350 degrees and bake 15 minutes longer. Let cool for several hours before cutting it or, if you wish to eat it hot, just break with your hands.

Yeast Breads

BASIC ROLLS

This is a yeast recipe, but it's a quick one. A yeast dough, divided up into small pieces to make rolls, cooks in a fraction of the time it takes for a yeast loaf to bake. Here's another tip: I once made these yeast rolls without letting them rise the prescribed amount of time. I usually allow about an hour to fix dinner. I started the rolls first, then let them rise for as long as I could afford without going over my total dinner prep time (15 minutes in this case). They turned out fine. So don't dismiss the idea of making yeast bread from scratch even on a busy night. You *can* have it, in the form of rolls. Use the rapid-rise variety of yeast for these rolls to save time.

1 ¼-ounce package active dry yeast

1 cup lukewarm water or water reserved from cooking vegetables

1 teaspoon salt

1 teaspoon honey

4 cups unbleached flour

light sesame oil

cornmeal

In a large mixing bowl, dissolve the yeast in the tepid water. Add the salt and honey. Let this mixture stand until the yeast begins to foam, about 5 minutes. Mix in 3 cups of the flour and mix thoroughly. Put the remaining flour on a bread board. Turn out the dough, roll it in the flour, and knead until smooth and elastic—about 15 minutes.

Grease the dough lightly with oil and put it in a clean bowl covered with a clean towel. Let rise in a warm, draft-free place until doubled in bulk (or for as long as convenient)—in about 1½ hours for standard yeast, about 30 minutes for rapid-rise yeast. Preheat the oven to 400 degrees. Punch down the dough and knead it again for a minute or so on the floured board.

Cut the dough into chunks and form into rolls by tucking the corners under. Set on a greased cookie sheet sprinkled with cornmeal. Bake until lightly browned, about 15 minutes.

Note: For a "hard roll" effect, do not preheat the oven. Set it at 400 degrees when you put the rolls in. Brush them with water when you put them in the oven and once again during baking. For a roll with no stretch marks, slash the tops lightly with a sharp knife before baking.

VARIATION

Cheese Rolls: When you form the rolls, flatten each chunk of dough enough to accommodate a 1-inch cube (or more, shredded) of very sharp cheese. Fold the dough around the cheese and pinch the seam well to close it. Bake as directed.

ZUCCHINI BUNS
Makes 24 buns

A great way to use up those big summer squashes, with thanks to Karen Parker.

3½ *cups flour*

1 *¼-ounce package active rapid-rise yeast*

1 *teaspoon salt*

1 *cup pureed zucchini, skinned and seeded*

¼ *cup water*

¼ *cup light sesame oil (available at health food stores)*

2 *tablespoons honey*

1 *egg*

Combine 1½ cups of the flour with the yeast and salt in a mixing bowl. Mix well. In a saucepan, heat the zucchini, water, oil, and honey until warm (not hot). Add to the flour mixture. Add the egg and blend until moistened. Beat by hand or with a mixer set at medium speed for several minutes. Add the remaining flour gradually, mixing by hand to make a soft, elastic dough. Transfer the dough to a clean bowl, cover it with a clean cloth, and let rise in warm draft-free place until doubled in bulk, about 30 minutes. Punch down the dough and knead for about a minute or so on a lightly floured board. Divide into 24 pieces and shape each into a smooth ball. Place in greased cake pans and allow to rise again, until doubled if possible. Preheat the oven to 375 degrees. Bake for 20 to 25 minutes, until golden. Remove from the pans and cool.

CORNELL TRIPLE-RICH ROLLS

The triple-rich bread recipe, developed at Cornell University, is defined by the addition of wheat germ, soy flour, and dry milk to a regular bread recipe to add nutrients, especially protein. The result is a hearty bread that makes a wonderfully nourishing roll, perfect for taking along in the morning for an on-the-go breakfast. For even heartier fare, substitute whole-wheat flour for half of the unbleached flour.

1½ *cups lukewarm water*

1 *¼-ounce package active dry yeast*

1 *tablespoon honey*

4 *cups flour*

2 *tablespoons wheat germ*

¼ *cup soy flour*

⅓ *cup skim milk powder*

1 *teaspoon salt*

1 *tablespoon light sesame oil*

cornmeal

Combine the water, yeast, and honey in a large mixing bowl. Let stand for 5 minutes. Sift the flour and add the wheat germ, soy flour, and dry milk powder. Stir the salt into the yeast mixture and add half the flour mixture, stirring constantly. Beat for 2 minutes by hand or with a mixer. Add the oil and 1 cup of the flour mixture. Mix in and turn onto a floured board. Knead thoroughly, 5 minutes or more, to make a smooth, elastic dough. Grease the dough and place it in a ceramic bowl covered with a clean towel. Let rise until doubled in bulk, punch it down. Let it rise again, until doubled if possible.

Preheat the oven to 350 degrees. Divide the dough into roll-sized pieces and shape by tucking the edges under. Bake on a cookie sheet dusted with cornmeal until lightly browned, about 15 to 20 minutes. The rolls are done if they sound hollow when their bottoms are tapped.

FOURTEEN

◇

Sweets

I don't think it's realistic to deprive kids of sweets altogether, and dessert *is* traditionally part of dinner in our culture. So in our house we do serve dessert—we've eaten our share of commercial desserts, but we've also made our share of less-sweet homemade treats.

I mentioned this earlier, and I'll say it again here: if you don't want your kids to eat sugar, don't eat it yourself. Somehow the kids will know what you've been up to and will want to join in. As with all other food habits, it just won't work unless everyone helps.

With that major caveat aside, desserts that are more or less wholesome—those with less sugar and more nutrients—are possible. Take carob, for instance—the only chocolate substitute I know of. While carob chips are not sugar-free by any means, they *are* caffeine-free and carob is a source of calcium. So try Carob Chip Cookies instead of chocolate chip. Some of the desserts in this section, like the ones made with kanten (agar-agar) or carrageen, are rich in minerals. And the fruit desserts offer their share of vitamins and fiber. So dessert can be another place to add essential nutrients.

Making desserts is also a good way to get kids into the kitchen and a great way to while away a rainy day. Once your child has baked with you a few times using a recipe you're comfortable with, you can make any of the cookie recipes together with ease.

BISCUIT COOKIES

A good first recipe for kids to make. Let them help with Buttermilk Biscuits (see recipe) and then use the scraps of dough.

scraps of dough from
Buttermilk Biscuits (see
recipe)

flour

1 tablespoon sugar

1 teaspoon ground
cinnamon

Preheat the oven to 425 degrees. Form the dough scraps into a ball. Dust a bread board with the flour. Let your child roll the dough out, using a real or play rolling pin. Help the child cut out shapes (you make sure the cutters are pressed down all the way before they are removed). You can coax a heart shape or a star out of a circle, but kids love to have their own cookie cutters in different shapes. Mix the sugar and cinnamon together. Sprinkle the cookies with it and transfer them carefully to an ungreased baking sheet. Use up the remaining dough in the same way. Bake for 5 to 10 minutes, but watch them—if shapes are small, they'll bake quickly. Cool before eating.

VARIATION

Thumbprint Cookies: Instead of cinnamon sugar, use sugarless fruit preserves as your sweetener. Cut or pat the dough into small circles (pat by making a small ball and flattening it), then let your child make a thumbprint in the middle. Fill the depression with sugarless preserves of different colors for a pleasing effect. Or fill the depression with a few drops of honey and a walnut or pecan.

OATMEAL COOKIES
Makes about 2 dozen cookies

Sugarless! Put these on your gift plates of holiday cookies to balance out the sugary ones.

3 *cups rolled oats*	1½ *cups apple juice*
1 *cup flour*	1 *tablespoon honey, barley malt, or rice syrup (optional)*
¼ *teaspoon salt*	
2 *tablespoons light sesame oil (available in health food stores*	*raisins and/or nuts (optional)*

Preheat the oven to 375 degrees. Mix the dry ingredients in a bowl. Add the oil and mix. Add the juice (plus remaining ingredients, if desired). If the dough seems too dry, add more juice. Drop by the teaspoon onto a greased cookie sheet and flatten slightly to ensure a crisper cookie. Bake until golden brown, about 15 to 20 minutes.

VARIATIONS

• Make the cookies without wheat flour for those with allergies. Use oat flour and add 1 tablespoon arrowroot flour or powder.

• Use pineapple juice instead of apple juice for sweeter cookies.

• To use leftover oatmeal, use 1 cup juice and 2 tablespoons honey or other sweetener.

CAROB CHIP COOKIES
Makes at least 12 cookies

Owen and his father started making their own chocolate chip cookies from scratch one long winter afternoon and have been doing it ever since. For this recipe we use carob chips, though of course you could substitute the same amount of chocolate chips. This recipe, based on a chocolate chip recipe, does feature butter and sugar; to substitute oil and a non-sugar sweetener, see Note.

½ cup (1 stick) unsalted butter

½ cup brown sugar

1 egg

½ teaspoon vanilla extract

1 cup flour

½ teaspoon baking soda

¼ teaspoon salt

½ cup carob chips

Preheat the oven to 375 degrees. Mash the butter in a mixing bowl until creamy. Add the sugar and mix thoroughly. Beat in the egg and vanilla. Sift the dry ingredients together. Combine the wet and dry ingredients and mix well. Add the chips. Drop by the teaspoon onto a greased cookie sheet. Bake for 8 to 10 minutes, until just golden.

Note: For the amounts of sugar and butter given here, substitute ¼ cup light sesame oil (available in health food stores), ¼ cup barley malt, honey, or rice syrup, and some fruit juice if needed for moistness or sweetness.

POPPY SEED COOKIES
Makes at least 12 cookies

Another recipe, this one courtesy of Steve and Nancy Doyne, that helps offset the sugar and butter of some other recipes. And these are delicious.

1 cup pastry flour

1 cup rolled oats, ground up in a blender or food processor

½ teaspoon baking soda

¼ teaspoon sea salt

¼ cup poppy seeds

⅓ cup rice syrup, barley malt, or maple syrup

⅓ cup light sesame oil

1 teaspoon vanilla extract

1 teaspoon rice vinegar

Preheat the oven to 350 degrees. Mix the dry ingredients, including seeds, in a bowl. Mix the wet ingredients in a separate bowl. Add to the dry ingredients and drop by tablespoons onto greased cookie sheet. Flatten slightly to ensure an evenly baked cookie. Bake for 10 to 12 minutes.

HOLIDAY SUGAR COOKIES

Makes about 18 cookies

These have no redeeming nutritional value at all. Their social value is that they are not drop cookies, but the kind you roll out and cut with a cookie cutter. So they provide you with appropriate shapes for holiday gift plates. Mix them up with the more wholesome cookies.

2 cups flour, sifted

1½ cups sugar

1 cup (2 sticks) unsalted butter, set at room temperature for 2 hours

1 teaspoon grated lemon zest

3 egg yolks

Combine all ingredients and mix together until thoroughly blended, using an electric mixer or your fingers. Chill the dough until firm, about 2 hours. Preheat the oven to 325 degrees. Take the dough in small portions, leaving most of it in the refrigerator, and roll it out on a very lightly floured board (or between 2 sheets of wax paper that have been sprayed with vegetable oil spray) to a thickness of ¼ inch (or a little more). Cut into shapes and transfer quickly to a buttered cookie sheet. Bake for 10 minutes or until barely golden (if you let them bake until their edges are browned, they will be too hard when cool). Remove to racks to cool.

Notes: For this recipe you need two things besides patience: (1) enough cookie sheets so that they have time to cool between batches and (2) wire racks to cool them on (available at any discount store). In addition, remember to keep checking the oven even while you're rolling out the next batch, to prevent burning them.

Some cooks recommend superfine granulated sugar if you can find it.

This is a tough recipe for kids to help with because the cookies are fragile. You do the rolling and moving. Let them do the cutting, supervised. You can also keep them occupied applying colored sprinkles to the unbaked cookies, but do this before you transfer them to the baking sheets or there will be burned sprinkles on the sheets.

NONGRAHAM PIECRUST

Makes a single crust for 1 9-inch pie

Designed for any pudding or jell-type filling, in response to the fact that those wonderful commercial graham crusts *do* contain saturated fat.

1 cup rolled oats, ground in a blender or food processor

1 cup wheat germ

1 cup ground walnuts or almonds

1 tablespoon sesame seeds

¼ teaspoon salt

¼ cup light sesame oil

2 tablespoons barley malt, rice syrup, or maple syrup

Put the dry ingredients into a 9-inch pie pan. Add the oil and work lightly with your fingers to mix. Pat it out to cover the pan's bottom and sides and drizzle lightly with barley malt or syrup. Use as you would a crumb crust.

Suggested fillings: Try 2 cups (or more) of *hot* Banana-Carrageen Pudding or Mint-Carob Pudding *or* 1 cup hot Kanten Gel plus 1 cup fresh sliced peaches or berries (see recipes in this chapter). Chill and serve.

NUTTY PIECRUST

Makes a single crust for 1 9-inch pie

A good crust for people with allergies because it contains no wheat. Wheat flour may of course be substituted for the oat flour.

1½ cups rolled oats, ground in a blender or food processor

½ cup oat flour

½ cup nut meal (grated or blended nuts)

¼ teaspoon salt

2 tablespoons light sesame oil

apple juice

Mix the dry ingredients in a bowl. Add the liquid ingredients, using enough juice to moisten thoroughly. Press the dough into a 9-inch pie pan, overlapping the edges by ¼ to ½ inch for shrinkage. Fill and bake at 350 degrees for about 30 to 45 minutes (baking time depends on filling); or bake for 10 to 20 minutes unfilled and fill when cooled.

Note: For a lighter crust, use more oil and less juice.

Suggested fillings: Fruit Custard Filling or Pumpkin Filling (recipes follow).

FRUIT CUSTARD FILLING
Makes 1 9-inch pie

CUSTARD:

1 *egg, beaten*

1 *cup plain yogurt*

1 *teaspoon vanilla extract*

1 *tablespoon honey*

FRUIT:

2 *cups sliced raw apples, pears, peaches, or other fruit*

1 *tablespoon brown sugar*

1 *tablespoon oat flour*

¼ *teaspoon salt*

Blend the custard ingredients. Mix the sliced fruit with the brown sugar, flour, and salt. Arrange it in an unbaked pie shell. Pour the custard over the fruit and bake as directed under Nutty Piecrust.

PUMPKIN FILLING

Another way to use up that Halloween pumpkin. Let the kids help mix this—they'll be fascinated to see the pumpkin they picked out at the farmstand continuing on its kitchen odyssey.

1½ *cups cooked pumpkin (see Note)*

1 *egg, beaten*

½ *cup plain yogurt*

¼ *cup barley malt or maple syrup*

¼ *teaspoon salt*

1 *teaspoon ground cinnamon*

Blend all the ingredients together and pour into an unbaked pie shell. Bake as directed under Nutty Piecrust.

Note: Use canned pumpkin from the supermarket if you don't have a pumpkin. If you do have one, split it, clean out the seeds, and bake, flesh side down, on a greased baking sheet at 350 degrees until you can pierce it easily with fork (at least 30 minutes). If you're using a jack-o'-lantern, bake it as soon after Halloween as possible. Check for mold first; it should be okay. Don't use the face part; just discard that and use the rest of the pumpkin. Unless it's a very small one, it should give you enough for a pie and Pumpkin Eater (see recipe). After baking, remove skin and puree flesh for easy storage.

KANTEN GEL OR MELLO

Rich in minerals, low in calories, fat- and cholesterol-free. A gelatin equivalent without the animal ingredients.

1 *bar kanten or the equivalent of agar-agar flakes (see Note; available at health food stores)*

3 *cups cold fruit juice*

ground cinnamon, cardamon, or ginger (optional)

Soften the kanten in 1 cup of the cold juice for 10 minutes. Then boil it in all 3 cups of juice until thoroughly dissolved, stirring with a wooden spoon. Add a large pinch of one of the spices if you like. Chill in individual dishes or use over fruit as the filling for a pie. Must be kept cold after the initial chilling, or it will melt.

Note: If you use the agar-agar flakes instead of the kanten bar, use about ¼ cup unless the package tells you otherwise. You may need to strain the mixture before jelling. Do so if it seems grainy. If the gel is too firm, use less kanten next time.

PEAR CRISP

Makes 4 servings

Use apple juice or white grape juice or a combination for this one, but don't use purple grape juice; it makes the pears turn color.

4 *ripe medium-sized pears, peeled, cored, and sliced*

juice of ½ lemon

¼ *cup rice syrup*

1 *tablespoon unbleached (wheat) flour*

¼ *teaspoon ground cinnamon*

¼ *teaspoon ground ginger*

1 *cup Homemade Granola (see recipe)*

½ *cup fruit juice*

unsalted butter or light sesame oil (optional)

Preheat the oven to 375 degrees. Sprinkle the pears with lemon juice and rice syrup and toss with the flour, cinnamon, and ginger. Spread in a thick layer in an 8-inch or 9-inch square baking dish. Top with a layer of granola and gently pour the juice over the granola to moisten. Dot with butter or drizzle lightly with oil if desired. Bake for 20 to 30 minutes, until the top is crisp and the pears are soft.

Note: Nuts or raisins may be added to the pears if desired.

FRUIT LEATHER

The homemade equivalent of the ever popular fruit rollups. Fruit leathers may also be bought at a health food store; they are made with pure fruit (no added sweeteners).

3 *cups sliced apples, pears, prunes, dried apricots, or berries*	pinch *salt*
	pinch *ground cinnamon*
water	*juice of ½ lemon*

Cook the fruit in water to cover until very soft. Puree in a food processor fitted with the steel blade or a blender. Spread no more than ¼ inch thick on a very well-greased cookie sheet with edges (grease the edges too). Leave in the oven set on the lowest temperature (for gas ovens, just the pilot light) for at least 6 hours or overnight. Cut into 3- by 4-inch pieces and roll up in pieces of wax paper. Store in a sealed container in the refrigerator or freezer until needed.

FRUIT BRITTLE

Makes about 8 cups

With many thanks to Mary Donhowe Conlow and her family, on whose recipe this is based.

½ *cup light sesame oil (available in health food stores)*	½ *cup ground almonds*
	½ *cup wheat germ*
⅔ *cup barley malt, honey, or rice syrup*	1 *cup chopped mixed dried fruit*
1 *cup rolled oats*	
½ *cup shredded unsweetened coconut*	

Preheat the oven to 350 degrees. Blend the oil and sweetener in a saucepan over low heat. Gradually stir in the remaining ingredients until the dry ingredients are well coated. Spread in a 9- by 13-inch baking pan. Bake for about 20 to 25 minutes, stirring occasionally, until lightly browned and bubbly. Spread the mixture in a thin layer on an ungreased cookie sheet. Chill until firm. Break into bite-sized pieces. Store in a sealed container in the refrigerator.

APPLESAUCE

Surely one of the most innocuous of desserts, and you can make it with the kids. Add to the adventure if possible by picking your own apples (find a farm in the weekend section of almost any paper when apples are in season).

apples, peeled and sliced (Granny Smith, Winesap, and Stayman are nice)

water

raisins (¼ cup per 3–4 apples)

½ teaspoon maple syrup per apple

ground cinnamon

Boil the apples with the raisins and syrup in water to cover until the apples are very soft. Dust the top of the apple mixture with cinnamon. Blend to a coarse consistency in a blender or a food processor fitted with the steel blade and chill. Drain off excess liquid, if any, and save for drinking or cooking. Excess applesauce may be frozen. Keeps in refrigerator, tightly covered, for about a week.

BANANA-CARRAGEEN PUDDING

Makes 4 to 6 servings

Carrageen or Irish moss is a mineral-rich seaweed that is native to the North Atlantic and is the basis of a very commonly used commercial thickener. Here you go right to the source. It is very digestible and in folk tradition is used for complaints of the stomach. The banana flavor makes this a mild, pleasant dessert.

2 *ounces carrageen (available at health food stores)*

cold water

2 *cups milk*

2 *tablespoons barley malt, honey, or maple syrup*

1 *teaspoon vanilla extract*

1 *ripe banana, mashed*

freshly grated nutmeg

Soak the carrageen in cold water for 15 minutes and discard the water. Bring the milk to a boil in a saucepan; add the carrageen, sweetener, and vanilla. Boil until the mixture is thick, stirring occasionally. Strain to remove carrageen. Blend with banana. Chill for at least 1 hour, in individual dishes if desired. To serve, sprinkle with nutmeg.

Allergy note: Make this dessert allergen-free by substituting a soy-based milk or fruit juice (apple, pineapple, or some combination thereof) for the milk.

MINT-CAROB PUDDING

Makes 4 to 6 servings

Again, carrageen is the thing that makes this pudding. Served without the Carob Syrup, it's a mild dish for convalescents.

2 ounces carrageen (available in health food stores)

cold water

2½ cups milk

2 tablespoons rice syrup, barley malt, or honey

½ cup Mint Tea (recipe follows)

1 teaspoon vanilla extract

Carob Syrup (optional; recipe follows)

Soak the carrageen in cold water for 15 minutes; discard the water. Bring the milk to a boil in a saucepan; add the carrageen, sweetener, Mint Tea, and vanilla. Cook until thickened, stirring occasionally. Strain to remove the carrageen and chill until set, at least 1 hour, in individual dishes if desired. Serve with Carob Syrup if desired.

MINT TEA

1 bag (1 tablespoon) mint tea

½ cup boiling water

Steep the tea in the boiling water for 5 to 10 minutes, until strong. Remove the tea leaves.

CAROB SYRUP

3 tablespoons carob powder

3 tablespoons barley malt or honey

¼ cup boiling water

Stir the ingredients to blend well. Serve hot or cold.

◆

CARROT CAKE

Makes 9 to 10 servings

This was our standard birthday cake until Owen was three. Now he gets to pick his own flavors, but at least we think we got him off to a reasonably healthy start.

2 *cups whole-wheat pastry flour or regular whole-wheat flour (if pastry flour is not available)*

2 *teaspoons baking powder (optional; see Note)*

½ *teaspoon baking soda (optional; see Note)*

¾ *cup barley malt or maple syrup*

1 *cup apple juice*

½ *teaspoon salt*

1 *teaspoon ground cinnamon*

3 *tablespoons light sesame oil (available at health food stores)*

2 *teaspoons vanilla extract*

½ *teaspoon freshly grated nutmeg*

2 *eggs (optional; see Note)*

½ *cup chopped nuts (optional)*

½ *cup raisins (optional)*

1½ *cups grated carrots*

Cream Cheese Icing or Tofu Cream Sauce (recipes follow)

Preheat the oven to 350 degrees. Combine the flour, baking powder, and baking soda. Mix well. Mix all other ingredients except icing or sauce and add them to the dry ingredients. Mix and pour into a greased and floured 9-inch square pan until about half full. If you have batter left over, use a second pan. Bake about 1 hour, testing with a toothpick after 50 minutes—if it comes out clean, the cake is done. Cool the cake in the pan. Frost with Cream Cheese Icing or serve with Tofu Cream Sauce (recipes follow).

Note: Baking powder, soda, and eggs may be omitted for a macrobiotic version of this cake, though it will be heavier.

Allergy note: The baking powder and soda may be left in and oat flour substituted for wheat, and the eggs omitted, for an allergen-free version. This cake too will be a little heavier. Also, those with allergies should note that pastry flour, even when made from wheat, is much lower in gluten than all-purpose flour.

CREAM CHEESE ICING

¼ *pound cream cheese*

¼ *pound ricotta cheese*

⅓ *cup honey or barley malt*

½ *teaspoon vanilla extract*

Blend the ingredients well and spread the icing on top of Carrot Cake. Chill and serve. Keep leftovers refrigerated.

TOFU CREAM SAUCE

1 *tablespoon agar-agar flakes (available at health food stores)*

1½ *cups water*

½ *pound tofu, boiled 5 minutes in water to cover*

1 *teaspoon vanilla extract*

1 *teaspoon fresh lemon juice*

½ *teaspoon grated fresh lemon zest*

⅓ *cup rice syrup or maple syrup*

¼ *teaspoon salt*

Simmer the agar-agar in the water for 10 minutes. Drain the tofu and blend it with the agar-agar mixture and remaining ingredients until smooth. Chill and serve with Carrot Cake.

POPPY SEED CAKE

Makes 12 servings

An especially good and wholesome recipe

2 *cups unbleached (wheat) flour*

1 *cup whole-wheat pastry flour*

1¼ *teaspoons salt*

¼ *teaspoon ground cinnamon*

½ *cup poppy seeds*

1 *tablespoon baking powder*

¼ *cup tahini (available at health food stores)*

¼ *pound tofu*

1 *cup maple syrup*

½ *cup light sesame oil (available at health food stores)*

1 *cup apple juice*

1 *teaspoon vanilla extract*

Tofu Cream Sauce (preceding recipe) or Raisin Tahini Icing (recipe follows) (Optional)

Preheat the oven to 325 degrees. Combine the dry ingredients and mix well. Blend the tahini and tofu together until fluffy. Add the remaining ingredients to the tofu mixture. Add to the dry ingredients and mix well. Bake in a greased and floured 9- by 12-inch pan for 45 to 55 minutes. Serve plain or with Tofu Cream Sauce (see recipe) or Raisin Tahini Icing.

◆

RAISIN TAHINI ICING

2 *cups raisins*

1 *tablespoon tahini (available at health food stores)*

Cover the raisins with water in a saucepan and bring to a boil. Boil for 10 minutes and drain, reserving 2 tablespoons of the water. Mix the raisins and reserved water with the tahini. Cool before icing Poppy Seed Cake.

◆

JUICESICLES

As simple to make as can be; a favorite dessert or treat for hot days. A child who is old enough to do so neatly can help pour the juice.

Use regular ice trays, or Popsicle-shaped forms if you have them. Fill with a favorite juice or with assorted juices for a rainbow of colors. If using ice trays, add sections of plastic straw, toothpicks, or Dixie spoons for handles. Allow to freeze until solid, usually a couple of hours. For a child's whole meal on a sweltering day, add them to a Fruit Platter (see recipe).

◆

FROZEN BANANA YOGURT BARS

Makes 8 to 10 bars

Again, ice trays may be used, although the Popsicle-shaped forms are nice for these.

1 *ripe banana, mashed*

1 *cup banana yogurt*

1 *cup yellow (or apple, pineapple, etc.) Juicy Juice*

Blend the ingredients well and pour into bar forms or ice trays and freeze.

AMASAKE

Makes about 2 quarts

You can buy amasake and amasake pudding in health food stores—look for them in the refrigerator or freezer section. Use liquid amasake in lieu of milk or milk shakes, as a beverage, as a treat, over hot or cold cereal, or in baking. To make your own, you'll need to buy *sweet brown rice* (labeled as such) and the *koji* starter culture in a health food store. After that, amasake is as easy to make as yogurt—much the same process, since it is natural fermentation that produces the nonalcoholic drink.

2 *cups sweet brown rice
(available in health
food stores), washed
and drained*

1–2 *cups rice koji
(available at health
food stores)*

3–3½ *quarts water*

Soak the rice in the water overnight. Bring to a boil in a large pot, reduce the heat, and cover. Cook over low heat until the rice is tender, at least 1 hour. Turn the heat off and let sit, covered, for 30 minutes. When the rice is cool enough to handle, turn it into a ceramic or glass bowl and mix in the koji with your hands. Let ferment for 6 to 12 hours, covered, in a warm place, as for bread or yogurt, mixing several times with a wooden spoon. To halt the fermentation, bring it to a boil, add the salt, and stir. Let cool. Blend in a blender or a food processor fitted with the steel blade for a creamy consistency. Refrigerate; keeps for 1 week.

AMASAKE PUDDING

Makes 6 servings

1 tablespoon agar-agar flakes (available at health food stores)

½ cup apple juice

1 teaspoon kuzu (available in health food stores) or arrowroot

pinch salt

1½ cups amasake (available at health food stores or see preceding recipe)

raisins or nuts (optional)

Soak the agar-agar in the juice in a saucepan for 15 minutes. Add the kuzu and stir to dissolve. Bring to a boil and stir until thick. Add the salt and amasake, plus raisins or nuts if desired, and refrigerate in individual cups or dishes. The pudding sets in about 1 hour.

RED, WHITE, AND BLUE PARFAITS

Makes 6 servings

Strawberries and blueberries conveniently come into season just about in time for the Fourth of July. Mix them up in this recipe and fill parfait glasses (or clear plastic tumblers) for a colorful dessert.

1 pint fresh strawberries, washed, hulled, and sliced

1 pint fresh blueberries, rinsed and cleaned

2 tablespoons honey

1 cup plain yogurt

1 pint vanilla Rice Dream (available at health food stores) or ice cream

12 vanilla wafers, crumbled

Put the strawberries and blueberries in separate bowls. Drizzle each with half the honey and add half the yogurt to each. Stir gently. Layer in parfait glasses, starting with strawberries, sprinkled with a little of the vanilla wafer crumbs, followed by a thin layer of Rice Dream or ice cream, followed by the blueberries, wafers, ice cream, strawberries, and so on. Top with wafer crumbs. Freeze for at least 1 hour.

PEANUT BUTTER PILEUPS
Makes 12 or more pieces

With thanks to Mary Noland and John and Michael Conlow, and the Greater Philadelphia Area Celiac Sprue Support Group; a delicious wheat-free treat to take along with you if your child has a gluten allergy and is going somewhere where cake or cookies will be eaten.

1 *cup peanut butter*

½ *cup sugar*

1 *egg*

½ *cup chocolate (or carob) chips*

Mix peanut butter, sugar and egg. Spread in a 9-inch pan and bake at 350 degrees for 10 minutes or until melted. Remove from oven. Sprinkle with chips, cover pan with foil, and allow to sit until chips have melted.

◇

FIFTEEN

Party Foods and
Play Foods

Kids' parties can be as simple or as fancy as you want to make them. To some extent that depends on how much the adults are going to be involved, because kids often like the simplest things best. Who hasn't discovered, at a one-year-old's birthday party, that it's the wrapping paper and boxes they love best?

For the very young, the one-year-olds, for instance, the best thing you can probably do about food is to keep it simple, keep it reasonably wholesome, and keep the sugar level down. Overexcited one-year-olds don't usually end up having a good time or letting anyone else have a good time. Simple sandwiches and a low-sugar cake such as Carrot Cake or Poppy Seed Cake (see recipes) can be a boon here.

From toddlerhood on, part of the fun of the party can be helping prepare, and that goes for the food too. Children love to be included, and it teaches them the skill of entertaining at a very basic level. So let them help you make the sandwiches, select the snacks, and decide what flavor of cake to have.

PARTY SANDWICHES

One nice idea for sandwiches that kids can make is finger sandwiches in geometric shapes—easy to make. Make up a number of sandwiches, using the spread of your choice, on plain sandwich bread; trim the crusts. Cut the square on the diagonal to form 2 large or 4 small triangles. Cut it lengthwise to make 3 or 4 rectangles. Cut it in half and in half again to make 4 squares. Use a round biscuit or cookie cutter for circles. Kids of two, three, and four who are learning their shapes will especially enjoy these. Of course you can also use regular cookie cutters for other themes—hearts and stars, dinosaurs, or other cutter shapes.

Party fare can also take the form of nonsandwiches, or rollups. See Chapter Eleven for ideas.

CHEESE PUFFLES
Makes 4 to 5 dozen

For this recipe I'm indebted to Gwen Rosvold, who makes it as a party snack in the classroom with her four- and five-year-old pupils. Kids like working the dough with their hands.

2 *cups unbleached (wheat) flour*	2 *cups grated sharp cheese*
1 *cup (2 sticks) unsalted butter*	4 *cups Rice Krispies*

Preheat the oven to 400 degrees. Cream the flour, butter, and cheese together in a large bowl. Add Rice Krispies and mix into a cohesive dough. Shape Puffles as small balls, using your hands. Bake until golden, about 10 to 15 minutes. Let cool.

SPICY PEANUT SPREAD

Makes about 1 cup

An idea that may sound strange but tastes good is this adaptation of an Indonesian dish.

⅔ cup peanut butter

¼ cup Hain's ketchup

1 teaspoon soy sauce

1 tablespoon fresh lime juice

pinch cayenne pepper

Blend the ingredients well and spread on crackers or toast points.

SPREADS FOR FINGER SANDWICHES OR CRACKERS

See Chapter Eleven for Cream Cheese–Veggie Spread, Minus-Mayo egg salad, and Sesame Chick-pea Spread (a junior version of hummus).

DEVILED EGGS

Makes 2 dozen halves

Another dish the kids can help with. Let them mash the filling and even fill the eggs.

12 eggs, hard-cooked and shelled

⅓ cup mayonnaise

1 tablespoon Dijon mustard

1 tablespoon rice vinegar

paprika

Halve the eggs lengthwise and carefully remove the yolks. Blend the yolks with the remaining ingredients until smooth and stuff the whites with the filling. Garnish with paprika.

OTHER SNACKS

* Peanuts and raisins in a mix

* Low-salt pretzels

* Popcorn with a little butter or salt

* Unshelled peanuts

* A mixture of spoon-size shredded wheats, nuts, and sunflower seeds

Note: No nuts for those under two (danger of choking in the excitement)—plain pretzels and spoon-size shredded wheats will keep them happy.

FRUIT BOWL

Cut up various fruits in season, mix together, and sprinkle liberally with fresh lemon juice to prevent browning. Top with a dusting of ground cinnamon and serve in a large bowl or part of a melon shell.

Possible fruit combinations: Cantaloupe, strawberries, watermelon, and blueberries; apples, pears, pineapple, orange or tangerine, and banana.

MYSTERY ROLLS

Buttermilk Biscuit dough (see recipe)

FILLING SUGGESTIONS:

ricotta cheese mixed with drained crushed pineapple
quartered hot dogs, Vienna sausages, or Tofu Sausages (see recipe) with mustard
cooked chicken chunks, grated carrots, and raisins

Preheat the oven to 350 degrees. Roll out the dough very thin (less than ¼ inch if possible), using a little dough at a time. Trim into 3- by 4-inch rectangles and fill with one of the suggestions. The filling should be placed down one of the longer sides of the rectangle, which is then rolled up. Seal the seam and the ends and bake for 10 to 15 minutes, until the dough is crisp. Allow to cool. Slice into thirds or serve whole.

Note: You can use packaged roll dough for this recipe if you're short on time or energy. Just roll it out so that you get some kind of rectangle to start with.

MAKE-THEIR-OWN PIZZA

Again, for party purposes, let 'em eat packaged dough. Get enough refrigerator biscuit or roll dough (the kind that comes in tubular packages in the refrigerator section of your supermarket) to make at least 2 pizzas per child. Good for kids of five or six and up.

refrigerator biscuit or roll dough

1 *16-ounce jar good-quality spaghetti sauce*

freshly grated mozzarella and Parmesan cheese, mixed

other toppings, such as green peppers, grated carrot, etc.

In advance of the party, roll out the biscuits or rolls very flat between sheets of wax paper and store on a cookie sheet in the refrigerator. When it's time to bake, set the oven at the temperature indicated on the dough package (usually 350 to 425 degrees) and pour the sauce into a bowl that can be reached by all. Set out the cheese and other toppings (anything you think the kids will like, or nothing if you think plain cheese is enough), give each child 2 pizzas on a paper plate, arm them with spoons, and let them make their own. You collect the pies, put them on baking sheets or whatever, and try to remember whose is whose.

Note: You can use English muffins instead of dough. Allow 1 muffin per child as the base for the pizza.

Sweet Things

You'll find cake and cookie recipes, some of which are quite low in sugar and some of which may be made without wheat flour, milk, or eggs, in Chapter Fourteen. As your child gets older, you may opt to go the bakery route, the store-bought mix route, or the store-bought ice cream roll route. Since this particular day comes only once a year, I think you should let your child decide.

For kids with allergies, or simply because you want to avoid dairy food, let me mention Rice Dream again. Get it from the frozen foods section of your health food store. It's the best of the nondairy ice cream clones as far as I can tell. It comes in vanilla, carob, and fruit flavors and is really delicious. It's made from amasake.

And of course you can always serve Juicesicles or Banana Yogurt Popsicles (see recipes). Just be sure the party child has input (after about age two) into whatever decisions you make.

PARTY IDEAS

Here are a few ideas about parties, by age group:

- For age one: Simply provide special refreshments, such as a low-sugar cake (Mary's Banana Bread, Carrot Cake, Poppy Seed Cake—see recipes) with a candle and ice cream or a substitute. At this age children don't really need organized entertainment. Paper goods, including a tablecloth, make for swift cleanup. Provide a snack for attending parents. If lunch is part of the scenario, simple quartered sandwiches and juice will suffice. If you're part of a play group, discuss whether or not birthday get-togethers will include gifts. Many parents at this stage feel their children already have more than enough toys.

• By age two, expectations are higher. Your child definitely knows about cake and ice cream. You may get away with a homemade, low-sugar cake, but it should be iced (try Carrot Cake with Cream Cheese Icing—see recipe). If you don't want to serve ice cream because you're avoiding dairy foods, try making a good-quality nondairy alternative like Rice Dream (available at health food stores) your birthday tradition. Children may be amused by a simple activity like decorating their treats bag with crayons, markers, stickers, or construction paper applied with a paste stick or tape. Go easy on sugar treats; avoid chocolate entirely at this age if possible. Again, if a meal is involved, keep it simple; make peanut butter, cream cheese, and/or tuna finger sandwiches, carrot sticks and fruit slices, and offer juice rather than soda.

  Nonsugar favors can include clickers, stickers, uninflated balloons, small boxes of crayons, pads of "stickups," small decorative magnets, raisin boxes, or Fruit Leather (see recipe). The treat bags may be decorated according to a theme or the individual child's fancy. Put names on the bags. Themes can include seasonal items, such as Halloween stickers, hearts, turkeys, spring flower cutouts, or patriotic stars and stripes. Other themes children love are clowns, bears, and dinosaurs. Games should be noncompetitive—a little singing and clapping or rolling a big ball from child to child (with children sitting in a circle) may be enough to round out the party.

• At age three the menu can stay much the same. Your child may be ready for a more sophisticated cake; chocolate may enter the picture. Use carob ice-cream (Haagen-Dazs has one) or carob Rice Dream (available at health food stores) if you want to avoid chocolate. Simple sandwiches, unsalted popcorn, peanut butter crackers, fruit, raw veggies (maybe with a simple dip), and pickles will satisfy three-year-old appetites, though corn chips will probably be met with enthusiasm. By now your child and peers are pretty well aware of what's available in the world of food. Try to hold the line on sweets. There's no need to complicate the occasion with candy treats. Even your supermarket can provide a wealth of inexpensive nonsugar favors, including balloons, pencils, small toys, magnets, and so forth. By all means keep using paper party goods wherever possible for easy cleanup.

Kids at this age still get a kick out of decorating treats bags. Encourage them to write their own names. They may also go for an additional activity, such as creating a head mask or body costume out of a large paper grocery bag (bugs, bears, monsters, Indian headbands, and robots are possibilities) and then having a parade. Whistles as a party favor are a great asset here, an instant hit for the kids and torture for the adults (have the parade right before the cake; that way the whistles can be rounded up and safely consigned to the treats bags for the trip home). Music for the parade can also include playing drums made of coffee cans or pots, singing and clapping, tunes from any instrument an attending adult can play, or a cassette of children's songs. Have the parade out in the yard to let off steam or around the kitchen table and out into the living room. By the way, cake and ice cream signal the end of the party, after activities and presents. The refreshments occupy the young, bring to a (screeching) halt all other activities, and guarantee rapt attention and good humor to end the party.

• By age four you may want to add more elegant fare, such as hot dogs (beef, tofu, or whatever), pizza, and chips or pretzels in baskets. Your child at this age should definitely be consulted about the food, especially the flavor of the cake *and* its icing. You can still hold the line on such items as soda and candy if you want to. One imaginative mother had large cookies instead of cake for her four-year-old's party. Guests iced their own cookies and then decorated them with an assortment of sprinkles and some small candies. You could do this with cupcakes too, but you'd better ask your child first, to be sure he or she agrees not to have a regular cake.

At this age it's really helpful if you can get everyone outside to blow off a little steam by running around. Noncompetitive activities include a peanut hunt, throwing a large ball around, or playing ring-around-the-rosy. If bad weather or the absence of a yard prevents an outdoor venture, you can do these activities inside, provided you prepare by battening down your breakables. A quieter activity is a hand and chanting game like "Let's go on a bear hunt" or singing games like "Heads, shoulders, knees and toes" or "This old man came rolling home."

• At ages five and six you may be seeking a change of venue, especially if you have a winter birthday to cope with. You gain excitement but lose the comfort and casualness of a home party. Still, some good options include fast-food restaurants that provide packages including food, party setups, favors, and sometimes a clown, old movies, or other entertainment; a gymnastics center that provides supervised gymnastics; roller skating or ice skating parties; or a community center that offers more space and perhaps some supervised activities. For summer birthdays, of course, there are pool parties.

For parties at home, a video with a blanket on the floor and popcorn for all may fill part of the time. You can also hire an entertainer—clowns, storytellers, or musicians are often available at a modest fee. You can even provide the "clowns" (nontoxic makeup for the children's faces) yourself. Children of this age like to participate, and they like people who can show them how to do things and let them get involved. One way to do so is to let them make their own English muffin pizzas. They will also enjoy making anything else you let them, including their treats bags, simple jewelry, or some other simple craft they can take home.

♦ Multiple parties. These are the bane of parents' existence. By the time your child is three you may be facing several celebrations—one at nursery school, one for friends, one for family. Just try to keep them simple (for your sanity) and as low-sugar and low-salt (for the children's sake) as possible. You are in charge of the food, so make the nursery-school treats applesauce cupcakes, have the family over for a simple supper, and can the candy at the kids' party.

Other Celebrations

Children love to celebrate, and I'm in favor of helping them do it. Seasonal preparations are discussed in Chapter Six because the kitchen (or hearth) is traditionally the center of these festive events. Simple, home-based traditions that children can be part of are food for their spirits just as much as home cooking is food for their bodies.

Again, you're the boss, so steer the food emphasis away from sugar and salt. At Halloween, for instance, the traditions you set in your house can emphasize the fun of making costumes or shopping for them together, cutting a jack-o'-lantern, or decorating the door with paper skeletons, pumpkins, or bats. If trick-or-treating makes you nervous, talk to friends about organizing a *simple* party instead. Have your child help prepare for it. Bobbing for apples and a costume parade are two traditional activities. Making monster masks out of grocery bags, making "jack-o'-lantern" apples or oranges with gumdrops as eyes and mouth (use toothpicks), or listening to Halloween stories (in books from your library) are other possibilities. And as for the pile of candy they will get (at school, at parties, from relatives—it's in the *air* at Halloween): No matter how you try, make some rules. Some of the rules I've heard include: your child can have as much as he can eat right now, and the rest you throw away; she can have three pieces now and the rest will be saved (in this case you can even sort through it after she goes to bed and throw most of it away, but this works only up to about age five);

or the child can have certain kinds, but that you're going to throw out or give away the other because they're worse for the child's teeth.

The candy problem exists during the Christmas season, on Valentine's Day, and around Easter too. Be firm. Again, put the emphasis on decorations, cooking preparations, and the meaningful aspects (stories, songs, rituals) of whatever holidays you choose to recognize. Invent or hand down your traditions and keep them as simple, low-tech, and participatory as possible. The glitz will catch up with us soon enough. In the meantime, the children really enjoy being part of the preparation. After all, getting there is at least half the fun.

Play Recipes

PLAYDOUGH

2 *cups flour*
1 *cup salt*
1 *tablespoon cream of tartar*
2 *tablespoons cooking oil (peanut oil makes for a nice aroma)*
2 *cups water*
   assorted food coloring (see Kids in the Kitchen)

Mix the dry ingredients. Add the wet ingredients and cook over medium to low heat until the playdough coheres and doesn't stick to sides of pan. Turn out on a clean board or other surface and knead. Let cool and store in an air-tight container. This can last over a month.

Note: If you want to have several colors of playdough at once, the ingredients must be subdivided and heated separately. Sometimes it's nice to have at least 2 colors to work with at once.

Kids in the Kitchen: Let your child decide on the color or colors and do the mixing and help with the kneading.

SALT DOUGH FOR ORNAMENTS

This is not intended as an edible dough. When baked, it's too hard to eat. When eaten raw in small quantities it would not make anyone sick, but it would be very salty.

Use this recipe for all holidays—make a midwinter mobile of hearts by tying several of the finished cutouts on a ribbon and hanging them in a window. Decorate them for Halloween too. You'll find cookie cutters for all seasons if you just keep an eye out at grocery stores, hardware stores, yard sales, party stores, craft stores, children's catalogs—collecting them can be a hobby for children. Use the ornaments as party favors.

1 *part salt*	4 *parts flour*
1½ *parts hot water*	

Dissolve the salt in the water. Add the flour and knead until smooth. Roll out on a floured board to about ¼-inch thick. Preheat the oven to 350 degrees. Cut out shapes and arrange on ungreased cookie sheets. Insert wires (see Note). Bake for 1 hour or more (up to 1½ hours), so that the dough is thoroughly dried. Let children paint the ornaments with poster paints or watercolors. When dry, you may varnish or shellac them (nail polish works too) for a more lasting ornament.

Note: For the wire loops, a spool of fine wire from a florist shop or craft shop or hardware store works well. Cut 1-inch lengths, fold in half to make a loop, and insert into top of cutout. This part of the process is best done by adults.

SQUASH OR APPLE TURKEYS

Fun to make for Thanksgiving centerpieces. A good activity for parties for kids at Thanksgiving time or to keep the children occupied at a family Thanksgiving gathering.

> *toothpicks*
> *small yellow crookneck squashes*
> *cranberries*

Stick a tripod of toothpick "legs" into the bottom of each squash for support. On the "back" end of the squash, make a fan of toothpicks and thread with cranberries for a tail.

Note: To make an edible version, use apples instead of squashes and large and small gumdrops and marshmallows instead of cranberries. Set up the apples as described. Thread the "tail" with small candles. Add a toothpick "neck" and a large gumdrop or marshmallow "head."

S I X T E E N

◇

Beverages

Start your children off right by not loading their systems down with unnecessary stuff in the beverage department, just as in the food department. For starters, your infant drinks breast milk or the best formula you can find. Don't hurry to introduce dairy beverages. When your child is old enough for juice, start with the mildest juices (apple, followed by pear and grape) and dilute them fifty-fifty with water.

And speaking of water, should you be drinking the water from your tap or buying spring water or distilled water?

First of all, distilled water should be completely pure H_2O, because of the distillation process. But that also means that minerals naturally occurring in the water, some of which are beneficial, have been removed. Ask your pediatrician or health care provider about the advisability of this for small children.

Your pediatrician can also advise you about the general healthiness of your local water (e.g., whether it should be boiled to kill bacteria before use in formula). In general, municipal water supplies are free of harmful bacteria, while well water sometimes is not. For more information on your local municipal water supply, visit your town or city manager's office and ask to see the printed analysis of the water supply. It should tell you how your water stacks up against federal standards. You are entitled to see it.

What about spring water? It may be the best or the worst choice. The trouble is, you don't know whether it came from an uncontaminated mountain spring (the best) or from one that has been contaminated by illegal dumping, for instance (the worst). You can write to the manufacturer on the label of any spring water in the store and ask for information about place of origin, type of processing, and mineral content.

Between the ages of one and two you can introduce your children to amasake (see recipe or get it at a health food store). It's as good as a meal for very little people on very hot days.

What about herb teas? There has been much concern that some herbs are too potent for regular use by anyone, let alone small children. Some herbs, on the other hand, are perfectly benign in small amounts and are even beneficial. I suggest that you do not casually feed herb tea to small children. If you want to know about specific herbs, write to a reputable manufacturer of herb teas, such as Celestial Seasonings.

APPLE TEA

For hot days you can mix bancha sun tea and apple juice to make a refreshing semisweet cold drink. Roasted bancha twigs contain a fair amount of calcium and can be made into tea as you could make any sun tea.

Put a tablespoon or so of bancha twigs (tea) into a clear glass or plastic jar, cover, and set in full sun for several hours (or all day). You can also do this with any herb tea (such as the noncaffeine Celestial Seasonings teas), mixing 1 part bancha tea with 1 part apple juice. Serve over ice with a stalk of mint if available.

PRUNE-GRAPE DRINK

I mentioned that prune juice is a good source of iron, so don't neglect this alternative. If it's too sweet, dilute it fifty-fifty with grape juice to make a palatable drink. Add a shot of seltzer if your kids are into fizz.

HOT MULLED APPLE CIDER

This is a nice hot drink for cold days.

Heat apple juice or apple cider with a couple of whole cloves, a sprinkling of ground cinnamon, and a couple of slices of lemon. Strain cloves out and serve in mugs, garnished with cinnamon sticks.

Another cold-weather favorite is cocoa. If the double whammy of dairy food plus caffeine-laden chocolate doesn't please you, there are soy-based alternatives. However, there are also studies that suggest that heated milk is more digestible than cold. Warm milk is also touted as a bedtime pacifier. In our house we do use Ovaltine or a carob-based powder instead of cocoa or hot chocolate mix.

◇

SEVENTEEN

Comfort Foods

When the kids are under the weather, it's a sign that the body is trying to shake off some kind of toxin, whether it's a germ or some kind of imbalance (eating too much, not enough sleep, change of weather). Whatever the case may be, you want to make things as easy as possible on the digestive system and the rest of the body, to promote healing. Fluids are always important. And what about food? It turns out there are good reasons why parents reach for the chicken soup and the ginger ale. Those things really are comfort foods.

Recipes that can make a sick kid feel better include things hot or cold that have a high liquid content and are mild. Sometimes foods that are mineral-rich are comforting too—they speed recovery and help the patient feel better by replacing minerals lost through perspiration, vomiting, or diarrhea. Here are some recipes for comfort foods, plus hints on adapting recipes given elsewhere in Part II.

Food

CHICKEN RICE SOUP

1 *quart Basic Chicken Stock (see recipe)*

½ *cup raw rice*

1 *cup water*

½ *teaspoon salt*

1 *small carrot, sliced into thin matchsticks*

Strain the stock to remove any onions, celery, meat, etc. Add the rice, water, salt, and carrot and cook over low heat until the rice is very soft, about 45 minutes. Pick out the carrots if your child doesn't want them today. Serve with bland crackers, preferably made with unsaturated fat.

CHICKEN OATMEAL SOUP

Follow the recipe in Chapter Twelve, removing the carrots if your child is up to only a little more than clear liquid. Oatmeal is soothing to the mucous linings of the stomach and digestive tract. Also, the ingredients in this soup are hypoallergenic, for those with colds.

BASIC MISO SOUP

Follow the recipe in Chapter Twelve, straining the soup to remove any vegetables, leaving a clear broth. Serve with udon noodles when your child is on the mend. Miso Consommé is also excellent for hot weather; the kanten in it adds minerals.

JUICESICLES

Follow the recipe in Chapter Fourteen and start with juicesicles made from apple juice; it's the mildest. Avoid citrus if your child has a stomach bug. Encourage citrus for a cold.

KANTEN GEL

Follow the recipe in Chapter Fourteen and start with the apple juice variety. Can also be frozen in ice trays with segments of plastic straws as sticks. Mineral-rich.

MILK TOAST

Makes 1 serving

Why does this traditional comfort food work for sick people? Well, it obviously won't work for everyone—don't contemplate it if your child has allergies. But heated milk becomes more digestible, releasing its supply of tryptophan for use by the body. The tryptophan in turn has a soothing and sedative effect, as does the warm liquid.

1 *cup milk, heated to boiling*

1 *pat unsalted butter*

2 *slices dry toast*

Pour the milk over the toast in a flat soup dish. Add the butter and serve warm.

Other useful foods for sick children include amasake, which may be drunk instead of milk when they have a cold. It is also a nourishing food for kids when they get past the clear liquid stage and are getting better. Custards are good at this time, too. Try Banana-Carrageen Pudding (see recipe).

Beverages

GINGER ALE

Adapted from Dian Dincin Buchman's wonderful book *Herbal Medicine*. She reports that ginger, much used in the Orient in cooking and medicine, is used in China even to combat certain types of poisoning. Ginger is hot to the tongue but cooling to the system. It helps ease all kinds of digestive discomfort.

1   *gingerroot, washed and chopped*

1   *pint water*

honey or rice syrup to taste

Perrier or sodium-free seltzer

Simmer the ginger in the water until the water turns a deep yellow color. Add honey or rice syrup to taste. Stir well. Cool. Strain out the ginger, add 1 part Perrier to 3 parts ginger water, and store refrigerated in a clean, tightly sealed bottle.

BANCHA-GINGER-PLUM DRINK

Inspired by Naboru Muramoto's *Healing Ourselves,* this drink is also a traditional remedy for various discomforts. It is good for the digestion but may also be used as a tonic to ward off a cold or other minor illness before it has a chance to take hold.

1   *umeboshi plum (available at health food stores), crushed between the fingers (remove pit)*

1   *chunk gingerroot, grated*

1 *tablespoon tamari soy*   4 *cups boiling water*
   sauce (available at
   health food stores)

1 *handful roast bancha*
   tea twigs (available at
   health food stores)

Put all the ingredients in a teapot and pour boiling water over them. Allow to steep for 10 minutes or so. The drink may be served very warm as soon as it has steeped or saved and reheated.

CAYENNE COLD REMEDY

This cold remedy, drawn from American folk medicine, sounds unappealing, but to a sore throat it is surprisingly welcome. Not for children under six. Don't offer more than ¼ cup at a time, or 1 cup within any 24-hour period.

1 *garlic clove, mashed*   2 *tablespoons honey*

1 *teaspoon cayenne*   2–3 *cups boiling water*
   pepper

Steep the ingredients in the water. Allow to cool to drinking temperature, but for best results drink while still very warm.

CINNAMON TEA

Dian Buchman also recommends cinnamon as an antinausea agent. She suggests that the following mixture be kept on hand:

3 *small cinnamon sticks*   1 *tablespoon freshly*
                                   grated nutmeg
8 *cardamon seeds*

Grind bark and seeds in a coffee or spice grinder; mix in nutmeg. Add ¼ teaspoon to 1 cup of hot tea for an adult, a tiny pinch to a cup of warm tea for a child. For a child, make the "tea" with hot water and a little honey—no tea leaves. Add the pinch of spices to the child's "tea," let sit a few minutes, strain, and serve.

Other Teas

It's a bitter drink, but dandelion tea is said to be a tonic for the digestive organs, including the liver, pancreas, and spleen. Buy it at a health food store.

As mentioned in Part I, mint is loaded with magnesium, which is used in commercial digestive aids. So brew your own mint tea (steep a tablespoon of leaves or 1 bag per cup of boiling water) and add a little honey.

Sources and Resources

Books and Publications

American Academy of Pediatrics Committee on Nutrition. "Nutrition and Lactation." *Pediatrics* Vol. 68, 3; Sept. 1981.

——— "Nutritional Aspects of Obesity in Infancy and Childhood." *Pediatrics* Vol. 68; 1981.

——— "Prudent Lifestyle for Children: Dietary Fat and Cholesterol." *Pediatrics* Vol. 78, 3; Sept. 1986.

——— "Toward a Prudent Diet for Children." *Pediatrics* Vol. 71; 1983.

——— "Vitamin and Mineral Supplement Needs in Normal Children in the United States." *Pediatrics* Vol. 66, 6; Dec. 1980.

Asthma and Allergy Foundation of America. *The Allergy Encyclopedia.* New York: New American Library, 1981.

Ballentine, Rudolph, M.D. *Diet and Nutrition: A Holistic Approach.* Himalayan Institute, Honesdale, Pa., 1978.

Brazelton, T. Berry, M.D. *Infants and Mothers.* New York: Delacorte Press, 1983.

Buchman, Dian Dincin. *Herbal Medicine: The Natural Way to Get Well and Stay Well.* New York: Gramercy Publishing Co., 1980.

"Calcium the Natural Way." *Consumer Reports,* May 1988.

"Food for Thought." *Consumers' Research,* Sept. 1987.

For Our Kids' Sake. Washington, D.C.: Mothers and Others, 1989.

The Gesell Institute of Child Development. *Your One-Year-Old,* New York: Delacorte Press. 1982.

Johns, Stephanie Bernardo. *The Allergy Guide to Brand Name Foods and Food Additives.* New York: New American Library, 1988.

Kirschmann, John D. *Nutrition Almanac.* New York: McGraw-Hill, 1979.

Pryor, Karen. *Nursing Your Baby.* New York: Simon and Schuster, 1973.

Smith, Lendon K. *Feed Your Kids Right.* New York: Dell, 1979.

———. *Foods for Healthy Kids.* New York: Berkley, 1984.

Books for Kids

Fritz, Jean. *George Washington's Breakfast.* New York: Coward, McCann, and Geoghan, 1969.

Hoban, Russell. *Bread and Jam for Frances.* New York: Harper & Row, 1964.

PLACES TO WRITE FOR PRODUCTS, FOR INFORMATION, OR WITH COMPLAINTS

PRODUCTS

Breast-feeding aids:

Mag-Mag battery-operated breast pump. Courier Health Care Inc., P.O. Box 1210, Agoura Hills, CA 91301.

Lac-Tote, Lait-Ette, 183 Florence Ave., Oakland, CA 94618.

Gerber Precious Care hand pump and electric pump. Available locally, or from Gerber Products Co., Fremont, MI 49412.

Natural baby foods:

Earth's Best, P.O. Box 887, Middlebury, VT 05753.

Growing Gourmet, 1320 Mt. Diablo Blvd., Suite D, Walnut Creek, CA 94596.

Simply Pure Foods Inc., RFD 3, Box 99, Bangor, Maine 04401. 1-800-426-7873.

Companies Supplying foods for those with allergy problems (gluten-free flour, dairy-free products, etc.):

Dietary Specialties, Inc., P.O. Box 227, Rochester, NY 14601.

Ener-G Foods, Inc., 6901 Fox Ave. South, P.O. Box 24723, Seattle, WA 98124.

For Our Kids' Sake.

A book available by mail order on pesticide hazards in foods. Write to Mothers and Others, Dept. D, 96652, Washington, DC 20090. ($7.95)

Compost bin and other gardening aids:
   Smith & Hawken, 25 Corte Madera, Mill Valley, CA 94941.

Nonelectric waffle iron and other kitchen tools:
   Williams-Sonora Catalog, Box 7456, San Francisco, CA 94120-7456.

Dinosaur cookie cutters, muffin and cake molds:
   Just for Kids, P.O. Box 901, Highland Park, NJ 08904.

Information

On allergies:
   American Allergy Association, P.O. Box 7273, Menlo Park, CA 94025.
   American Academy of Allergy, 611 E. Wells St., Milwaukee, WI 53202.
   Celiac Sprue Association/USA Inc., 2313 Rocklyn Drive, Des Moines, IA 50322.
   The Greater Philadelphia Area Celiac Sprue Support Group, 1243 Glen Burnie Lane, Dresher, PA 19025. This is an especially active chapter of CSA/USA, which among other things is responsible for the survey of fast-food restaurants used in this book, and also has reports on products from such major companies as Campbell Soup, Procter & Gamble, Knouse, Nestles, Hershey, Ralston-Purina, Kellogg's, and Oscar Mayer.
   Gluten Intolerance Group, P.O. Box 23053, Seattle, WA 98102.

On breast-feeding, prenatal care, infant health and other health areas:
   American College of Nurse Midwives, 1522 K St. NW, Suite 1000, Washington, DC 20005. 202-289-0171.
   Center for Science in the Public Interest, 1501 16th St. NW, Washington, DC 20036. 202-332-9110.
   Couple-to-Couple League, P.O. Box 111184, Cincinnati, OH 45211. 513-661-7612. An interfaith organization also offering information on natural family planning and teen chastity.
   Consumers' Union, 2001 S St. NW, Suite 520, Washington, DC 20009. 202-462-6262.
   Environmental Defense Fund, 1616 P St. NW, Suite 150, Washington, DC 20036. 202-387-3500.
   Healthy Mothers, Healthy Babies. 409 12th St. SW, Washington, DC 20024-2188. 202-863-2458. A coalition of 90 national organizations addressing maternal and infant health; consumer, government, and voluntary groups working together.
   International Childbirth Education Association, P.O. Box 20048, Minneapolis, MN 55420. 1-800-624-8660. Bookstore offers catalog on books covering breast-feeding, pregnancy, childbirth, child care, et al.

LaLeche League International Inc., 9619 Minneapolis Ave., Franklin Park, IL 60131. Consumer, environmental information.

March of Dimes, 1275 Mamaroneck Ave., White Plains, NY 10605. 914-428-7100. Prenatal nutrition.

National Resources Defense Council, 1350 New York Ave. NW, Suite 300, Washington, DC 20005. 202-783-7800.

COMPLAINTS

On the Quality of the Food Supply:

Environmental Protection Agency, 401 M St. SW, Washington, DC 20460.

Food and Drug Administration, 5600 Fishers Lane, Rockville, MD 20857.

U.S. Department of Agriculture, 14th and Independence Ave. SW, Washington, DC 20250. 202-479-3800. You may also contact your state and federal legislators and your state environmental agency.

On Unsafe Produce:

These are major supermarket chains you can write to about the need for safe produce—organic, local, or grown under the Integrated Pest Management System:

American (Acme, Alpha Beta), 124 N. 15th St., Philadelphia, PA 19101. 215-568-3000.

IGA, 18000 Horizon Way, Mt. Laurel, NJ 08054.

Kroger, 1014 Vine, Cincinnati, OH 45202. 513-762-4000.

Safeway, 201 Fourth St., Oakland, CA 94660. 415-891-3267.

Supermarkets General (Pathmark), 301 Blair Rd., Woodbridge, NJ 07095. 201-499-3000.

APPENDIX B

Breast-feeding Hints

1. If you're a working mother, there are now many mechanical aids available to help you. These have appeared or become common only in the past few years, which clearly seems to indicate that the working nursing mother is a phenomenon on the rise. So, you're not alone. Things you may want to get your hands on: the Mag-Mag battery-operated breast pump. It's more efficient than hand pump, and probably a must if you're going to pump away from home; from Courier Health Care Inc. Also, the Lac-Tote, a cooler designed to store and transport your pumped milk; from Lait-ette. Gerber also produces a very good quality hand pump and an electric breast pump kit. Both go under the label Precious Care. (For addresses, see Appendix A.)

2. Feed yourself. Your milk supply won't maintain itself if you don't maintain yourself. You need extra calories, and good-quality ones. Keep dried fruit, nuts, or a sandwich on your night table to replenish yourself after night feedings.

3. You need extra liquid. That's what the breast milk is, after all. There won't be any if you don't drink enough for yourself *and*

the baby. Drink a glass of water after each feeding. If milk supply is a problem, especially in hot weather, your liquid intake should be a prime suspect.

4. Avoid stress as much as possible. Stress is the enemy of your milk supply. Get rest whenever and wherever you can—catnaps, lie down and doze during feedings, put your feet up, daydream while nursing if you can, sneak away during lunch at work to be with your baby if possible. If not, sneak away and lie down or have a walk outdoors.

5. Storing pumped milk: Keep it chilled until you get it to the baby or your freezer. It will keep, frozen, for at least a month. But to freeze it, you have to chill it first. If you add your warm milk to a frozen supply, you risk thawing and spoilage.

6. For more efficient and comfortable breast feeding, change positions while nursing. Changing positions helps empty all parts of the breast evenly and that prevents possible undrained milk from causing an infection. Good complementary positions: The obvious front one, like all the Renaissance madonnas; the so-called football hold, in which your baby's feet are behind you, his/her legs and torso are under your one arm, his/her head is at your breast, face up, and your free hand is under the back of the head. This is the exact opposite of the front position. The third position is lying down on your side and nursing from the lower breast. Great for sleeping while nursing. The trick is to use about four pillows: One for your head (your lowermost arm goes under it); one behind you to keep you from rolling back, one for your upper knee to rest on; one for behind the baby, who is lying facing you, so your uppermost arm can rest comfortably. No kidding—this one only works if you're securely propped, but it's worth the trouble to get the snooze.

7. If you do get an engorged, inflamed or infected breast, *don't* stop nursing. Use heat to get the milk to drain: a hot water bottle, hot shower, compress or heating pad (be careful not to burn your baby with the latter). Then just nurse in every position until the irritation is released. If you do need an antibiotic, get one that

won't adversely affect the baby. They do exist, so that's not a reason to stop nursing. Stopping is the worst thing you can do to help ease an inflammation.

8. For cracked or sore nipples, sunlight is the best healer. I always wondered how the books expected us to get it. Next best are a sun lamp, an incandescent lamp held near the breast, or a minute or so of direct hot air from a hair dryer on the exposed breast. Avoid bras as much as possible, especially synthetic ones. Wear loose clothing. Use Eucerin ointment, vitamin E, or Masse Breast Cream on the nipple. Just be sure your baby doesn't ingest too much of same.

9. Remember that your baby eats what you eat. Spicy foods may cause gas and discomfort; medication, caffeine, nicotine, or any other drug passes right through to the baby; colic results in some babies from cow's milk (so if your baby is a crab and won't burp or sleep, you might want to experiment by cutting out dairy food for a few days or a week). If you don't use dairy food, get an alternate calcium supply.

10. In an emergency, if anxiety or stress cuts into your milk supply, there is a synthetic hormone on the market that mimics the milk-releasing effect of the body's natural hormone oxytocin. One brand name for the synthetic hormone is Syntocin. Get a prescription phoned to your pharmacist from your health care provider (or your baby's). Insist on this help—it does work.

11. Remember that everyone's different. Listen to all the good advice people want to give you, then pick and choose what works for you.

12. If you need support, look for local chapters of La Leche League, the International Childbirth Education Association, or the American Nurse Midwives Association (see Appendix A).

APPENDIX C

◇

Allergies

The key to dealing with food allergies is to find substitutes. Some of these are mentioned in the recipes; others will become obvious as you work with the alternatives. For alternatives to wheat flour, see the list below. Also remember that good-quality pastry flour, low in gluten, may be okay if your child's allergy is not to wheat but to gluten. For more information on gluten-free products, see Appendix A. Other routine substitutions include arrowroot powder for eggs as a thickening or binding agent; other liquids for milk (these may include soy milk if there are no soy allergies, or nut milk, or juice, stock, water, etc.); goat or sheep cheese (or goat milk, goat milk yogurt) instead of products made from cow's milk.

Some recipes obviously have eggs or milk so much at their center that they are best avoided altogether. But most recipes in this book can be adapted with little fuss to avoid the most common food allergies.

WHEAT FLOUR SUBSTITUTES

For 1 cup wheat flour, substitute:

½ *cup barley flour*

1¼ *cups rye flour*

1 *cup rye meal*

1⅓ *cups ground rolled oats*

½ *cup rye and ½ cup potato flour*

⅔ *cup rye and ⅓ cup potato flour*

⅝ *cup rice flour and ⅓ cup rye flour*

⅞ *cup rice flour*

⅝ *cup potato starch*

½ *cup rice flour and ½ cup potato starch*

The other strategy for dealing with allergies is to use a rotation diet under the supervision of a health care provider. With a rotation diet, known allergy-producing foods may be eaten, but not every day. If your child has multiple allergies, this approach is worth looking into.

The following list of recipes and their conversions to more or less allergen-free status may be of some help.

First baby foods (Chapter Nine): Check Part I for information on avoiding allergens early on. Make yogurt from goat milk, but be sure it's from a certified source. Buy wheat-free bread and cereal.

Breakfast recipes (Chapter Ten): See the "Allergy note" under Cinnamon French Toast and Wheat-free Pancakes.

Lunch recipes (Chapter Eleven): Buy wheat-free breads for sandwiches. If your child has an allergy to peanuts, use sesame butter instead of peanut butter. Remember that feta cheese and chèvre are not cow's milk cheeses (feta is sheep or goat; chèvre is goat): Use them for Cream Cheese-Veggie Spread, mixing in goat milk yogurt or

Basic Vegetable Broth (Chapter Twelve) for creaminess. Look for egg-free mayonnaise at health food stores.

Soup recipes (Chapter Twelve):   Most soup recipes are fine to use. Exceptions: Avgolemono; Quick Egg-Drop; Chicken Noodle; Cream of Tomato; Cold Green Pea (the last two just because they're hard to make properly without dairy products, but you may want to look them over). For Potato Soup, omit the yogurt or use goat milk yogurt; use oil instead of butter. For Pumpkin Eater Soup, use oat flour. Use Basic Vegetable Broth instead of milk. For "Wolf" Soup you may omit the corn.

Salad recipes (Chapter Twelve):   Use a simple oil and rice vinegar dressing. Use quinoa pasta. For Kale-Corn Salad, substitute cooked millet for corn. For Bulgur with Chick-peas, use cooked millet instead of bulgur. For Coleslaw with Buttermilk, use feta cheese and water blended to a creamy consistency instead of buttermilk.

Entrees recipes (Chapter Twelve):   In general, make substitutions for milk, cheese, eggs, and flour. Avoid tacos (corn and wheat), tofu recipes if there are soy allergies, and spoon bread (contains corn, eggs, and milk). For Basic Mashed potatoes, substitute soy or goat milk for the milk. For Meat Loaf recipes, make your own bread crumbs from wheat-free bread. For Brunswick Stew, omit the corn. Omit Soufflé-Stuffed Peppers; for Stuffed Red Peppers omit the eggs and cheese. Add cooked millet to vegetables and mix in some feta or chèvre for flavor. For Ratatouille Rarebit, omit the sauce. For Easy Tofu Lasagne, you can make a substitute casserole with layers of tomato sauce, squash, quinoa pasta, goat milk or sheep milk cheese, and tofu if there are no soy allergies. For Little Pies, wrap the filling in crêpes made with rice flour and arrowroot. For Corn Bread Pie, top the pie with nonwheat bread crumbs mixed with non-cow's milk cheese. For crêpes, use rice flour, omit the egg, and increase the liquid slightly; add 2 teaspoons arrowroot powder. Use oat or rice flour and stock in the sauce and omit the yogurt. For Stuffed Potatoes, omit the milk and use feta cheese. For Colcannon, use non-cow's milk and substitute oil for the butter.

Bread recipes (Chapter Thirteen): See the Wheat Flour Substitutes list. Use water or juice instead of milk. Use 1 teaspoon arrowroot powder per egg. Don't forget to add a good pinch of baking soda to neutralize acids in fruit juice. Avoid yeast breads if your child has a yeast allergy.

Sweets recipes (Chapter Fourteen): Use flour substitutes as needed. With this simple substitution all cookies except Biscuit Cookies and Holiday Sugar Cookies can be made easily and enjoyed. Carrot Cake and Poppy Seed Cake are designed to avoid eggs and milk. And don't forget Rice Dream (available in health food stores).

INDEX